SHOP TIPS

SHOP TIPS

FROM AMERICA'S BEST WOODWORKERS

**EXPERT ADVICE
ON MAKING THE MOST
OF YOUR SHOP TIME
AND TOOLS**

Reader's
Digest

THE READER'S DIGEST ASSOCIATION, INC.
Pleasantville, New York/Montreal

Library of Congress Cataloging-in-Publication Data has been applied for.

ISBN 0-7621-0189-X (paperback)

American Woodworker is a registered trademark of RD Publications, Inc.

Reader's Digest and the Pegasus logo are registered trademarks of The Reader's Digest Association, Inc.

4 6 8 10 9 7 5 3   paperback

EDITORS: Jeff Day, Kenneth S. Burton, Jr., David Schiff, Robert A. Yoder, Bob Moran, Roger Yepsen

COPY EDITOR: Barbara Webb

COPY MANAGER: Dolores Plikaitis

ADMINISTRATIVE ASSISTANT: Susan Nickol

OFFICE MANAGER: Karen Earl-Braymer

ART DIRECTOR: Michael Mandarano

BOOK DESIGNER: Peter A. Chiarelli

COVER DESIGNER: Sue Gettlin

COVER ILLUSTRATORS: Glenn Hughes, Heather B. Lambert

INTERIOR ILLUSTRATORS: Glenn Hughes, Heather B. Lambert, Frank Rohrbach

INDEXER: Ed Yeager

Printed in the United States of America.

If you have any questions or comments concerning this book, please write to:

Reader's Digest
Illustrated Reference Books Editors
Reader's Digest Road
Pleasantville, NY 10570

You can also visit us on the World Wide Web at: http://www.readersdigest.com

CONTENTS

INTRODUCTION

Before the civil war, the kind of information found in this book was everywhere. The world was full of woodworkers. Some made chairs, some made boats, some made wagons, and some made houses, but all of them worked wood, and all of them learned their trade from a master. Bits of knowledge—like how to get a board truly flat—flowed from one generation to the next.

Not so anymore. Few chairs are even made of wood. With the industrial revolution, woodworking has largely become the province of the amateur, working alone in a basement or garage. Skilled in some other profession, the amateur rediscovers woodworking as he goes. New problems arise with every project. Somewhere, someone has already solved the problem, but that someone, whoever he is, is working alone. His secrets will probably die with him.

That's why we wrote this book. We went to every woodworker we know—amateur and professional—and asked each to share hints, tips, and shortcuts that have made his job easier. Then we wrote to every craft guild we could find. In the end, we got over 1,000 responses. The best tips are in this book, along with longer articles about dust collection, cutting joints, building the perfect bench, and other important woodworking topics.

The woodworker's of America supplied the core of this book. The Delaware Valley Wood Carvers Club, in particular, was a great help in compiling the carving chapter. But in addition, many woodworking editors contributed something of their woodworking background to this book. Rob Yoder carefully researched and provided a vision for this book. Bob Moran edited part of the book and launched a complicated package of letters to woodworkers. The editors at *American Woodworker* magazine contributed their knowledge, and their readers contributed tips. David Schiff edited and organized the longer entries; Ken Burton cheerfully edited much of what was left. Roger Yespen, Jr., who edits like no one I know, helped with the final edit. And if much of the work was technical, our administrative assistant Sue Nickol went boldly where no man has gone before. Without her, these tips would still be a huddled mass in a forgotten filing cabinet.

Despite this input some of the truly valuable tips never made it into the main text. When I was learning the trade, for example, I asked Jack Larimore, a Philadelphia cabinetmaker who taught me much of what I know, whether there was a particularly good day of the week for woodworking. "Yesterday," he said. "Yesteryear." Edwin Ruppert, a cabinetmaker whom I met while working with Jack, offered more general advice: "Find out what work you do best; then do that work in an environment you love."

Bob Ingram, a Philadelphia woodworker who has forgotten more about woodworking than most of us will ever know, advises: "Buy low. Sell high. Do the least amount for the best result, which will translate into the highest returns. Maximize your liabilities."

And finally, Ernie Conover, father of the Conover lathe, tells us: "A file makes a jail stay shorter." We're not sure how he knows this.

I think I have learned as much as I ever will about this craft from Jack, Bob, and Edwin. From this book, I hope you will learn at least one thing about woodworking that Bob has forgotten.

Jeff Day
Editor

1 LAYOUT AND MEASUREMENT

PENCIL POINTERS

Use a harder-than-average pencil like a #4H when laying out cuts and joinery. It will stay sharp much longer and make a more precise mark. Use a standard #2 pencil, sharpened not quite as much, for other marks. It won't dent or scratch the wood and will erase or sand off more easily.

Kenneth S. Burton, Jr.
Allentown, Pa.

FINDING LAYOUT LINES

Use white-leaded pencils to mark dark woods like walnut.

Kenneth S. Burton, Jr.
Allentown, Pa.

LIGHT UP THE MARK

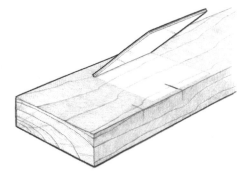

A mirror small enough to fit in your shirt pocket reflects an amazing amount of light. A layout mark that is nearly invisible will jump right out at you when the mirror is held at the right spot and angle. Even the polished back of a chisel can be a great aid.

David Page
Swarthmore, Pa.

HANDY LAYOUT FLUID

A felt-tipped permanent marker works as well as machinist's layout fluid for laying out marks on machines or tools. Rub the marker over the whole area where you need to scribe a mark, let dry for about 30 seconds, and scribe into the ink. Remove the ink with steel wool when you're finished.

Robert Pauley
Decatur, Ga.

ACCURATE LAYOUTS

Pencils dull quickly when marking wood, and the lines become wider. To avoid having to keep track of which edge of the pencil line represents the real mark, scribe the layout lines with a sharp awl, utility knife, pocket knife, or special layout knife. A scribed line is uniformly thin and very precise.

Nick Engler
West Milton, Ohio

KNIFE LAYOUT STOPS SPLINTERING

When laying out cuts in plywood, score the lines with a utility knife. The saw blade is then less likely to lift the veneer, chipping and tearing it. The resulting cleaner cut is particularly noticeable when cutting dadoes in plywood.

Nick Engler
West Milton, Ohio

RECYCLED LAYOUT KNIFE

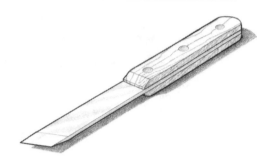

For precise layouts, you need a layout knife. But you don't need to pay a fancy price for one. You can pick up an old paring knife at a flea market for next to nothing and regrind the blade to suit your own preferences. A popular shape is shown in the drawing.

David Page
Swarthmore, Pa.

MARKING GAUGE TUNE-UP

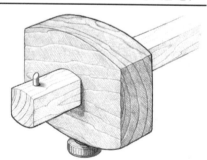

Marking gauges come with awl-type points that don't make a very precise line. They're also usually too long. Improve your marking gauge by filing the point to a shorter, rounded-tip knife edge as shown.

Ric Hanisch
Quakertown, Pa.

VERSATILE MARKING GAUGE

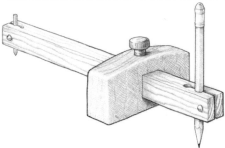

You can make your marking gauge more versatile by drilling a hole in it to hold a pencil. Drill the end opposite the scribing point and saw a kerf as shown. Drive in a screw so you can tighten the grip on the pencil. When a scribe mark won't do, you can stick in your pencil and use the pencil end of the gauge.

Simon Watts
San Francisco, Calif.

MARKING GAUGE FOR CENTERLINES

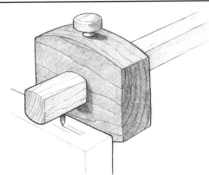

To scribe a centerline on a board with a marking gauge, estimate the gauge setting and mark the board from both edges. If the two marks do not coincide, estimate the setting to mark halfway between the first two marks and try again. If your two new marks still don't coincide, a third try should put you right on the money.

Ric Hanisch
Quakertown, Pa.

CENTERING JIG

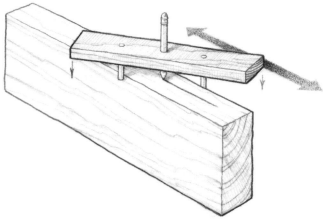

You can make your own centering jig for drilling or marking. Bore three evenly spaced holes in a straight line through a piece of scrap wood. The distance between the outer holes must be greater than the width of the stock you want to center on. Glue short dowels in the outer two holes (a diameter of ¼ inch is appropriate, but use whatever you have). For marking, the center hole should be sized to hold your pencil snugly. For centering a drill bit, the center hole must be the same diameter as the drill bit. To use the jig, place it on the stock so the dowels are over the edges, and twist it until the dowels touch the edges. You can slide it along to mark a centered line.

J. A. Wilson
Lexington, Mass.

QUICK COMPASS

To draw a large arc, more or less freehand, hold a pencil in your hand and pivot your arm at the elbow.

Rick Wright
Schnecksville, Pa.

TAPE MEASURE TURNED NOTEPAD

Have you ever noticed how easy it is to erase pencil marks from plastic laminate? A wet thumb will do it. I peeled off the label from my tape measure and glued a round scrap of plastic laminate in its place with contact cement. Now whenever I measure anything, I've got a handy spot to jot down the numbers.

Chris Carey
Houston, Tex.

DIMENSIONS IN FEET AND FINGERS

How often have you needed a tape measure but didn't have one with you? You can measure with sufficient accuracy for many purposes using your own body dimensions. Memorize your height from the floor to the top of your kneecap, from the floor to your navel, from floor to nose, and overall height. For widths, memorize your arm span to the tips of your fingers, elbow to finger tip, total hand span from the tip of your thumb to the tip of your little finger, the width of your palm, and so forth. The more dimensions you can carry in your head, the more accurately you can size up a piece of furniture you'd like to reproduce.

Ralph S. Wilkes
Branchport, N.Y.

MEASURING TO INSIDE CORNERS

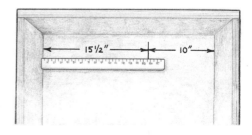

To determine the distance from one inside corner to another, first measure out from one corner and place a mark at an easily added measurement like 10 inches. Then measure from the other corner to the mark and add 10 inches to the measurement.

Daniel C. Urbanik
Washington, Pa.

SPACING SLOTS OR HOLES

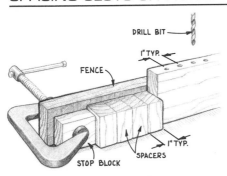

To make a series of identically spaced slots or holes, begin by making a set of spacer blocks equal in length to the spacing of the desired slots or holes. Use a stop block on your radial arm saw fence or miter gauge fence to make the identically sized spacer blocks. To make the slots or holes, position the stock for the first slot or hole with the aid of a stop block. Insert a spacer block between the stop block and the stock for the second one, insert two spacers for the third one, and so on.

Ben Erickson
Eutaw, Ala.

STORY BOARD FOR SHELF SUPPORTS

Bore uniformly positioned holes for shelf supports with the aid of a story board, which has holes drilled

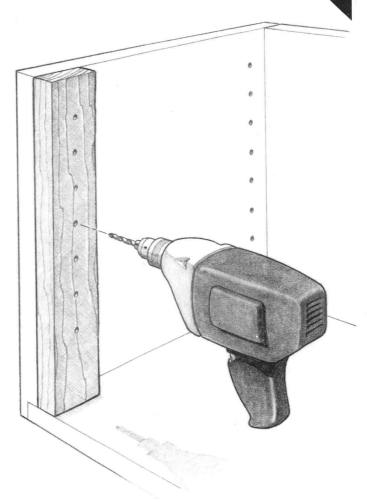

in it every inch or so to guide the bit. If you make a lot of projects with adjustable shelves, choose hardwood or even aluminum or steel to make an especially durable board. Hold the story board in each of the four corners of the cabinet, and bore the shelf support holes through the holes in the story board. The shelves will rest uniformly on their supports, with no annoying tip or rattle.

Rick Wright
Schnecksville, Pa.

SQUARE CHECK

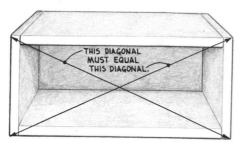

To check whether a rectangular object or assembly is square, measure the diagonals. If the two diagonals are the same length, the rectangle has truly square corners. But there's a catch: The opposite sides of the rectangle must be equal in length. If a cabinet top is a trifle narrower than the cabinet bottom, the four corners can never all be square at the same time.

Jeff Greef
Soquel, Calif.

QUICK DIVISION

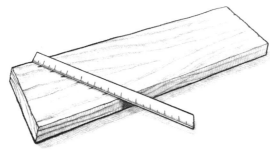

To quickly mark off equal divisions on a board for dovetails or other joints, place a rule diagonally across the surface so you can mark off the number of divisions in whole numbers. For example, to divide a board into seven equal parts, place the zero mark on one edge of the board and place the 7-inch mark on the other edge. Make a pencil mark at each inch mark—1 through 6—to divide the board.

Bill Bigelow
Surry, N.H.

BISECT AN ANGLE WITHOUT A COMPASS

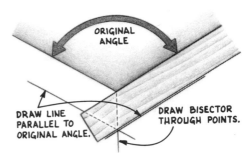

I have a very simple method for bisecting angles for mitering moldings. First I rip a board so I'm sure its edges are parallel. Then I lay the board along one leg of the angle and trace along it, drawing a line parallel to that leg. Next, I lay the board along the other leg of the angle. I draw a line parallel to that leg, which intersects the first line I drew. Finally, I connect the intersection of the two lines with the point of the original angle. The method is particularly useful for mitering baseboards in a room with odd angles.

J. A. Wilson
Lexington, Mass.

DRAWING PARALLEL LINES

Tape two standard pencils together to draw parallel lines ⁹⁄₃₂ inch apart. Tape a spacer between the pencils for lines spaced farther apart. This is a particularly handy way to lay out lettering for carved signs or carved decorations on panels.

Rick Wright
Schnecksville, Pa.

TRANSFERRING ANGLES

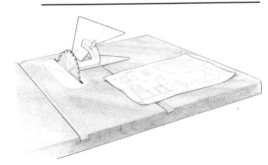

I adjust my table saw bevel angle, miter gauge angle, and other angle adjustments on machines without actually measuring the angles. I set a draftsman's adjustable triangle to the angle as drawn in the plans. I then adjust the blade tilt or miter gauge to the adjustable triangle. If I'm working by hand, I transfer the angle directly to the stock.

Ric Hanisch
Quakertown, Pa.

FIGURING THE RADIUS OF AN ARC

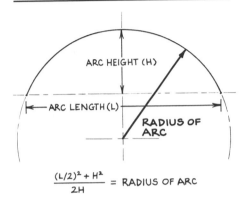

$$\frac{(L/2)^2 + H^2}{2H} = \text{RADIUS OF ARC}$$

Now and then you must lay out an arc (part of the circumference of a circle) knowing only the length and height of the arc. To calculate the radius, add the square of half the length (or L) to the square of the height (H), then divide this sum by twice the height. That is to say:

$$\frac{\left(L/2\right)^2 + H^2}{2H} = \text{Radius of the arc}$$

If, for example, you must lay out an arc that is 96 inches from end to end and 36 inches high:

$$\frac{\left(96/2\right)^2 + 36^2}{2 \times 36} = 50$$

The answer, 50, is the radius of the arc.

Nick Engler
West Milton, Ohio

LAYING OUT LARGE ARCS

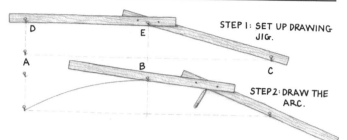

STEP 1: SET UP DRAWING JIG.

STEP 2: DRAW THE ARC.

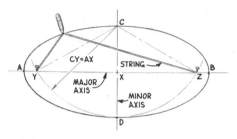

When an arc has a very gentle curve, it may be easier to lay it out from the span and rise instead of from the radius. You'll need two sticks and a few nails. First lay out the span, AC; the midpoint, B; and the rise, E, directly above B. Next add D directly above A so that AD also equals the rise. Drive nails partway in at A, C, D, and E. Take two sticks, each a few inches longer than EC, and nail them to each other, one along DE and the other along EC as shown. Nail the sticks securely so the angle between them doesn't change. Put your pencil in the angle where the two sticks join. Slide the sticks against the nails at E and C to trace one half of the arc. Hold the sticks against A and E to trace the other half.

Angelo Rotondo
Pueblo, Colo.

DRAWING AN OVAL

To draw an oval, first decide on its length and width, known as the major and minor axes. Draw these two axes, perpendicular to each other and crossing at their centers. Label the ends of the major axis A and B,

and the ends of the minor axis C and D. Label their intersection X. Adjust a compass to the distance AX. With the point of the compass at C, strike an arc through AB near each end. Label the two intersections Y and Z. Drive a small nail at Y and another at Z. Tie a piece of string into a loop that, when pulled taut, will be equal to AZ in length. Put the point of a pencil through the knot, put the string around the two nails, pull the string taut, and draw the oval, dragging the string around the nails as you draw.

Nick Engler
West Milton, Ohio

A PERFECT OVAL

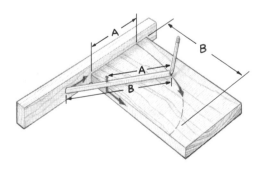

To draw a perfect oval (ellipse) of a given length and width, I make a template of one quarter of the ellipse, as shown in the drawing. Cut a stick to length B, which is half the length of the oval. Drive a nail at A, which is half the width of the oval from one end. Put a straightedge against the board. Keep the near end of the stick in contact with the straightedge, and the projecting nail in contact with the edge of the template stock. Hold a pencil against the other end of the stick and move it to draw a quarter of an oval.

J. A. Wilson
Lexington, Mass.

CALCULATING PERFECT PENTAGONS

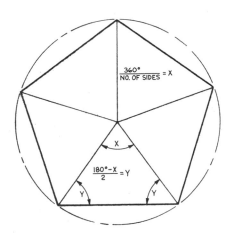

When making a five-sided box or frame, it's easier and faster to calculate the angles than to draw them out. Picture the figure you are trying to make as a series of triangles that come together at a common point, as shown in the drawing. The sum of the interior angles of these triangles will always be 360. If you divide this figure by the number of sides in the piece you want to make (in this case, five), you will get the number of degrees in the interior angle of one of the triangles (X). In the example in the drawing, the figure would be 72. The three interior angles of a triangle must always add up to 180, so the two outside angles (Y) must add up to 180 − 72 = 108. Since these two angles are equal, each one must be 108 divided by 2, or 54. To cut the pieces to form a pentagon, you would cut five pieces of equal length, each with a 54-degree miter at the ends. You can use the same calculation for a figure with any number of sides, provided they are equal in length.

David Firth
Amherst, Nova Scotia

FINE-TUNING STAVES AND RING SEGMENTS

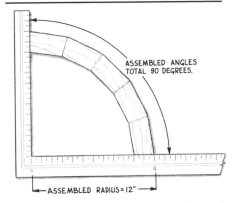

Staves for coopered panels and wedges for segmented rings must be very accurately cut. If they aren't, minor errors will accumulate and the final assembly will be obviously flawed. If the angle of the edges is off by a little bit, the last piece will have a big gap on either the inside or outside of the assembly. If the width of the parts is off by a little bit, the diameter of the assembly will be off by quite a bit.

To get the parts just right, first adjust the saw as well as you can by calculating the angles and widths, or by drawing the assembly full-sized and measuring the drawing. Cut enough parts out of scrap so that when assembled, they'll form a 90-degree angle. Assemble them and check the total angle with a square, then fine-tune the angle adjustment and recut them until they assemble to form a perfect 90 degrees.

To fine-tune the width, assemble the scrap parts and draw lines extending the outer edges until they intersect. This intersection is the center of the circle that the parts will assemble into. If the radius of this circle is too small, make the parts wider and vice versa.

C. E. Rannefeld
Decatur, Ala.

DRAWING A FAIR CURVE

To draw a fair curve (that is, smooth and true), find a thin, knot-free, straight-grained strip of wood and bend it to follow the line you require. Then trace along its edge. You can hold this spline in place with weights or small nails driven alongside it. If you need to make several pieces with the same curve, use the spline to draw the curve on a piece of thin plywood. Saw the plywood to

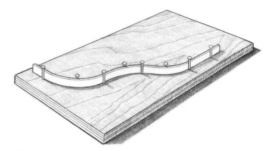

shape, smooth the edge with a spokeshave, and trace it onto your stock. If some parts of the curve need to have a much smaller radius than others, you can plane the spline thinner in these areas.

Ric Hanisch
Quakertown, Pa.

HOLDING A SPLINE
TO DRAW A CURVE

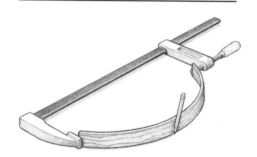

The next time you hold a spline to a desired curve with two of your hands and wonder how you will now hold a pencil to draw the curve, try clamping the spline lengthwise in a bar clamp. The more you tighten the clamp, the sharper the curve in the spline. The pressure of the clamp will hold the spline in place so you can modify the curve with one hand and draw the line with a pencil in your other hand.

Simon Watts
San Francisco, Calif.

BOTTLE-TOP CIRCLE TEMPLATES

A good collection of bottle tops and aerosol can caps makes a very handy, easy-to-use set of circle templates for laying out shapes on wood.

Walter J. Morrison
Northport, N.Y.

REINFORCED PAPER PATTERNS

If you need to trace a paper pattern several times, apply cheap, wide masking tape to the back side before cutting it out. The reinforced pattern will be much stiffer and more durable.

Stan Watson
Palm Springs, Calif.

LAYING OUT ON GLASS

When cutting glass to an unusual shape, first draw the shape on white paper. Lay the glass on top of the drawing and score the glass along the line just below the glass. This is a lot easier than marking the glass itself.

Royce W. Stafford
Jefferson City, Mo.

EVEN OVERHANGS

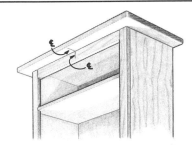

To get perfectly even overhangs when installing a top on a cabinet case, don't measure the overhangs at all. Mark the centerlines of the top and case and line them up.

Daniel C. Urbanik
Washington, Pa.

GREAT MATERIAL FOR PATTERNS

Scraps of plastic laminate make great patterns for woodworking projects. They're rigid, stable, just the right thickness, and easily shaped. You can cut the laminate with a band saw, sheet metal shears, or heavy-duty scissors. Smooth the edges and fine-tune the shape with a rugged abrasive like sandpaper used for floors.

Ben Erickson
Eutaw, Ala.

ALUMINUM FOR TEMPLATES

Use ¼-inch-thick aluminum for router and shaper templates that you expect to use a lot. You can shape it with carbide tools. Aluminum will long outlast hardwood plywood or hardboard, and if you accidentally hit it with a router bit or shaper cutter, you won't damage the cutter or create sparks.

Jeff Greef
Soquel, Calif.

HARDWARE LAYOUT

When tracing around hinges, strike plates, and similar hardware to lay out their mortises, scribe lightly with a sharp layout knife. If you need to

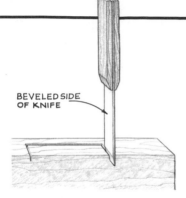

BEVELED SIDE OF KNIFE

deepen the lines, remove the hardware and deepen the lines with the knife bevel toward the waste side of the line. The crushed wood fibers that give the line width will be removed as the mortise is cut.

Jeff Greef
Soquel, Calif.

RECORD YOUR CHANGES

If you're like me, you make many changes to a design as you build it the first time. Some are small detail

Labeling Parts

Which is the top? Which is the jointed edge? Which is the face? Is this the left side or the right? Simple questions, until you face a pile of project parts and you aren't quite sure what you had in mind when you milled them.

For me, the key to keeping parts oriented are two simple, traditional marking systems. The first mark that gets lots of use in my shop is a large V. When I have selected the order of boards to be edge-glued for a tabletop, for example, I mark a V across them as shown in *Marking Out a Tabletop*. This makes it obvious which board goes where during glue-up. If I will be gluing up more than one top, I mark the first one with one straight line across all the boards, as shown in the drawing. If there will be two tops, I use two lines, and so on.

The other mark I use is the line with a scribble. *Marking Out Legs* shows how the scribble helps me keep four table legs in order. Before I taper or otherwise shape the legs, I select the outside faces. The scribbles

MARKING OUT A TABLETOP

MARKING OUT LEGS

identify the outside faces, and by making them closer to the top of the legs, I know which end is up. At this point, I usually haven't decided which will be the front legs and which the back legs. I'll make that decision when I see how the legs look with the aprons and top.

Marking Out a Door Frame shows how this scribble can provide a wealth of infor-

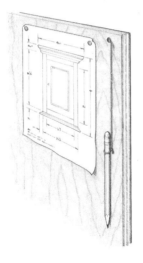

changes, some are changes to major dimensions. I pin my drawings to a piece of plywood or hardboard and keep a good pencil tethered to the board. As I make changes or work out details, I record them on the drawing so I can reproduce the project exactly and won't have to reinvent the best procedures.

David Page
Swarthmore, Pa.

---

mation. First, you must understand that I always try to orient lumber so that the inside of the tree is the outside face of the work—I call this the show face. As a result, as soon as the stock is planed to thickness, I already know how the parts will be oriented. *Choosing the Show Face* shows what I mean.

Once I've planed the wood, I joint one edge—the edge that will be on the inside of the frame. I then make a mark on the out-

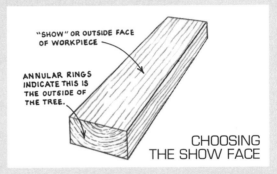

"SHOW" OR OUTSIDE FACE OF WORKPIECE

ANNULAR RINGS INDICATE THIS IS THE OUTSIDE OF THE TREE.

CHOOSING THE SHOW FACE

side face at the jointed edge. Now I know, for example, that this is the outside face of the left stile. Since the scribble also tells me which is the inside edge, I automatically know which is the top of the stile and which is the bottom. Having made my mark, I run the stock through the table saw with the jointed edge against the fence. I now have four clean surfaces, and by assembling them with the mark facing me and toward the center of the door, I know that I'm assembling the frame correctly.

—*FRANK KLAUSZ*
Klausz is a professional woodworker in Pluckemin, N.J.

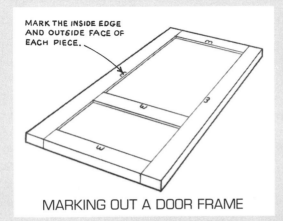

MARK THE INSIDE EDGE AND OUTSIDE FACE OF EACH PIECE.

MARKING OUT A DOOR FRAME

CHALK 'EM UP

Use blackboard chalk to label parts as you lay them out on rough stock. You can even mark the finished dimensions on the parts so you don't have to constantly refer to the drawings. The chalk is easy to see on rough lumber, easy to remove from surfaced lumber, and cheap.

David Page
Swarthmore, Pa.

STICK-ON PARTS LABELS

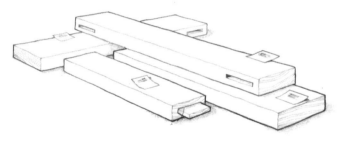

In any large woodworking project, keeping track of all the parts becomes an organizational problem. I don't like to write on the wood, because it involves an additional cleanup step later. I find it easy to keep track of my parts by labeling them with 3M Post-It Notes, sold in pads at office supply stores. These little paper note sheets use an adhesive that will not mar the wood, so no cleanup is necessary.

Alan McMaster
Brighton, Mich.

IRON-ON PATTERNS

You can transfer patterns—such as carving or band saw patterns—onto wood by copying the pattern on a photocopying machine, placing the copy face down on the wood, and ironing the back of the paper to transfer the pattern to the wood. Of course, the pattern will be a mirror image of the pattern in the book. Patterns may be enlarged or reduced on some copying machines.

Bill Bigelow
Surry, N.H.

LAYING OUT PARTS

When laying out the parts for a project, always lay out the longest parts first. You can easily edge-glue greater widths for wide parts, but scarfing boards to join them end to end to obtain greater length is far more difficult.

Ben Erickson
Eutaw, Ala.

MARKING SURFACES

When cutting out parts for a project, be sure to mark either the fronts of all the parts or the backs. It doesn't matter which, as long as you're consistent. Then, when machining the parts or laying out joinery, be sure to keep the same surface of the stock against the fence or table of the tool. That way, any small error in the tool adjustment will affect all of the pieces in the same way.

For example, if a rail and stile are to be flush when joined with a mortise and tenon, lay out and cut both the mortise and tenon by referencing the front surface of the pieces.

Kenneth S. Burton, Jr.
Allentown, Pa.

TRIANGULAR MARKING

When gluing up boards into a wide panel, first arrange them to find the best grain match or pattern, then mark them with a big triangle as illustrated. You can now joint the edges, apply glue, or even set them aside while you work on other parts of the project, and still put them back in the same arrangement. If I'm arranging boards for more than one panel, I double or even triple one or both of the lines so that the boards of one panel can be distinguished from those of another panel.

Kenneth S. Burton, Jr.
Allentown, Pa.

COMPENSATING ERRORS

A small error in setting the jointer fence square to the table can accumulate over the many jointed edges in a glued-up panel. The result is a

curved panel. Avoid this by jointing the boards so that any error is self-correcting instead of accumulating.

Arrange the boards the way you intend to glue them up, then mark the top surface of every other board with an X. Mark the intervening boards with an O. When you joint the edges, always keep the Xs against the fence and the Os away from the fence.

Kenneth S. Burton, Jr.
Allentown, Pa.

THE KING OF SHIMS

I find that playing cards of known thickness come in handy when shimming a specific amount. You can find the thickness of a single card by dividing the thickness of the deck by the number of cards; mine are 0.012 inch each. Three of them are approximately ¹⁄₃₂ inch (0.036), five are ¹⁄₁₆ inch (0.060), and so on. A decimal-to-fraction conversion chart is a handy accessory to the deck of cards.

William Guthrie
Pontiac, Mich.

TROUBLE-FREE STOPS

When making stops for positioning wooden parts in jigs or on fences, bevel or point the end of the

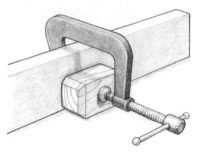

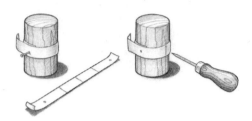

stop that will contact the wood. This gives sawdust a place to escape so that the wooden part contacts the stop and not an accumulation of sawdust.

Nick Engler
West Milton, Ohio

MICRO-ADJUSTABLE STOP BLOCK

To make a finely adjustable stop block, thread a bolt into a snug (but not tight) hole in a block of wood. Since the bolt acts as the actual stop, any debris that collects will slip under the stop, rather than ruining your cut.

Trebor Narom
Onaled, N. Mex.

SPACING AROUND A CYLINDER

To lay out equal segments around the circumference of a cylinder, wrap

a strip of paper around the cylinder and keep it in place with a single pin where the strip overlaps. Remove the strip and divide the distance between the pin holes into equal parts. Replace the strip around the cylinder and prick through the paper into the cylinder at each of the marks.

Percy W. Blandford
Stratford-upon-Avon, England

COPYING SHAPES ONTO PAPER

The usual pattern-transfer job in the shop involves copying a shape from paper onto wood. Occasionally, you may need to copy a pattern from wood onto paper. To do so, drive brads along the line to be copied. Cut off the brads as close as you can to the wood surface with diagonal wire cutters. (If you need to remove the nails, cut them to a length that you can grab later with pliers.) This will leave a small wedge-shaped end of the brad sticking up. Lay out your paper over the pattern and press it down over the brads. The projecting tips of the brads will punch a mark onto the paper. Connect the punch marks with a flexible rule or spline.

Simon Watts
San Francisco, Calif.

HAND TOOLS

COPING WITH HOT BLADES

The main reason coping saw blades break so often is that the friction on these thin blades causes heat to build up, weakening the metal. To solve this problem, I have two coping saws. I use one to cut an inch or so into the wood, then switch to the other, alternating this way through the cut. This may seem a little cumbersome, but it's a lot faster, not to mention cheaper, than ruining blades. My blades last for weeks before they get dull—instead of minutes before they overheat and get ruined.

Roy Moss
Rio Rancho, N. Mex.

KEEPING THE EDGE ON YOUR TEETH

The spines supplied with cheap plastic folders make great guards for hand saw blades. One spine is about right for a tenon saw or backsaw; for a longer saw, use two spines end to end.

Ben Erickson
Eutaw, Ala.

BOOT-HEEL SCRAPER

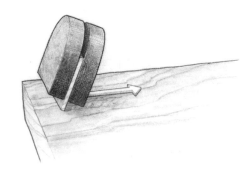

To scrape wood, hold a piece of glass between a pair of rubber heels. The glass stays put, and you have a large surface to hold onto.

J. E. Terzich
Hibbing, Minn.

SCRAPING A SMOOTHER SURFACE

A scraper will smooth a rough wood surface much faster and with less effort than sandpaper. But unlike sandpaper (which is available in many different grits), you can get only one degree of smoothness with a scraper, right? Wrong! You can control how smooth a scraper cuts by changing the size of the burr on the edge. The smaller the burr, the smoother the scraper will cut. To alter the size of the burr, regulate the amount of pressure applied to the burnisher when sharpening the scraper. For a smaller burr, apply less pressure.

Nick Engler
West Milton, Ohio

GLASS SCRAPERS

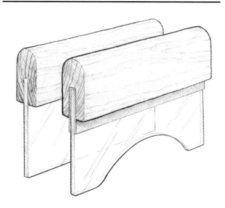

Everybody knows that glass is sharp, but few people realize that it can be made into an excellent scraper. I get free scraps of window glass from the local hardware store and then make a holder for them by sawing a slot in a piece of hardwood. If the kerf is too wide, I bind the edge of the glass with masking tape before inserting it. With a bit of practice, I've found that I can cut freehand curves in the glass to match a piece of trim or molding.

Donald Kinnaman
Phoenix, Ariz.

GOUGE SCRAPER

Smoothing the inside of a cove in a mitered corner is impossible with sandpaper. I scrape the cove instead. My special tool? A turning gouge. Just stand it on end, or come into the wood at a low angle, whichever works best.

Jeff Greef
Soquel, Calif.

BURNISHER FROM WRIST PIN

Wrist pins from auto engines make ideal burnishers for putting a burr on hand scrapers and cabinet scrapers. They're very hard and can be highly polished. You can find wrist pins at junkyards and engine repair shops. They come in a variety of sizes. Look for hollow wrist pins so you can add a pair of handles.

H. Wesley Phillips
Greer, S.C.

UPHOLSTERER'S HAMMER SAVES FINGER

It's tough to hit small tacks and brads with a full-sized hammer without hitting your fingers, too. I've tried holding the little nails with pliers, but that gets awkward. An upholsterer's hammer works much better. It's magnetized, so it holds the tacks for you.

David Page
Swarthmore, Pa.

NAIL HOLDER

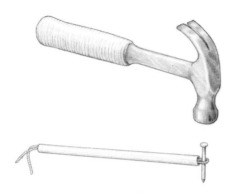

If your fingers can't reach to hold a nail where you need to start it, hold the nail with a loop of string through a soda straw. Slip the nail through the loop and pull the string tight to hold the nail.

Alice and Robert Tupper
Canton, S.Dak.

CHISELING OUT DOVETAILS

When I clean out corners of half-blind and full-blind dovetails, I find a skew chisel helpful. The angled edge gets into the corners that a straight chisel can't.

Gerald R. Randolph
Danbury, Wis.

WORN NAILSET BECOMES A PUNCH

When the tip of your nailset becomes too blunt to stay on the nail head, don't throw it away. Grind it to point and use it as a punch. Because the tip is already tempered, it will hold a point for a long time.

Ralph S. Wilkes
Branchport, N.Y.

SHOP ANVIL FROM RAILROAD RAIL

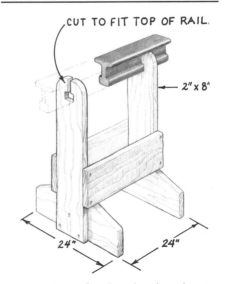

A section of railroad rail, at least a foot long, makes a handy anvil. It can be used for riveting, peening, forming metal, and many other purposes. You

The Virtues of the Scraper

HAND SCRAPER PROFILES

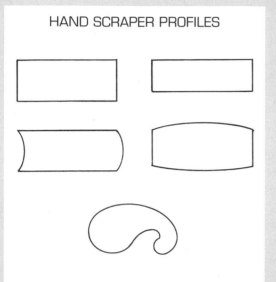

times in history people made them of flint, obsidian, bone, shell, glass, copper, and bronze. Steel scrapers are the modern version. The edge is turned over with a burnishing tool to form a hook. In use, the blade is sprung into a curve by pressure from both thumbs, to control depth of cut. This simple tool is called a hand scraper. The most common scraper is a thin rectangular piece of steel, but there also are shapes to fit the contours of your workpiece.

Cabinet scrapers work on the same principle but employ a cast-iron frame with a handle on each side, similar to a large spokeshave. The sole is flat, and a steel blade, also with a hooked edge, is clamped in place and held at a constant angle. Instead of thumbs, an adjustable wing screw springs the blade into a slight curve. Again, the degree of curvature determines the depth of cut.

I've always found machine sanding to be the most boring aspect of woodworking—with all the noise, I can't even console myself with public radio. However, the majority of woodworkers lean heavily on electric sanders. They plug in the orbital, insert a nice new sheet of 80-grit, and go for it. Peering through the dust storm a few minutes later they see that the planer or saw marks are gone, but in their place is a swirl of circular scratches. That requires going after them with 100-grit; then more dust, more sandpaper, finer and finer grits . . .

In my view, it's sheer perversity to start smoothing a wood surface by inflicting deep, cross-grain scratches and then removing them by making more. Scrapers offer another option, one that is cheaper, more healthful, and much quieter.

Scrapers are ancient tools. At various

CABINET SCRAPER

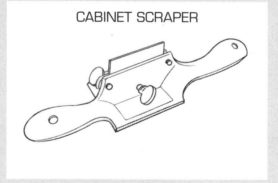

There's another small difference between hand scrapers and cabinet scrapers. Hand scrapers have square cutting edges, so you can turn a burr on both sides of each edge. But cabinet scrapers have beveled cutting edges, so you can turn only one burr on each edge. To learn how to make these burrs, see "Sharpening a Hand Scraper" on page 62 and "Sharpening a Cabinet Scraper" on page 64.

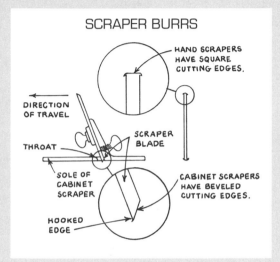

SCRAPER BURRS

HAND SCRAPERS HAVE SQUARE CUTTING EDGES.

DIRECTION OF TRAVEL

THROAT

SCRAPER BLADE

SOLE OF CABINET SCRAPER

CABINET SCRAPERS HAVE BEVELED CUTTING EDGES.

HOOKED EDGE

Most people build projects with lumber that has been surfaced in a thickness planer. Finishing involves removing the parallel ridges left by successive cuts of the planer knives. This is a job quickly done with a well-tuned scraper. The tool is especially useful on kiln-dried hardwoods, such as oak and maple, because they are just too brutally hard to plane by hand. Even the rough surfaces left by band saws and circular saws can be made smooth with a couple of passes of a cabinet scraper. This tool works best when skewed slightly to the direction of travel. You'll find that the finished surface is clean, is free from dust, and has the kind of sheen you never get with an orbital sander. Cabinet scrapers are especially useful when surfacing a large area—a tabletop, for exam-

ple. The great advantage of a scraper is that, unlike planes, the hooked edge seldom tears up the grain. You can use a scraper to smooth inlaid work, marquetry panels, and the tangled grain found in burls and crotches. In skilled hands, scrapers can also smooth end grain or awkward surfaces such as corners, where there is an abrupt, 90-degree change in grain direction.

Apart from sharpening, scrapers need little maintenance. With frequent use, especially on abrasive woods such as teak, you may find that the cabinet scraper's iron sole becomes rounded or even slightly hollow. The best way to flatten it is to use a drywall abrasive mesh known as Fabricut.

Fabricut is made by 3M and is widely available in hardware and paint stores. Lay a sheet of the 120-grit mesh on a piece of ¼-inch plate glass. Flush away the metal particles with plenty of fresh water while rubbing the sole of the scraper back and forth on the mesh. When the new, shiny area extends over the whole sole, it is again truly flat. Wipe the tool dry with a soft rag and put a few drops of oil on the bare metal surface. Don't let the blade get rusty, or the edge will become pitted so that it scars a surface instead of smoothing it.

You need skill and experience to get the best performance out of a scraper, but in the long run it will save you time. In addition, it reduces noise, airborne dust, and the expense of relying exclusively on sandpaper.

—*SIMON WATTS*
Watts is a professional woodworker and author in San Francisco, Calif.

can clamp it upside down to your bench vise, or mount a 2- or 3-foot section in its own stand as shown. Make the stand of 2 × 8 stock with the rail 32 to 36 inches off the ground, depending on your height. I filed a slight rabbet in one edge of mine so I can use it to set circular-saw teeth. I hold the body of the blade flat against the rail and use a punch and hammer to set the teeth.

Ralph S. Wilkes
Branchport, N.Y.

SHARP FILES

Files can become dull as much from banging against each other as from use, so don't lay them on top of each other in a drawer. Instead, keep them sharp by storing them upright in a file block. Make the block from a piece of wood at least 3 inches thick. Drill a series of 1-inch holes in the top to hold files and rasps.

David Page
Swarthmore, Pa.

HAND JOINT
FOR STRONG PANELS

If the jointer is not perfectly sharp, it tends to compress and burnish the wood. The surface fibers are weakened and the burnishing keeps glue from penetrating. As a result, machine-jointed edges tend to fail over time. When it is critical to make a strong edge-glued joint, shoot the joint with a hand plane.

Ric Hanisch
Quakertown, Pa.

JOINTER-PLANE JOINTER

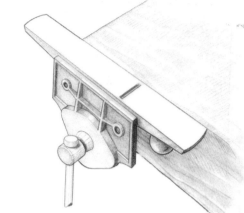

Here's a way to joint pieces of wood that are too short to be run safely over the jointer. Flip your hand jointer plane upside down and clamp it in your bench vise. Now you can pass the wood over the plane to joint the edge. It's a good idea to use a push stick so that you don't nip your fingers on the blade.

Alan McMaster
Brighton, Mich.

HOW TO KNICK YOUR
FRESHLY SHARPENED
PLANE IRON

Here's the best way I have found to undo a careful sharpening job: Embed a bit of grit in the edge of the board by leaning it on end on the floor. It's worked for me in the past. I have since become very careful in handling pieces ready for the plane. Brushing off the board won't get out that embedded grit, and a single hard particle will make a tiny notch in the blade. Hit that grit once, and you'll have a tiny raised line following your plane stroke. Keep those boards clean!

Ric Hanisch
Quakertown, Pa.

ICE PICK IN THE SHOP

While ice picks are no longer in daily use, you can occasionally find one at a garage sale or antique sale, sometimes even in a hardware store. If you run across one, buy it. You'll find it has dozens of uses around the home and workshop. You can use it as a marking tool, as a drill center, even to "predrill" softwood.

Ralph S. Wilkes
Branchport, N.Y.

TRULY SQUARE

What is the standard of square in your shop? Consider buying a steel machinist's square, which is accurate to tolerances beyond those you'll ever need for woodworking.

Jeff Greef
Soquel, Calif.

CHECKING THAT A SQUARE IS SQUARE

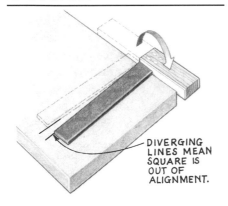

DIVERGING LINES MEAN SQUARE IS OUT OF ALIGNMENT.

To check that a square is square, place the base against the edge of a board and draw a line along the blade. Flip the base 180 degrees and draw another line over the first. If the lines diverge, your square isn't square.

Nick Engler
West Milton, Ohio

ADJUST YOUR FRAMING SQUARE

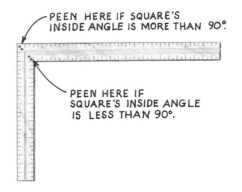

PEEN HERE IF SQUARE'S INSIDE ANGLE IS MORE THAN 90°.

PEEN HERE IF SQUARE'S INSIDE ANGLE IS LESS THAN 90°.

Careful as you may be, eventually you will drop your framing square onto the floor. When you do, it may get bent slightly out-of-square. Here's a way to repair the damage. If the square's inside angle is less than 90 degrees, use a punch to peen a small depression near the square's inside corner. Check the angle. Peen again, next to the first depression. Continue doing this until the angle is correct. If the inside angle is more than 90 degrees, peen near the *outside* corner of the square.

Bob Moran
Emmaus, Pa.

Tuning Hand Planes

I love the look of a surface that has been prepared for finish with a hand plane. There's a quality that can't be matched by the scratching of abrasives, no matter how fine the grit. Besides, making shavings is a lot more healthful and a lot more fun than making dust.

Hand planing to a finish-ready surface requires planes which have been tweaked to optimum performance. Any plane, new or old, can benefit from careful adjustment of a few critical factors. Learn how these factors influence the functioning of a plane, and you'll be able to shop for a good one.

Checking for a Flat Sole

A plane with a twisted, cupped, or bowed sole will give you nothing but frustration. Twist is a problem you'll rarely encounter in a steel-bodied plane, but it is not uncommon with wooden planes. To check the sole, use two straight winding

sticks, each about ¼ to ⅜ inch square by about 12 inches long. Lay the sticks on the inverted plane as shown, and sight across them to make sure they are parallel.

You can use sandpaper to remove twist from a wooden plane. Tape a piece of sandpaper to a flat surface, such as your table saw. Remove the iron, and run the plane on the sandpaper until you expose new wood on the entire bottom.

Next check the plane to see whether it's cupped. Lay a straightedge across the width of the plane and look for light between the plane and straightedge. Check in several places.

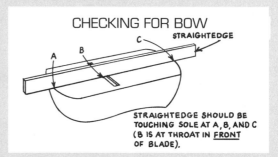

CHECKING FOR BOW

STRAIGHTEDGE

STRAIGHTEDGE SHOULD BE TOUCHING SOLE AT A, B, AND C (B IS AT THROAT IN <u>FRONT</u> OF BLADE).

Now make sure the sole isn't bowed. Retract the plane iron, and lay a straightedge along the sole from front to back as shown in *Checking for Bow*. There are three critical areas which should all lie in the same plane. At the throat—in front of the plane iron— the sole should be in contact with the straightedge. If you see light, that critical part of the sole is not doing its job of regulating the depth of cut. When planing thin panels, if your plane keeps grabbing the

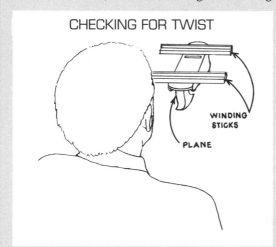

CHECKING FOR TWIST

WINDING STICKS

PLANE

work even when set for a very shallow cut, the problem probably lies in the contour of the sole at the throat.

Late-model planes with this problem were probably finished at the factory on a belt sander. They may be good enough for planing the edge of a door but are unsuitable for fine cabinetwork. Older planes generally have flatter soles. Once you understand what to look for, you can examine a plane's sole in the store or flea market by holding it up to the light and observing the reflection off the sole at the throat. You can flatten the sole with silicon carbide on a glass plate lubricated with water, but this is extremely tedious. Do it once, and you'll look for planes without this defect. Wooden-soled planes can also suffer from this problem due to wear of the sole at the throat. The bottom can be flattened, unless the throat opening becomes too large for fine work. A new sole can be applied or a new wear block can be inlaid at the throat.

Checking Plane-Iron Support

The plane iron must be firmly supported. The slightest play in the plane iron will cause its setting to change and it may "chatter." The cap lever of a steel bench plane clamps the plane-iron-and-chip-breaker sandwich to the frog as shown in *Anatomy of a Hand Plane*. In block planes, the cap iron holds the plane iron directly to the plane body. The wedge of a wooden plane performs the same function. In each case the plane iron must be evenly clamped along a line close to its working edge. If

this condition is not met, the plane iron may twist out of its set position or vibrate during use, producing chatter marks. If these symptoms occur, examine the surfaces that hold the plane iron in position. I have been able to improve the fit to the plane iron on newer planes by filing rough or uneven spots that cause spotty contact with the plane iron. When assembling a plane after sharpening, blow out any debris which has collected on these surfaces. Chips of wood trapped under the plane iron can cause uneven pressure.

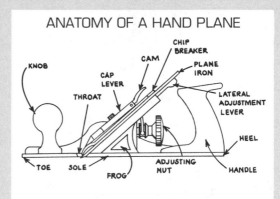

ANATOMY OF A HAND PLANE

Checking the Plane Iron and Chip Breaker

After repeated sharpening, the edge of the plane iron may become out-of-square with the sides of the plane iron. It's time to square the edge again when the sideways adjustment is no longer enough to compensate.

(continued)

Tuning Hand Planes—*Continued*

Most bench planes have chip breakers which are clamped to a slotted plane iron with a screw. The chip breaker reduces tear-out in wood with changing grain direction by turning the shaving upward and breaking it, thereby reducing its tendency to pull out a thicker splinter from a level below the surface. In order to function, the entire length of the chip breaker's edge must be in contact with the back of the plane iron. Shavings will catch in any gaps and quickly clog the throat of the plane. It is well worth a few minutes to file and smooth the edge of the chip breaker so that it can divert the shaving without snagging it.

For most planing, the chip breaker can be set ⅟₃₂ to ⅟₁₆ inch behind the edge of the plane iron. If tear-out still occurs, reduce the distance to the edge to as little as ⅟₆₄ inch. I don't keep the setting this small, because I feel additional resistance as the plane removes shavings.

Determining the Angle of the Cutting Edge

In bench planes, the iron is installed with the bevel down. This means the cutting angle is fixed at the angle at which the plane iron is held in the plane. On block planes and shoulder planes, the iron is installed with the bevel up. As a result, the bevel angle does affect the cutting angle. On bevel-up planes, the cutting angle is the sum of the bevel angle and the angle at which the iron is held in the plane.

Experimentation is the best way to determine the bevel angles appropriate for your requirements. I like to keep the guide on my grinder set at about 33 degrees for all my plane irons. This gives me a cutting angle of about 55 degrees for my standard block plane and 42 degrees for my low-angle block plane. In practical terms, low cutting angles slice across end grain more smoothly and cut with less resistance along the grain. High cutting angles make for more resistance but are less likely to produce tear-out.

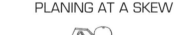
PLANING AT A SKEW

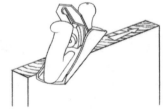

FLATTEN PLANE SOLES

If you are having trouble getting good results with a hand plane, it is possible that the sole is not flat. Flatten the sole with coarse emery cloth. Put the emery cloth on a piece of plate glass. First adjust the plane blade so that none of it extends beyond the sole. Then push the plane across the emery cloth and glass as if you were planing it. After

Keep in mind that cutting angle is measured perpendicular to the plane iron. When you move the plane along at an angle to its axis, you are effectively reducing the cutting angle, as shown in *Planing at a Skew*. In practice, this means you will get a smoother cut across end grain by angling the plane to the direction of movement. This can help in knotty areas, too. For more information on sharpening plane irons, see "Sharpening Edge Tools" on page 58.

Setting the Plane Iron

Be careful when you put the blade back into a plane. A light bump against a metal part will put a nick in your razor edge. Whether your plane has a wooden wedge or a lever mechanism, try to put the right pressure on the plane-iron clamp. Make it tight enough to keep the plane iron positioned but loose enough for easy adjustment.

The amount of opening at the throat can influence the cutting action. Coarse work with heavy shavings requires a wide throat. For fine work, a narrower throat can help give a smoother cut. The adjustable frog on steel bench planes lets you reduce the throat opening. Some block planes have two-part soles that enable throat adjustment.

Adjusting the Cut

With the plane iron clamped in place, you're ready to adjust the cut. I'm usually trying for an even cut (except when back-beveling a door), and this requires an even plane-iron projection. I like to examine the iron by looking from the back of the plane and catching a reflection from a light source. A bright line shows whether your setting is even. Make a trial pass at a board. Tap the front of a wooden plane to make the cut deeper, or the back to retract the blade. Is the thickness of the shaving consistent from side to side? Tap the upper edge of the plane iron to the side, or use the side adjustment lever if your plane has one, to make the cut even.

Steel soles can develop enough friction with the wood to make planing less pleasurable. Try drawing an S on the sole with a bit of paraffin to put the glide back in your stroke. The surface that appears in the wake of a well-tuned plane will justify the effort it takes to maintain and propel this traditional tool.

—*RIC HANISCH*
Hanisch is a woodworker in Quakertown, Pa., who has written numerous articles about woodworking.

pushing a little while, the high spots will have a dull sheen. Keep going until the sheen is uniform. If you have trouble judging the sheen, tint the sole with machinist's bluing.

Continue pushing the plane across the emery cloth. When you've sanded off all the bluing, the plane is flat.

Jeff Greef
Soquel, Calif.

DOUBLE BEVEL GAUGE

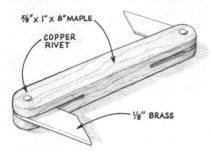

⅝" x 1" x 8" MAPLE

COPPER RIVET

⅛" BRASS

When measuring compound angles, it is very handy to have two bevel gauges in one. Boat builders have used such a tool for centuries. Make your own from a length of hard maple and some sheet brass. Use rivets for pivots.

> *Jim Tolpin*
> *Port Townsend, Wash.*

CUTTING PERFECT HINGE MORTISES

When making mortises for butt hinges, cut the sides with a chisel, but use a *router plane* to shave the bottom. This simple hand tool cuts a mortise, rabbet, dado, or any other recess to a uniform depth. It can also be used to shave the faces of tenons when fitting mortise-and-tenon joints.

> *Nick Engler*
> *West Milton, Ohio*

PREVENTING RUST ON SMALL TOOLS

To keep rust from forming on tools that you keep in enclosed spaces (such as tool boxes, drawers, or cupboards), keep a block of *camphor* with the tools. The camphor slowly evaporates and deposits an oily film on the metal surfaces. This, in turn, protects the surfaces from moisture and prevents rust from forming. Camphor is available in blocks or tablets from most drug stores.

> *Nick Engler*
> *West Milton, Ohio*

WAX THOSE TOOLS

Rub metal planes, hand saws, and power tools with paste wax to make the job go more easily and to prevent rust.

> *Ernie Conover*
> *Parkman, Ohio*

PROTECTING THE TIPS OF CHISELS

Protect the cutting edges of chisels by storing them in a canvas chisel roll or by covering the tips with loose slips made of cloth or leather. Do *not* use plastic tip protectors or the dipped polyethylene tip that may have come with the tool. Unlike leather and cloth, plastic does not allow moisture to evaporate. If even a small amount of moisture accumulates inside the plastic, or if the temperature in the shop fluctuates and the metal surfaces "sweat," the covered tips of the chisels will rust.

> *Nick Engler*
> *West Milton, Ohio*

Using Winding Sticks to Ensure a Flat Surface

You can joint the cup out of a board, or assemble a door or panel frame with tight and square joints, and still end up with a warped surface. The simplest way to check that a workpiece is flat is to lay the piece on a perfectly flat and clean workbench. The warp announces itself by forcing an up-turned board or assembly to rock on a flat surface.

Unfortunately, I can't remember the last time I saw a perfectly flat workbench in my shop. And at any rate, workbenches tend to disappear under jigs, hand tools, and hardened glue drippings. All is not lost, however. To check for warp quickly and accurately, I make up a pair of winding sticks.

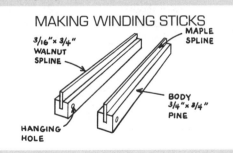

MAKING WINDING STICKS

3/16" x 3/4" WALNUT SPLINE

MAPLE SPLINE

BODY 3/4" x 3/4" PINE

HANGING HOLE

I begin by cutting grooves along two pieces of dry, straight-grained softwood as shown in *Making Winding Sticks*. Then I glue a thin spline of hardwood into the groove. The wider base makes the sticks stand up, while the thinner splines ensure greater accuracy. To make the sticks highly visible against one another, I make the splines from woods of contrasting colors, such as walnut and maple. It's important that the top of each spline be parallel to the bottom of each base. It's also crucial for both sticks to be the same height. To ensure both of these

conditions, I run the assembled sticks spline-up through my planer at the same setting.

I coat my sticks with varnish or shellac. This makes them pretty and helps keep them clean. But most important, it helps keep the sticks themselves from warping. Still, it's a good idea to check that your sticks are true before you use them. To do this, place one spline on top of the other and make sure they are in contact along the entire length.

I keep two sets of winding sticks handy: a 16-inch set for testing boards, and a 30-inch set for doors and panels. To use the winding sticks, place one at either end of the board or frame to be tested. Be sure to orient the sticks parallel to one another and perpendicular to the edge of the test piece. If the sticks aren't parallel, you won't get an accurate assessment of the twist. Sight across the sticks—I find it easier to sight the dark-splined stick against the light one. If any warp is present, the tops of the splines will clearly be in different planes. Note that the ample length of the sticks magnifies the degree of error, allowing you to see a twist as slight as $\frac{1}{10}$ degree.

—*JIM TOLPIN*

Tolpin is a professional woodworker and author in Port Townsend, Wash.

USING WINDING STICKS

SIGHT ACROSS THE WINDING STICKS TO SEE IF THEIR TOP EDGES ARE IN THE SAME PLANE.

NO-CLOG FILES

Soft, nonferrous metals like brass and aluminum will clog a file pretty quickly. Rub your file with a piece of chalk, and you'll find the file teeth won't clog as quickly.

Lazlo Spectrum
Tucson, Ariz.

IN QUEST OF THE PERFECT PLIERS

Flea markets are a good place to find unusual pliers that either are no longer made or are overpriced at hardware stores. Gas fitter's pliers are good for opening cans. Carpenter's pinchers are exceptional for removing nails.

Ernie Conover
Parkman, Ohio

QUICK TEST FOR TOOL HARDNESS

A metal file is a quick test for tool-steel hardness. If the file "skates" across the tool instead of digging in, the tool is Rockwell 55 or harder.

Ernie Conover
Parkman, Ohio

CIRCUIT TESTER TELLS THE SHOCKING TRUTH

A neon circuit tester (90 volts to 300 volts) is a good addition to your tool box. They cost about two dollars. If you are worried that a tool is not grounded, touch one tester lead to the tool and the other end to a ground. If the tester lights up, beware, you have a hot one. If you are working in wet conditions and are worried about shock hazard, touch one lead to the plugged-in tool and hold the other lead between two fingers. The neon has enough resistance that, at worst, you will feel only a tingle. But if the light lights up, you know that you are in for a real jolt if you touch the tool.

Ric Hanisch
Quakertown, Pa.

NAIL-PULLING WEDGE

This wedge is useful when pulling nails—especially large ones. Slide the wedge forward as you extract the nail so the fulcrum stays close to the head. It works equally well with a wrecking bar.

Robert Tupper
Canton, S.Dak.

Making and Using a Scratch Stock

Aspiring woodworkers often marvel over the fine border inlays, special moldings, and reeding and fluting that typify eighteenth- and nineteenth-century furniture. These details were all created with a simple tool called a scratch stock. Today, the router has largely supplanted this ancient technology. But in many instances, the scratch stock can be just as effective, if not more so, than its noisy, electric counterpart. What's more, you can make one with a number of different cutters for a fraction of the cost of one new router bit.

Make your scratch stock from a block of hardwood 1½ inches square × 8 inches long. Carve or turn one end on the lathe into a comfortable handle as shown in *Scratch Stock*. Cut away part of the other end to make the blade holder and create the fence. Make sure the fence cut is square to the axis of the handle as shown. Split the blade holder with a single saw kerf. Then drill three holes along its length for the tightening bolts. With three holes, you should have the flexibility to lock a blade anywhere along the length of the holder.

Make the blades from discarded handsaw blades. You can usually find old saws at flea markets for a dollar or two. Cut the desired profile(s) with a jeweler's saw, and refine the profile with a file. Make the edges square to the face of the blade. Some suggested shapes are shown in *Possible Blade Profiles*.

POSSIBLE BLADE PROFILES

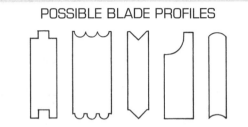

To use the scratch stock, slip the desired blade into the holder the appropriate distance from the fence. Lock it in place with a carriage bolt and wing nut. Start with just a little bit of the blade exposed. Draw the stock down the workpiece, guiding the fence along the piece's edge as shown in *Using a Scratch Stock*. Expose more of the blade as the depth of cut increases.

—*Christopher J. Semancik*
Semancik is a professional woodworker and boat builder in Kempton, Pa.

SCRATCH STOCK

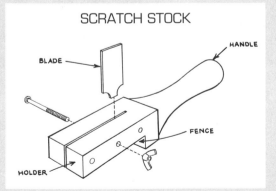

BLADE

HANDLE

FENCE

HOLDER

USING A SCRATCH STOCK

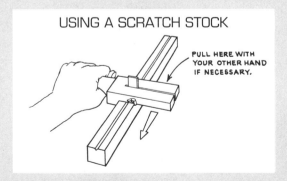

PULL HERE WITH YOUR OTHER HAND IF NECESSARY.

3 CLAMPING AND GLUING

QUICK 'N' EASY SPRING CLAMPS

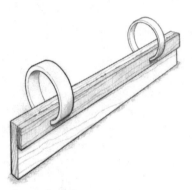

Saw 2- or 3-inch-diameter PVC pipe into rings an inch or so wide and then cut them open. They'll provide about 8 pounds of pressure when opened about an inch. They may not be as convenient as one-handed spring clamps, but since you'll get more than a hundred of them from a 10-foot length of PVC pipe, at least the price is right.

Tom Whalen
Cohoes, N.Y.

WOODEN WEDGE CLAMP

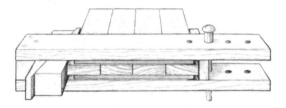

If you're like me, you never have enough clamps during assembly of a piece of furniture.

Here's a device I often use when joining boards edge to edge. I attach the end of two long 1 X 2 strips firmly to each side of a 2-inch block. At the other end, I drill holes for a ½-inch bolt.

In use, the assembly goes over the job, then a flat piece of wood goes against the bolt to prevent marking the wood. To tighten the "clamps" I drive two wedges, with slopes about 1 in 6, into place against the block. Hammered in from opposite sides, the wedges exert as much force as any screw clamp. An added bonus of this device is that you can keep the glued boards flat by inserting spacers under the strips—something you can't do with an ordinary bar clamp.

Percy Blandford
Stratford-upon-Avon, England

ANOTHER WOODEN WEDGE CLAMP

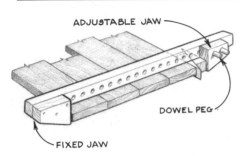

ADJUSTABLE JAW

DOWEL PEG

FIXED JAW

Long bar clamps are expensive and you need a lot of them. Here's an alternative you can make in your shop from any hardwood. I like to use maple because it's stable and extremely strong.

The bar is a 2 × 2-inch piece, cut to any length you desire. Make the jaws 2 × 4 × 6 inches; then taper them from 4 inches at one end to 2 inches at the other. Glue and screw the fixed jaw to one end of the bar. Drill two ¾-inch-diameter holes on 2-inch centers in the adjustable jaw. Drill matching holes in the bar, using the jaw as a drilling template. Make sure the top of the jaw is flush with the top of the bar when you drill. Cut along the diagonal of a 2 × 2½ × 6-inch piece of hardwood to make the wedges. Make the pegs for the adjustable jaw from 6-inch lengths of ¾-inch-diameter dowel.

To use the clamp, just position the adjustable jaw as close as possible to the edge of the work and tap the wedges into place with a mallet.

Jeff Greef
Soquel, Calif.

DOOR-SPRING CLAMPS

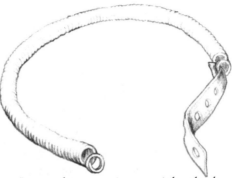

Long door springs with cloth straps attached to one end make good clamps for chairs, frames, and cylinders.

Bill Bigelow
Surry, N.H.

FIREHOSE CLAMP

To pull a stave-joined column together, forget about band clamps. Wrap a 1½-inch-diameter by 50-foot fire hose around the column like a barber pole. Make an overhand knot at each end and cap one end. Adapt the other end to fit on an air compressor, and pump it up to about 60 pounds per square inch. Leave the compressor on until the glue sets. It's a good idea to wrap the column in waxed paper so the hose doesn't get glued to the column.

Besides being cheaper than band clamps, this method is faster and will not dent the column.

Ben Erickson
Eutaw, Ala.

CLAMPING AT AN ANGLE

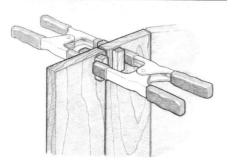

Here's the clamping method I use for gluing up splined boards that are at a slight angle to each other. I glue cardboard to both sides of each piece and then glue plywood blocks to the cardboard. Then I use spring clamps to hold the staves together.

Simon Watts
San Francisco, Calif.

AN EXTRA CLAMP

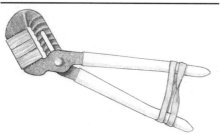

When we need just one or two more small clamps to finish a job, we use channel-lock pliers with stout rubber bands on the handles.

Alice and Robert Tupper
Canton, S. Dak.

BENCH-MOUNTED C-CLAMP

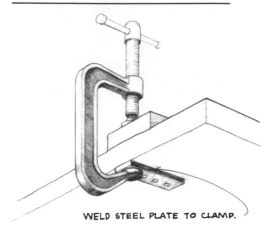

WELD STEEL PLATE TO CLAMP.

I use a fixed C-clamp mounted to my work table to hold parts in jigs and fixtures. It takes the place of expensive toggle clamps and is easy to use one-handed.

I weld a 1 × 5-inch length of ¼-inch-thick steel plate on the fixed end of the clamp. I usually locate the centerline of the plate on the centerline of the clamp. I predrill and countersink the plate for three or four #12 flathead screws, which fasten the plate to the underside of the table.

A 5- or 6-inch C-clamp such as a Jorgenson #175 or #176 offers plenty of throat depth. A battery of these clamps along one edge of the bench is great for laminating.

Patrick Warner
Escondido, Calif.

TURNBUCKLE AND CHAIN CLAMPS

I don't have clamps that will span more than 6 feet, so I use turnbuckle and chain clamps when I need to span

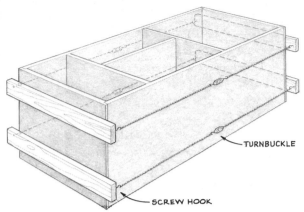

TURNBUCKLE

SCREW HOOK

long distances. Each clamp consists of two 2 × 4s cut about 6 inches longer than the width of the piece I'll clamp. I thread a screw hook into each end of the 2 × 4s as shown in the drawing. A length of chain runs from each screw hook to a turnbuckle. Twist the turnbuckle to tighten the chains and clamp the piece together.

As long as opposing 2 × 4s remain flat against the project, you'll know equal force is being applied on both sides. For a case such as the one shown, I'd use the turnbuckle and chain clamps along the length, and bar or pipe clamps to press the shelves into their dadoes.

Tom Groller
Palmerton, Pa.

NO-CLOG GLUE-BOTTLE CAP

For years I've confronted the problem of keeping the spout of my glue bottle flowing freely. I've solved the problem by drilling a hole through an electrical twist-on connector and pushing a 1½-inch roofing nail through the hole. The connector twists on the glue bottle spout, seals the opening, and prevents glue from hardening around the spout. The nail keeps the spout open.

Lyle E. Bohrer
Beaumont, Tex.

CAP HANG-UPS

Seal a tube of airplane cement, liquid solder, or whatever by putting a screw eye or screw hook in the opening. This tightly seals the tube, is easy to remove, and provides a convenient way to hang the tube on the wall. This is also a handy solution if you lose the cap to a plastic glue bottle.

Ralph S. Wilkes
Westport, N.Y.

GLUE-BOTTLE TOP SWAP

Replace the top of your glue bottle with a top from a liquid detergent bottle. The new top closes tight and there's no separate cap to come off and get lost.

Brian L. Otto
Chesterton, Ind.

PROTECT SURFACE WHEN GLUING CRACKED BOARD

When gluing a cracked board, it's difficult to keep glue off the board's face while working it into the crack. This causes a problem because glue seals the pores of the wood, so stain and finish will not penetrate.

Avoid the problem by applying masking tape close to each edge of the crack. If the crack is curved, use short pieces of tape, following the curve, or trim the tape with scissors. Some glue will squeeze out when the board is clamped. The squeeze-out will be on the tape instead of the wood, so you can easily remove it along with the tape after the glue has dried.

Ralph S. Wilkes
Branchport, N.Y.

GLUE CLEANUP BUCKET

Cut the top off a 1-gallon plastic milk jug to make a handy water bucket for cleaning up glue. Leave the handle so the bucket will indeed be handy.

Jeff Greef
Soquel, Calif.

CLEAN UP GLUE WITH A RAZOR BLADE

Clean glue squeeze-out from tight corners with a razor blade. Use a scraping action while the glue is still wet. Then wash the area of the workpiece with hot water and a rag.

Jeff Greef
Soquel, Calif.

WAXED-PAPER GLUE BARRIER

Put waxed paper between any parts you don't want to stick to each other during a glue-up. For example, put waxed paper between a curved form and bent laminations and between the laminations and the clamping cauls.

Jeff Greef
Soquel, Calif.

THE LAST STRAW

When glue squeezes out on the inside corner of a joint, you have some choices. You can smear it all over trying to wipe it up; you can risk tearing out wood fibers by letting it dry first and then chiseling it off; *or* you can scoop the glue up with a plastic straw. Push the straw into the corner just enough to make it conform to the joint but not enough to collapse the straw, then slide it along, scooping up the glue.

Robert L. Eskridge
Vandenberg AFB, Calif.

WAIT A BIT
BEFORE REMOVING GLUE

Let yellow glue squeeze-out semi-harden for 40 minutes or so and then skim it off with a chisel. This is more effective than wiping wet glue with a wet rag—wiping smears the glue into the grain to interfere with your finish. It's also a whole lot easier than scraping fully cured glue off the work.

Ric Hanisch
Quakertown, Pa.

PLYWOOD PROTECTS
BENCH FROM GLUE SPILLS

Cut a piece of cheap ¼-inch plywood to the same area dimensions as your workbench. Put the plywood on the bench during glue-ups to protect the bench from spills and drips.

Jeff Greef
Soquel, Calif.

PREVENT CLAMP STAINS

When bar or pipe clamps contact yellow glue or other water-based glues, they leave a dark stain on the work. Sometimes this stain can go fairly deep, especially in open-grained woods such as oak. To prevent this, put masking tape along the bars or pipes where they would come in contact with glue.

Jeff Greef
Soquel, Calif.

NO-HANDS CLAMP PADS

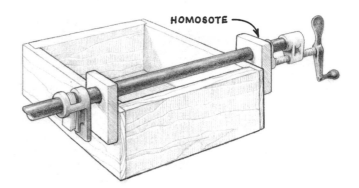

HOMOSOTE

You've got a bar clamp stretched across a project, with a scrap of wood under one jaw to protect the project. You reach to put a scrap under the other jaw. The clamp slips. The first scrap falls to the floor. Valuable glue-up time slips away.

Here's an easy way to avoid this common scenario. Cut squares of Homosote or similar fibrous building board. Drill the pieces to fit over your clamp pipes or cut them to fit bar clamps. Place two of these pads on each clamp between the jaws. Now you know your clamp pads will stay in place during the next glue-up.

Ralph S. Wilkes
Branchport, N.Y.

STYROFOAM CLAMP PADS

When laminating curved surfaces, I use 1- or 2-inch-thick Styrofoam as clamp pads. The pads form to the radius of the curved surface, resulting in even clamp pressure.

Brian J. O'Connor
Wolverine, Mich.

NO-SLIP CLAMP

When I use my bar clamps at an angle, I prevent the clamps from slipping with foam tape that has adhesive on both sides. It helps protect the wood, too. If necessary, a little naphtha removes leftover tape.

Margaret Scally
Albuquerque, N. Mex.

KINDER, GENTLER CLAMPS

To prevent metal clamps from marring wooden workpieces, cover the faces with leather. Cut a piece of leather slightly larger than the clamp face, and glue it to the clamp with epoxy.

Nick Engler
West Milton, Ohio

REMOVABLE CLAMP PADS

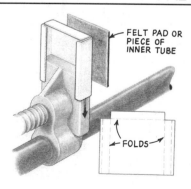

FELT PAD OR PIECE OF INNER TUBE

FOLDS

Glue-ups have been a lot less awkward since I made these removable pads for my bar clamps. I made them from sheet metal, cut as shown and bent around the clamp jaws. I protect the work with felt that I've fastened to the pads with rubber cement. Pieces of inner tube would make great pads, too.

Ralph S. Wilkes
Branchport, N.Y.

VISE-JAW CUSHIONS

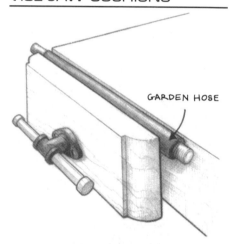

GARDEN HOSE

I protect dowels and threaded rod from vise jaws by slipping them into a piece of discarded garden hose before clamping them in the vise. Rubber automotive heater hose works for larger diameters.

Walter J. Morrison
Northport, N.Y.

ALTERNATE TREE CENTERS ON WIDE PANELS

When making wide panels by gluing boards together, alternate the direction of the annual rings. The

rings, visible in the end grain, show which way each board will warp. (The board will warp opposite the curve of the rings.) If five or six boards all cup in the same direction, the effect can be enough to make problems. Alternating the rings reduces the overall effect.

Jeff Greef
Soquel, Calif.

KEEP GLUE-UPS IN PLACE

To glue up awkward shapes that may slide under clamp pressure, drive small brads into one of the faces to be glued. Nip off the ends of the brads, leaving about 1/16 inch protruding. When the glue faces are clamped, the brads will prevent sliding.

Ric Hanisch
Quakertown, Pa.

USE BROWN GLUE FOR LONGER OPEN TIME

Use brown glue (urea-formaldehyde) instead of yellow glue (alaphatic resin) when you have a large glue-up with many parts that must go together all at once. Brown glue has a much longer open time than yellow glue, which sets after about 20 minutes.

Jeff Greef
Soquel, Calif.

SHAKE GLUE BUBBLES AWAY

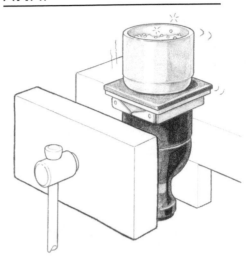

To get the bubbles out of plastic resin glue, clamp your orbital sander gently in a vise. Then hold the glue pot on the machine as it runs. The vibration from the sander will bring the bubbles and unmixed powder to the surface.

Kenneth S. Burton, Jr.
Allentown, Pa.

ONE STEP AT A TIME

Instead of juggling legs and aprons during a table glue-up, assemble the table in halves. First glue and clamp an apron between the front legs. Then glue and clamp the other apron between the back legs. Allow the glue to dry, and then glue the remaining aprons between the assembled leg pairs.

Ben Erickson
Eutaw, Ala.

ALIGNING BOARDS THE EASY WAY

When gluing up panels, it's nearly impossible to get all faces exactly flush. Whenever I am gluing up panels that aren't wider than my planer's capacity, I leave the stock ⅛ inch over final thickness when I glue it up. After removing the clamps, I scrape off the squeeze-out with a paint scraper. Then I run the panel through the planer two times on each side, taking ¹⁄₃₂ inch with each pass. The result is a flat panel that needs no hand planing and little scraping. For panels that are wider than my planer, I glue up sections that will go through the planer. Then I plane the sections to final thickness before gluing the sections together.

Tom Groller
Palmerton, Pa.

TWISTED CABINETS

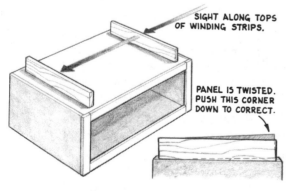

SIGHT ALONG TOPS OF WINDING STRIPS.

PANEL IS TWISTED. PUSH THIS CORNER DOWN TO CORRECT.

A case can be square and still be racked, or twisted. Old-timers called such cases out-of-wind (rhymes with *bind*) and knew they could be the devil to install doors and drawers in. They checked their cabinets with winding strips.

To make winding strips, cut two strips exactly the same width and about 20 inches long from contrasting woods. Put a strip near one edge of a surface, and put the second strip near an opposite edge. (Which surface you choose depends on the assembly. The top surface is usually the handiest.) Sight across the top edge of one strip at the top edge of the other strip. If the corner of one strip is higher than the corner of the other strip, loosen the clamps, and gently press down on the high corners of the assembly. When you've pushed the corners into alignment, tighten the clamps and recheck.

M. S. Langley
Detroit, Mich.

A SLIGHTLY DIFFERENT TWIST

Doors can be out-of-wind, too. I check them using two 24-inch rulers from my machinist's square. Put a ruler on each rail, and sight across them, just like winding sticks. If a corner of one ruler is higher than the corner of the other strip, loosen the clamps and gently twist the door until the strips align. Tighten the clamps and recheck. You'll find the door is least likely to twist if the center of each clamp screw is aligned with the center of the door.

Malden Rand
Huntington, W.Va.

GLUING CIRCULAR SEGMENTS

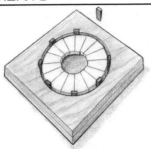

I cut a circle in a piece of ¾-inch plywood to make a jig for gluing together segments of a circle for rings or frames. The diameter of the hole should be about ⅛ inch to 3/16 inches larger than the diameter of the circular segments.

Clamp the plywood jig on a piece of ¾-inch plywood with waxed paper between to keep the segments from sticking to the plywood underneath.

Assemble the segments inside the circle, then push or drive small wooden wedges between the jig and the segments. The wedges push each segment toward the center and close up the gaps between segments.

C. E. Rannefeld
Decatur, Ala.

CLAMPING WOOD EDGING

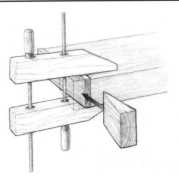

If you want to install edging on a shelf or counter and don't have any edging clamps, try small, wooden handscrews instead. Apply the edging strips and then position the clamps, leaving a gap of about ½ inch between the screws and the edging strip. Tap wedges into the gap until you see glue squeezing out. If the edging is slightly wider than the countertop, toe in the clamp slightly.

Dave Sellers
Emmaus, Pa.

INJECT-A-DOWEL

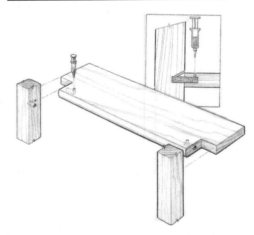

I needed invisible support for the front edge of a stair tread in a modernistic staircase, but there was no way to assemble the structure with a dowel. So I bored matching holes plus a ⅛-inch injection hole and a vent hole, then injected epoxy to fill the cavity. When the epoxy cured, I had a hard plastic dowel right where I needed it.

Trebor Narom
Onaled, N. Mex.

HOT-SPOT GLUE

Tired of the frustration of gluing small pieces of wood in hard-to-clamp places, I developed this technique: Spread glue on both surfaces to be joined, but leave a small area bare. On this area, apply a spot of hot-melt glue. Hold the two parts together for a few seconds until the hot glue grabs. Don't put any strain on the joint until the glue has cured.

Manuel Avalos
Doylestown, Pa.

VACUUM BAGGING ON THE CHEAP

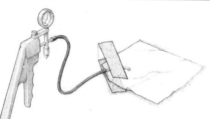

No need to blow your bait and beer money on a $400 vacuum pump. For small projects—veneering jewelry boxes, for example—I use a Ziploc resealable freezer bag attached to a hand-operated vacuum pump. These simple pumps (Mityvac is one brand) are made to bleed brake systems, cost around $30, and are available in most auto-parts stores. To make a leakproof seal where the tube enters the bag, snip one corner off the bag, insert the tube, and lay a piece of duct tape underneath it, sticky-side up. Put another piece on top and firmly flatten everything out.

Michael Chilquist
Pittsburgh, Pa.

MITER-CLAMPING BLOCK

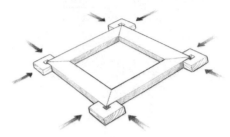

These clamping blocks let you clamp miters with bar or pipe clamps placed parallel to the edges of the frame. Make them from 2- or 3-inch-square blocks of plywood or solid wood. Be sure to notch out the little space to prevent crushing the outside corner of the miter.

Jeff Greef
Soquel, Calif.

LEAVE LEEWAY WHEN EDGE-BANDING

When edge-banding plywood, cut the banding ⅛ inch wider than the thickness of the plywood. This will allow you a little room for error as you glue the banding in place. Once the glue has dried you can easily trim the banding flush with a hand plane.

Kenneth S. Burton, Jr.
Allentown, Pa.

TRIMMING WOODEN EDGING

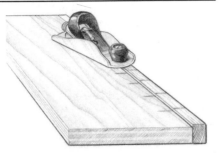

Solid-wood strips are often glued to the edges of plywood shelves or tabletops. Because it's often difficult to align the strips perfectly with the plywood, cabinetmakers usually glue on strips a bit wider than the plywood. But planing them flush with the plywood can be a problem. If you plane too deeply, you'll cut through the face veneer on the plywood. To avoid this, I draw several short pencil lines across the glue joint, as shown. I watch these lines and stop planing as soon as they disappear.

James Schenfield
Dayton, Ohio

BUMP EXTRACTOR

Anyone working with laminates knows how annoying it is to discover a lump under the surface. I use an old hacksaw blade as a "bump extractor."

Here's how it works: I smooth out the hacksaw teeth on a grinder and then grind a hook at one end of the blade as shown. If a lump shows up, I heat the end of the blade with a torch, slip it in between the laminate and the substrate, and grab the alien particle. It works every time.

Brian Gillespie
Newfoundland, N.J.

CLAMPLESS GLUE BOND

When clamping small pieces of wood in hard-to-reach places, you can still get a good glue bond without a clamp. Put glue on the block, put it in position, and slide it back and forth so it travels about an inch. Apply hand pressure as you slide it. It will begin to grab, and sliding will get more difficult. Stop the block where you want it, and you have a good glue bond.

David Page
Swarthmore, Pa.

SHOP-MADE GLUE SCRAPER

Here is a very effective glue scraper you can make from a piece of old planer or jointer knife. Cut a piece of hardwood to about 2 X 2 X

6 inches. Shape it on the band saw for a comfortable grip, and round-over the top edges with sandpaper. Cut a kerf in one end to snuggly hold the knife. If you don't have an old planer or jointer knife, you can grind a bevel onto any piece of steel that's about ⅛ inch thick.

Jeff Greef
Soquel, Calif.

GLUING UP POLYGONS

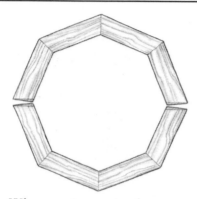

When trying to make a many-sided project, whether flat like a picture frame or coopered like an architectural column, tiny angle errors accumulate and become a big error when all of the parts are brought together. Instead of fiddling endlessly with impossibly fine adjustments of each angle, I glue up the parts in two halves. I then plane the mating surfaces to fit before gluing the two halves together to make the whole.

Glenn Hughes
Emmaus, Pa.

SLIPPING BAR CLAMPS

When the adjustable ends of your bar or pipe clamps begin to slip after much use, flip the angled plates that provide the grip. The edges of the plates get rounded with use so they no longer grip. Flipping them gives you fresh, sharp edges. To flip the plates, remove the stop pin on the end of the bar and remove the adjustable end. Carefully remove and flip the plates, noting the position of the spring. Replace the end and stop pin.

Jeff Greef
Soquel, Calif.

SUBSTITUTE FOR LONG CLAMPS

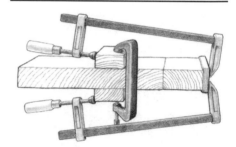

When your glue-up is longer than your clamps, or when there is no place on the work to locate the opposite end of the clamp, use this clamping arrangement to pull parts together. Use a C-clamp to secure a cleat on the top surface and one below. Then use bar or pipe clamps between the cleats and edge of the workpiece as shown. To keep the glue-up flat, always use the long clamps in pairs, one above and one below.

Jeff Greef
Soquel, Calif.

CLAMPING-BLOCK POSITION IS IMPORTANT

RAISE OR LOWER CLAMP BLOCKS TO ELIMINATE BOWING.

If a door or frame begins to bow during glue-up, raising or lowing the clamp blocks may solve the problem. The position of the pads affects where the pressure is applied. If the ends near the clamps are rising, lower the clamps, and vice versa.

Jeff Greef
Soquel, Calif.

ADJUST CLAMPS TO SQUARE CABINET

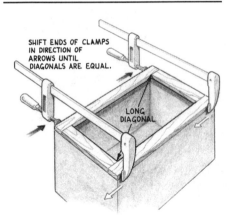

SHIFT ENDS OF CLAMPS IN DIRECTION OF ARROWS UNTIL DIAGONALS ARE EQUAL.

LONG DIAGONAL

During glue-up, check that your cabinet is square by measuring its diagonals. They should be equal. If not, adjust the clamps until they are. Here's how. Loosen the clamps and tilt them so they're all sloping in the same general direction as the long diagonal. As you retighten the clamps, the pressure will squeeze the long diagonal, shortening it and bringing the cabinet into square. Check your measurements as you're tightening the clamps, and double-check them once you're done.

Jeff Day
Perkasie, Pa.

NO-STICK CLAMP BLOCKS

When gluing up a tabletop, I've always put ¼-inch blocks between the clamps and the tabletop. This both protects the surface and also raises the boards, centering pressure along the edge of the boards. Sometimes the blocks stick and take a piece of the table with them when I pry them loose. To prevent this, I now use blocks make of Plexiglas or pre-finished plywood paneling.

Ben Erickson
Eutaw, Ala.

PUT A BAR CLAMP IN REVERSE

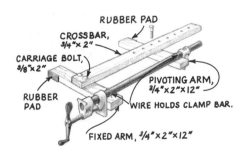

RUBBER PAD

CROSSBAR, ¾"x 2"

CARRIAGE BOLT, ⅜"x 2"

PIVOTING ARM, ¾"x 2"x 12"

RUBBER PAD

WIRE HOLDS CLAMP BAR.

FIXED ARM, ¾"x 2"x 12"

Here's a handy device for putting your bar clamps in reverse so you can use them to gently disassemble furniture for repair. The device has a fixed arm secured to a crossbar with two *(continued on page 48)*

What You Should Know about Animal Hide Glue

Animal hide glue is the oldest wood glue. It has been found on objects excavated from the tombs of the ancient Egyptian pharaohs. Animal hide glue can be made by cooking almost any animal skin, but in modern times cowhides are usually used.

Until the mid-twentieth century, hide glue was the most common choice for furniture and many other wooden objects. After the introduction of white glue in the early 1950s, hide glue fell out of favor because it requires more effort to use. Hide glue must be prepared in advance, is applied hot, and should be thrown out after about a week (sooner if the weather is hot). Once prepared, hide glue is like meat—it spoils. Clumps of bacterial growth develop in the glue, the odor worsens, and the glue doesn't cure as hard. In contrast, white and yellow glue require no preparation, can be applied at room temperature, and have a shelf life of several years.

Characteristics of Hide Glue

Despite the difficulties using hide glue, many furniture restorers and musical instrument makers like it for two reasons. Hide glue has a quick initial grip, and it can be redissolved for reuse.

Hot animal hide glue bonds in two steps. The initial grip occurs when the glue cools to about 95 degrees Fahrenheit. The bond becomes total when all the water evaporates out of the glue. The initial grip allows you to glue two pieces of wood together without clamps. Simply apply the glue to both surfaces and rub the pieces together to work out all the excess glue. When the glue cools to 95 degrees, the pieces will stick. Position them the way you want, and let the glue cure to complete the bonding. The glue blocks you see on the inside corners of old cabinet furniture were positioned with this "rub joint" technique. It's not uncommon to see glue blocks still in place after 200 years.

A rub joint can be used to replace broken carvings, pieces of veneer, and other parts that would be difficult to clamp. Neither white nor yellow glue offers enough tack to make this type of glue bond possible.

Once the liquid glue cools below 95 degrees, it gels and becomes unworkable. So you have to work fast or keep the air and wood very warm while you are applying the glue.

Not only does hide glue dissolve initially in hot water, it redissolves in hot water—even after a century or more. Because of this, you can apply new hot hide glue over old hide glue and the two will melt together. You can therefore reglue old furniture without removing all the old glue first, as you must if you are using any other kind of glue. Simply remove the loose and powdered glue from the joint, apply the new hot hide glue, and reassemble. (If you use any other glue, wash off all the old hide glue first with hot water, let the wood dry thoroughly, then apply the glue and reassemble.)

You can also release the glue bond in old joints that haven't come apart by injecting hot water or steam into the joint or by heating the joint with a heat gun or blow dryer. This is rather involved, in most cases. An easier technique is to inject denatured alcohol into the joint using a syringe. The alcohol will cause the glue to crystallize, allowing you then to knock the joint apart using a leather or plastic mallet.

Using Hide Glue

Most hide glue comes in solid (flake or pearl) form. You heat the glue with water to liquefy it to the thickness of white glue. Use a ratio of about 3 cups of water to 1 pound of glue, but make only as much as you can use in a few days. Let the glue soak in the water for 30 minutes before applying the heat. Heat the glue to at least 130 degrees Fahrenheit, but don't let it boil.

The glue will remain liquid as long as you keep it above 130 degrees. When the glue cools, it gels, and you will have to reheat it to use it. You can buy a special electric glue pot to heat the glue. Or you can simply put a small pot or jar containing the glue into a larger pot of water that you keep hot on a stove.

If a skin forms on the glue (due to contact with the cooler air), stir it back in. It won't weaken the glue significantly. But the glue will become thicker, due to water evaporation, and you'll eventually need to add more water. It's good practice to hold the moisture in and prevent the skin from forming by keeping the container covered when you're not using the glue. A plastic coffee-can lid works well as a cover.

Hide glue often smells like rotten meat when it is heated. Many people find this odor offensive enough that they don't use the glue. The odor is caused by bacteria that weren't removed when the glue was manufactured. The sole remaining American hide-glue factory, Milligan & Higgens, takes extra care to clean their glue, and it thus has very little odor. You can buy small quantities from The Olde Mill Cabinet Shoppe, RD 3, Box 547-A, Camp Betty Washington Road, York, PA 17402.

Liquid Hide Glue

Hide glue is also available at many hardware stores in liquid form. Liquid hide glue contains gel depressants to keep the glue liquid at room temperature plus preservatives to keep the glue from rotting for about a year. Don't use the glue past the expiration date stamped on the container.

Liquid hide glue can be redissolved just like hot hide glue, but it doesn't have an initial grip, it doesn't fuse with old hide glue unless applied hot, and it weakens in hot, humid weather. Its advantage over hot hide glue is its long open time (even longer than white glue's), which makes it easier to use when there are many parts to be glued simultaneously.

—*BOB FLEXNER*
Flexner is the author of Understanding Wood Finishing, *published by Rodale Press. He is a professional wood finisher in Norman, Okla., and has written extensively on the topic.*

carriage bolts. The pivoting arm is attached with one carriage bolt. Drill several holes in the crossbar so you can adjust the device for different situations. Position rubber pads as shown to protect the workpiece and to keep the device from slipping. The clamp's bar slips through wires at the ends of the arms to keep it in place. Make the device from hardwood so it will be strong.

Ralph S. Wilkes
Branchport, N.Y.

CLAMPING RACK FOR PIPE CLAMPS

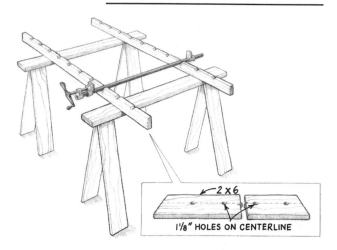

2 X 6

1⅛" HOLES ON CENTERLINE

Make a clamping rack for pipe clamps by drilling 1⅛-inch holes every 8 inches or so along the centerline of a 2 X 6. Rip the two-by in half, creating a pair of supports with matched half-circles that serve to cradle the pipes, keeping them aligned, level, and evenly spaced.

Jim Tolpin
Port Townsend, Wash.

ANOTHER PIPE-CLAMP RACK

Gluing up can either be a pleasant experience or a nightmare. Clamp arrangement and planning ahead can mean the difference between success and failure.

I've developed a sawhorse-type clamp rack that holds ¾-inch pipe clamps upright and at equal spacing during glue-ups.

To make the tops of the racks, I edge-glue two 5-foot lengths of 2 X 6, then drill equally spaced 1-inch-diameter holes down the center. Then I rip the piece down the middle.

Lee Maughan
Panaca, Nev.

CLAMPING AID

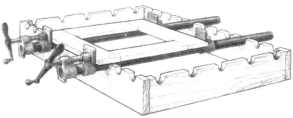

I keep my pipe clamps level, parallel, and properly spaced for glue-ups by arranging them in notches in a frame, as shown. I cut the notches ¾ inch deep, so the upper surface of the pipes remain above the surface of the notched frame.

Mark McClain
Rawlins, Wyo.

GETTING GLUE INTO DOWEL HOLES

To get glue into dowel holes, use a piece of dowel whittled down to fit easily into the hole.

Jeff Greef
Soquel, Calif.

ROLL ON THE GLUE

Spread glue over large areas with a paint roller and tray. Cheap disposable rollers for applying construction adhesive are available at hardware stores.

Jeff Greef
Soquel, Calif.

GET GLUE INTO HARD-TO-REACH PLACES

Use a syringe and needle to get glue into hard-to-reach places such as splits and splintered tear-outs.

Jeff Greef
Soquel, Calif.

GLUE SPREADER

We often spread glue with an old credit card that we've notched along one edge with pinking shears. For a

thinner layer of glue, we just nick the edge of the card with the pinking shears to make smaller notches.

Alice and Robert Tupper
Canton, S. Dak.

GLUE BLOCKS FOR MITERED CORNERS

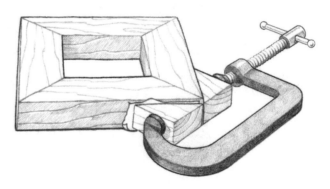

Glue mitered corners with the help of 45-degree blocks. Glue the blocks in place with a piece of grocery bag paper between the block and the case. Clamp across the blocks to close the miter. After the glue dries, pop the block off with a chisel. Sand or scrape off the paper that remains on the case. Put the glue on the block, rather than on the case, to make cleanup easier.

David Page
Swarthmore, Pa.

Glues Used in Woodworking

Type	Primary Usage	Positive Qualities
Yellow Aliphatic Resin (Carpenter's Wood Glue)	General-purpose wood glue. Most commonly used for laminations and joint assemblies. For interior structures only.	High strength (stronger than the wood) with setup times less than an hour at room temperature. Resistant to high humidity, cleans up with water, and sands relatively easily.
White Aliphatic Resin (Elmer's Glue-All)	General-purpose wood, paper, and fabric adhesive. Commonly used to attach paper to wood, canvas to tambour slats, and wood veneers to substrates.	White glue is closely related to yellow glue. Both glues share similar strength, setup time, and humidity resistance. But unlike yellow glue, white glue remains slightly flexible when fully set up, so that it maintains strength as joints flex.
Cross-Linked Aliphatic Glue (Titebond II)	General-purpose wood glue. Used to laminate and join wood in projects that may come into occasional contact with water or be subjected to high humidity.	Retains high strength and creep resistance, even when subjected to short periods of total submersion in water. Exhibits some strength over gaps of less than $1/32$ inch. Setup time is slightly faster than for other aliphatics.
Hide Glue	Traditionally used for nearly all types of wood product construction. Now used primarily for furniture restoration and assembly of musical instruments.	Sets up to high strength, yet easily comes apart when lightly steamed—a plus for instrument makers and fine furniture builders facing delicate repairs. Bonds to old hide glue (useful for restoration work). Unlike other glues, it takes stains similarly to wood. Long shelf life.
Urea-Formaldehyde (Weldwood's Plastic Resin Glue)	Before the introduction of epoxy, this was the glue of choice for exterior applications. Still a good alternative to epoxy for joining and laminating wood in outdoor furniture and boat fittings.	Waterproof in most exterior applications (excluding immersion in hot water). Powder must be mixed with water, though proportions are not very critical. Long working time (up to 20 minutes). Tan-colored glue line is relatively inconspicuous.
Epoxy	The most common glue product in use today for assembly of exterior wooden structures and for joining dissimilar materials.	Completely waterproof and extremely strong, even when joining poorly prepared or highly dissimilar surfaces. Does not lose strength over a gap. Some epoxies can achieve full strength in unusually wet and cold conditions. Can be mixed with a variety of fillers and pigments to achieve different consistencies and colors. Requires only enough clamping pressure to hold objects together.
Cyanoacrylate (Super Glue)	Now widely used in model making, construction of miniatures, and small-scale repair work.	Small amount of product forms an extremely strong bond that sets up almost instantaneously. The joint is waterproof and some formulations are strong across a gap. The glue line is nearly invisible.
Hot-Melt	Most often used by woodworkers to temporarily hold small wood components in position for fastening. It's also commonly used to bond cardboard or thin slats of wood when forming mock-ups and layout templates.	Hot-melt glue sets up in seconds and can bond two dissimilar or poorly surfaced materials. It is completely waterproof.

NEGATIVE QUALITIES	SPECIAL CAUTIONS
Allows joints subjected to moisture changes to creep over time. Lacks strength over a gap—joining surfaces must be tightly fitted and securely clamped. Working time is 15 minutes or less. Exhibits a short shelf life—less than a year. Fails if immersed in water.	Overclamping can squeeze out too much of this relatively thin glue, weakening the joint. Glue squeeze-out must be thoroughly removed from wood—it will not take a stain or finish. This glue is nontoxic.
Lacks gap-filling strength and has a relatively short shelf life (though somewhat longer than yellow glue). Tends to run more than yellow glue, which makes it more difficult to use in vertical applications. Joints must be tight and well clamped. The flexible glue line is difficult to sand.	Because white glue is even less resistant to moisture than yellow glue, avoid using it on objects that might come in any contact with water or damp conditions. This glue is nontoxic.
Like other aliphatics, this glue requires relatively tight-fitting surfaces clamped until the glue sets up. Working time is 5 minutes or less. The glue has a limited shelf life.	While highly moisture resistant, this glue is not considered by the manufacturer to be totally water-proof. Not recommended for exterior conditions. Nontoxic.
Slow setup time; requires relatively high air temperature (70°F plus). Lacks strength across gaps. Will fail in high humidity. Glue must be warmed to at least 140°F for application.	Because hide glue takes up to 24 hours to reach full strength, assembled parts must be handled carefully after unclamping. Nontoxic, though you may not like the smell.
To reach full strength, surfaces must be tightly clamped for 12 to 24 hours. Relatively thick glue line is not strong across gaps.	Because this glue contains formaldehyde, it should be kept away from the skin. Avoid inhaling fumes. If not thoroughly mixed, lumps can increase width of glue line.
Resin and hardener must be carefully measured and mixed to ensure full strength. Overclamping can squeeze out a thin glue line, weakening joint. Most formulations require clamping and setup times of 2 to 24 hours. This solvent-resistant glue is difficult to clean up. Epoxy is a very expensive glue.	This glue is toxic—keep it off your skin and avoid breathing fumes. Exposure causes allergic reactions in some people. Five-minute epoxies are good for small repairs and small moldings but are not strong enough for load-bearing situations.
Open working time is very short—measured in seconds. While the joint is strong, it is brittle, and impact may cause failure. The shelf life is less than a year (unless kept refrigerated). Very expensive and too volatile for use on large surfaces.	This glue instantaneously bonds skin as well as wood, and a special solvent is required to free yourself. Acetone can be used, but it is slow. Fumes irritate eyes and can cause allergic reactions in some people.
Although it can bond across a gap, hot-melt does not offer much strength. The glue is messy and difficult to clean up.	Hot-melt glue is hot enough to burn you and must be applied with caution. Not strong enough to permanently join wood without mechanical fasteners.

—*JIM TOLPIN*
Tolpin is a professional woodworker and author in Port Townsend, Wash.

MASKING TAPE TO THE RESCUE

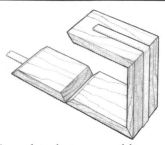

I used to hate assembling mitered boxes, because the pieces slipped during glue-up. Then I discovered masking tape. Stretch the tape, sticky-side up, across your workbench. Put the box parts on the tape in order—front, side, back, side—so that the miters touch. Now you can simply fold the pieces up so they form a box. Apply glue, and clamp in a band clamp.

Jeff Day
Perkasie, Pa.

MORE ON TAPE

If you don't have enough clamps to glue a long strip of molding onto a cabinet, apply pressure with masking tape. Simply stick the tape to one face of the cabinet, stretch it over the molding, and stick the tape to another face of the cabinet.

Rob Yoder
Quakertown, Pa.

A STICKY SOLUTION

Running crown molding around a built-in cabinet can be tricky. If you have trouble nailing the molding to the ceiling, attach it with construction adhesive instead. This adhesive comes in a caulking gun tube, and it works even if the ceiling has been painted. Put a bead of adhesive on the molding surface that will contact the ceiling. Press the molding into place, then nail the molding to the cabinet. Angle your nails slightly upward so they will push the molding into the ceiling. Use a putty knife to scrape off any adhesive that squeezes out. An added attraction: The adhesive fills any small gaps between the ceiling and the molding.

Glenn Bostock
Rushland, Pa.

CLAMPING FRAMES

It's easy to rack drawers, stiles and rails, and other assemblies out-of-square while clamping. To prevent this I use plywood gluing frames. Just cut a piece of ¾-inch plywood a little shorter and narrower than the assembly you will glue up. Make sure this base is square. Then screw plywood fences to two adjacent sides. Put the assembly in the frame, and clamp across the fences to the opposite side of the assembly. You can also clamp the assembly down to the base to make sure it remains flat. With a little practice, you can use the frames to glue up two or three frame-and-panel assemblies at once. Before clamping, stack the assemblies on top of each other in the frame with waxed paper between them.

Edwin Sheriff
Birmingham, Ala.

FINISHING TOUCHES

We all know that glue on a door panel means tragedy. The door sticks in the frame and eventually cracks. But waxing the corners creates problems of its own. A little extra wax in the wrong places will ruin the finish. Instead of waxing, I prefinish the entire door panel. Glue won't stick to the finish, and I've got a nicely finished panel to look at while I work.

Rob Yoder
Quakertown, Pa.

YOUR DRAWERS, SIR

Lots of people check to make sure their cabinets aren't racked but then forget about the drawers. Best time to check is before the glue dries. About 10 minutes after clamping up the drawer, remove the clamps and slip the drawer in its opening. If the drawer doesn't sit flat, push down gently on the high corners. Check for twist again. Once you've got it right, there's no need to reclamp. The dovetails will hold the drawer together.

David Page
Swarthmore, Pa.

CAULS COUNTER BOWING

Pressure from clamps can make a wide glued-up panel bow. Applying

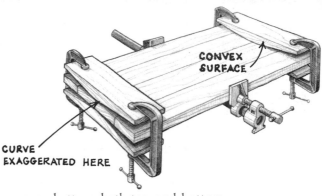

CONVEX SURFACE

CURVE EXAGGERATED HERE

convex battens both top and bottom will counter this pressure. Give the cauls a coat of paste wax to keep the glue from sticking.

Jeff Day
Perkasie, Pa.

QUICK-CHANGE VISES

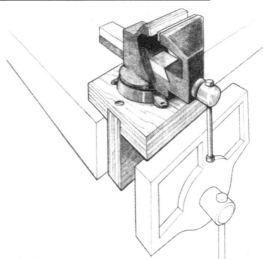

I had no room to mount a machinist's vise on my workbench, so I mounted the vise on a T-shaped wooden base. When I need the vise, I clamp the base in the jaws of my woodworking vise.

Clarence H. Fraley
Loyall, Ky.

Clamps

If you have done any woodworking at all, it is a good bet that you have used some kind of clamp to help you do it. Clamps are a woodworker's third hand—holding pieces of wood together while you glue or otherwise fasten them together. Wielding the power of the threaded incline, clamps can also force stubborn pieces of wood into alignment or move entire assemblies into square.

Today, there are almost as many types of clamps as there are ways to use them. In general, however, these tools fall into five categories: sash, throat, spring, band, and vise clamps. Sash and throat clamps are the real workhorses in the shop, holding and drawing together components of all sizes and functions. Spring clamps offer a quick and gentle hand for holding small components in position to be glued or fastened. Band-type clamps do the oddball stuff, drawing together assemblies of varying shapes or sizes. Finally, vise clamps hold miter joints in position while you fasten them together.

Sash Clamps

Sash clamps include the ubiquitous pipe clamp—probably the clamp most commonly found in a woodworker's shop. This pipe clamp works by enclosing the wood between two pressure points: a stop that slides along the pipe and a screw head fixed to one end. Because these fittings can be installed on any length of pipe, the width capacity of a pipe clamp is unlimited. The use of a pipe for the sash bar lends another nice attribute—it can be bent to accommodate a curved lamination. A throated variety of pipe clamp accommodates thicker stock.

For heavy-duty clamping, such as pulling together thick hardwood boards edge to edge, a steel I-beam sash clamp provides more force and rigidity than a pipe clamp. Unfortunately, the fixtures are locked to the I-beam, permanently limiting the capacity to the length of the I-beam. Some sash clamps feature bars made from square aluminum extrusions—a lightweight alternative that provides ample strength for many applications. Because aluminum does not react with glues and wood resins, these clamps do not stain the wood as steel bars often do. However, aluminum clamps aren't strong enough for some jobs; I wouldn't use them to edge-glue large panels.

Another variety of sash clamp, called a Wedgegrip jaw clamp, operates in an entirely different way than the standard pressure-point clamp—it squeezes the parts together between a wedge and a screw head. Because the bar does not have to carry a pressure point to the opposite edge of the work, the clamp need only be about a foot long. As a result, these clamps are lightweight and easy to handle. They are very convenient for gluing up large face frames.

Throat Clamps

Throat-type clamps include sliding-bar "speed clamps," fixed-throat C-clamps, and wood-bodied handscrews. Because they have no bar to support and help align the wood, throat clamps are rarely used for

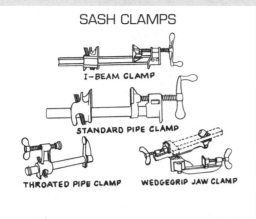

SASH CLAMPS

I-BEAM CLAMP

STANDARD PIPE CLAMP

THROATED PIPE CLAMP   WEDGEGRIP JAW CLAMP

SLIDING-BAR SPEED CLAMP   K-BODY CLAMP   GUITAR MAKER'S THROATED CLAMP

DEEP-THROATED SLIDING-BAR CLAMP

EDGE CLAMP

QUICK-GRIP   WOOD-BODIED HAND SCREW   C-CLAMP

THROAT CLAMPS

sion of the throat clamp goes one step further, by sliding to the stock and then clamping down tight with a one-handed operation.

Among the specialty sliding-bar clamps are K-body clamps. They feature broad, nonmarring jaws with flat, parallel surfaces—perfect for clamping together case assemblies. To protect the fragile and valuable parts of musical instrument assemblies, the jaws of guitar maker's throat clamps are made from cork-covered wood. The cam-action clamping head provides a firm but sensitive feel to the clamping pressure, reducing the risk of overtightening. Deep-throated varieties of sliding-bar clamps allow you to apply pressure up to 12 inches away from the bar.

A throat-type clamp standard is the common C-clamp. These are quick to apply, once you get the hang of spinning them open or closed with one hand, and extremely durable and powerful. They come in all sizes, from 1-inch openings to 10 inches or more. A specialized version adds a second screw head, turning the tool into an edging clamp.

Finally, the traditional wood-bodied handscrew has hardwood jaws that go easy on the stock, while their broad contact surfaces can exert enormous clamping pressure. The double opposed-threaded screws speed up opening and closing the clamp, and they allow the jaws to be set at angles other than parallel—a feature you won't find in other clamps.

edge-gluing thin stock. They are suited to exerting a high force over a limited surface area; drawing the parts of a joint together is one typical application.

Speed clamps well deserve their name. The screw head slides to the stock, requiring only a quick twist on the screw lever to snug down the clamp. The Quick-Grip ver-

(continued)

Clamps—Continued

Spring Clamps

When just a bit of clamping pressure is needed to hold small or awkwardly shaped parts, a spring clamp is often the perfect tool for the job. Be sure to only use spring clamps with protective plastic coatings on the jaw tips to minimize marring. These clamps are available in a wide range of sizes, with openings spanning from less than 4 inches to a full foot.

A specialized form of spring clamp, called a miter clamp, pulls together miter joints. The sharply pointed tips of the clamping ring dig into the wood and force the pieces together. Finish nails may be driven into these holes after the clamps are removed.

Band Clamps

When conventional sash or throat clamps will not do the job, the next tool to come out of the toolbox is often a band clamp. With the webbing run out and strung around the object, a racheting winch then draws the banding tight. This clamp can handle most any shape or size of object. A drawback is that all points under the webbing receive equal pressure—if certain areas need more clamping strength, they may not get it with the band clamp alone.

Specially designed band clamps are used to draw mitered frames together. The webbing carries three adjustable corner blocks, while the fourth block is permanently fixed to the winch handle. Although this clamp pulls the corners snugly together, it cannot ensure that the assembly is flat, and it

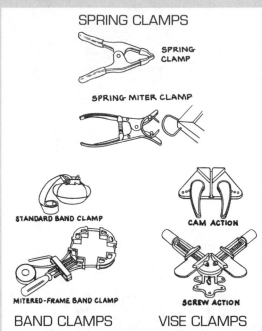

SPRING CLAMPS

SPRING CLAMP

SPRING MITER CLAMP

STANDARD BAND CLAMP

CAM ACTION

MITERED-FRAME BAND CLAMP

SCREW ACTION

BAND CLAMPS   VISE CLAMPS

should be used along with weights and a level support surface.

Vise Clamps

Another clamp designed to draw together miter joints consists of a double-headed vise. This clamp holds one corner of a frame together at a perfect 90-degree angle, allowing you to nail it before moving on to the next corner. Some varieties feature a cam-clamping action rather than a screw action, making them quicker to use. While most of these clamps are designed to mount on the workbench, others are portable, allowing you to move the tool rather than the entire frame—a distinct advantage when assembling larger frames.

—JIM TOLPIN

4
SHARPENING AND GRINDING

FLATTENING SHARPENING STONES

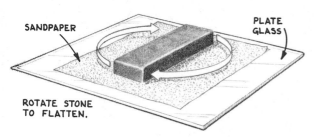

SANDPAPER

PLATE GLASS

ROTATE STONE TO FLATTEN.

To restore a flat surface to a worn sharpening stone, grind it on a piece of 120-grit wet/dry sandpaper. Lay the sandpaper on top of a piece of plate glass, flood it with water, and grind away. When the stone's face has a very even appearance, you're done.

Ernie Conover
Parkman, Ohio

KEEPING WATERSTONES FLAT

You can keep waterstones flat by rubbing them against each other after every few uses. Do this only with stones of nearly the same grit, and use plenty of water. You'll quickly learn to feel when they're flat.

Ric Hanisch
Quakertown, Pa.

TUPPERWARE TO THE RESCUE

After putting up with a wet mess for several years, I finally hit upon this system for storing and using my waterstones. I place each in its own Tupperware container, half-filled with water. I then place the containers on a tray that has a cleat screwed
(continued on page 60)

Sharpening Edge Tools

Every woodworker needs to know the three phases of edge preparation. There isn't one right way to do it, but there are some general principles which can help establish efficient sharpening practices.

Grinding

Grinding is for removing material quickly, when you need to remove a chip or need to change the shape of an edge or the angle of a bevel. Some grinders use the edge of the grinding-stone wheel. This produces the slightly concave bevel known as a hollow grind. Other grinders use the side of the wheel, which yields a flat bevel. In any case, the trick to grinding is to keep the steel cool. It is absolutely critical to have stones that will allow cool grinding. For more on grinders and stones, see "A Look at Grinders" on page 68.

High-speed dry grinders are the quickest, both to remove metal and to overheat. Even a clean, sharp stone will overheat a blade if you try to remove metal too quickly. An obvious sign of overheating is a blue oxide layer which appears in an instant at the edge of the tool—just the place where it is critical to keep the correct temper. Use a light touch, keep the tool moving across the stone, and have a can of water handy to dip the blade every few seconds.

If all of your bevel grinding is at the same angle, you'll never need to adjust the tool rest. If you want to readjust the tool rest to match a bevel on a tool, adjust by eye to make the flat of the bevel tangent to the arc of the wheel. Holding the tool in contact with the wheel, turn the wheel by hand about a quarter-turn. Check the scratches on the bevel. If the scratches are centered between the edge and the back of the bevel, the tool rest is set correctly. The tool rest that comes with most grinders is too small to hold a blade at a consistent angle. Make a wood or metal replacement which answers your needs.

Honing

The grooves left by a coarse grinder are replaced by the finer scratches of one or more bench stones. Oilstones and waterstones get their names from the lubricant used to float metal particles that would otherwise clog the abrasive. Keen edges can be obtained with either. I prefer waterstones because they cut fast, and there's no chance of getting oil on my projects. Waterstones are soft, so they need frequent attention to keep them flat. To do this, I work the faces of two stones together after every few sharpening sessions. A figure-eight motion works well, and you'll be able to feel the stones moving smoothly together once high spots have been leveled. I keep my waterstones in a water-filled plastic container with a lid, which prevents evaporation and mosquito hatches.

The aspect of honing that takes the most practice is keeping the tool bevel *flat* on the stone. The large bevel on a thick, wide blade is easier to keep in flat contact with the stone than the small bevel on a thin, narrow blade. There are wheeled clamping devices that can help maintain an angle on the smallest of chisels and engraving tools. You must be well balanced to center your weight over the bevel. A right-handed person will use the left hand close to the front of the tool, pressing down on the blade directly above the bevel; the right hand grips the tool farther back and guides the stroke. Work the whole surface of the stone, keeping it well lubricated. Reduce downward pressure on the backstroke, but don't break contact with the stone. Examine the bevel as you work it. Honed areas will show up distinctly from the ground areas. When the honed area extends across the length of the edge, feel gently for the wire edge, which will be bent over toward the back of the blade as shown in *Feeling for a Wire Edge*. The wire is produced when the material right at the cutting edge becomes so thin that it bends like foil and turns back. The final sharpening step, polishing, is designed to delicately remove the wire edge.

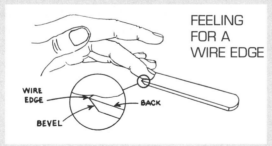

FEELING FOR A WIRE EDGE

WIRE EDGE

BACK

BEVEL

Polishing

A really sharp edge has two polished surfaces that meet at an acute angle. The bevel surface is renewed each time you sharpen, but the back of the blade needs to be flattened and polished only once—when you first sharpen it. Unless it becomes damaged, the back of the blade will need only that initial honing.

Polish with your finest stone—Arkansas or ceramic if you use oil, or a 6,000- or 8,000-grit waterstone. Alternately work the back and the bevel, being careful to keep them flat on the stone. If you have to lift the blade to make contact at the edge, this shows that the surface was rounded during honing and needs further honing to be flattened. If the bevel and back are flat, the wire edge will come cleanly free of the edge and can sometimes be seen in one length on the stone.

The final step is to strop the edge. A piece of smooth leather with polishing compound works well. I like to use the palm of my hand for plane blades. The blade is always drawn backwards from the edge when stropping, with the face almost parallel to the strop. A few strokes should leave you with an edge that will shave a hair from the back of your wrist.

An ax is sharp enough for hacking trees straight from the grinder, and a plane will work fine on the edge of a door after the honing stage. But you should go all the way through polishing when preparing chisels and planes for joinery. There's nothing quite like the whisper of a polished blade easing a tissue-thin shaving from a plank of your favorite wood. With experience, you'll be able to judge when it's time to rehone by the sound your plane makes or by a glance at the edge in good light. A dull blade shows a bright reflection from the flat where the edge ought to be.

—*RIC HANISCH*
Hanisch is a woodworker in Quakertown, Pa., who has written numerous articles about woodworking.

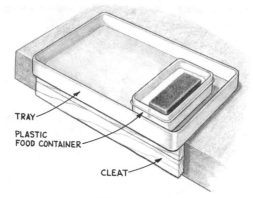

TRAY

PLASTIC
FOOD CONTAINER

CLEAT

WATERSTONE BOARD

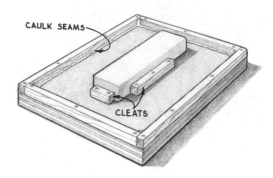

CAULK SEAMS

CLEATS

underneath. The cleat hooks over the edge of my bench and holds it in place. I use the stones right in the containers. Any mess is contained by the tray.

> *George Hayduke*
> *Moab, Utah*

BEWARE OF SNAKE OIL

Sharpening oil prevents a stone from becoming clogged, by floating away the fine particles of steel and stone that result from the sharpening process. That's all the oil does, and any light oil will do it. Before you pay for a can of special "honing" oil, consider that a can of 10W motor oil will probably do the job for far less.

> *Nick Engler*
> *West Milton, Ohio*

MAKING YOUR OWN SNAKE OIL

For a low-cost honing oil that works as well as any on the market, mix equal parts of 30W nondetergent motor oil and kerosene.

> *Morgan Ingalls*
> *Walnut Grove, Mo.*

You can make waterstones easier and less messy to use with this simple holder. Tack and glue ½-inch-square pieces of wood around the edges of a sheet of plywood. Caulk all of the inside corners so water won't leak out. Tack additional pieces of wood to the plywood to block the sharpening stone in place. Now you can sharpen right on your workbench without getting water all over.

> *Jeff Greef*
> *Soquel, Calif.*

FASTER-CUTTING OILSTONES

I clean my oilstones with a blast of WD-40, squirted from a spray can through a plastic extension tube. The resulting fresh, sharp abrasive works faster. I also use WD-40 instead of oil to float away the swarf while sharpening.

> *Arthur Guilmette*
> *Westport, Mass.*

SHARPENING V-PARTING GOUGES

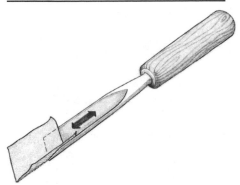

Of all my carving chisels, I find the V-parting gouges the hardest to sharpen. Honing the inside of the tip is really tricky. What I've found works best is to fold a square of 600-grit wet/dry sandpaper in half and dress the inside of the chisel with it. A drop or two of oil on the chisel makes the paper last longer. You can then use the paper on the outside bevels, or dress them on your regular sharpening stones.

Roy Moss
Rio Rancho, N. Mex.

WHEN IS IT SHARP?

You can tell when you've properly sharpened a chisel or plane iron by simply looking at it. Look directly at the cutting edge under a bright light and tilt the chisel back and forth. If a small burr is still on the edge, it will reflect a line of light back at you. A tiny nick in the edge will reflect a bright spot. If the edge reflects no light, it's sharp.

Nick Engler
West Milton, Ohio

SHARPENING ROUTER BITS

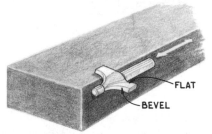

You can touch up the cutting edges of router bits by honing the flat side of the flutes. Don't try to sharpen the bevel; it is too easy to throw the bit out of balance.

For steel bits, any sharpening stone will work. But for carbide-tipped bits, only a diamond-based abrasive will cut the hard material. Lay the flat side of the flute on the stone, and hone with a back-and-forth movement. Apply pressure mostly along the cutting edge and give each flute an equal number of strokes.

Jeff Greef
Soquel, Calif.

HOW MANY ENTOMOLOGISTS DOES IT TAKE TO SHARPEN A CHISEL?

Knowing what a cutting edge looks like at different stages in the sharpening process can help you get sharper edges more efficiently and consistently. A pocket microscope—the type that's shaped like a fountain pen—will allow you to examine the edge in detail at each stage. It's also good for looking at bugs.

Ric Hanisch
Quakertown, Pa.

A QUICK, MAKE-DO SCRAPER EDGE

You can use a fine file to do a quick job of sharpening a scraper. File the edge flat and square with it, as usual. But skip the polishing and burnishing that are part of the usual scraper sharpening routine. The filed edge will produce a reasonably fine cut.

Jeff Greef
Soquel, Calif.

HOLD YOUR TEMPER

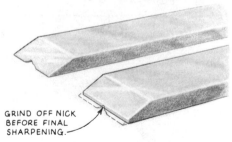

GRIND OFF NICK BEFORE FINAL SHARPENING.

It's easy to overheat a cutting tool if you have to grind it a lot to change the bevel or remove a nick. A thin

Sharpening a Hand Scraper

When you must work with figured woods or veneer, a hand scraper is a must. Woodworkers also tend to reach for the hand scraper whenever a gnarly spot resists hand planing.

Straighten the Edge with a File

Clamp the scraper in a bench vise with the edge up and level. Go over the edge with a fine-to-medium mill file that's long enough to hold at both ends, as shown in *Filing the Edge*. The idea is to remove the old work-hardened hook and create a flat, square surface. The face of the file must be held perpendicular to the scraper in such a way that the file contacts the whole length of the scraper edge during the stroke. With a sharp file a few passes are sufficient. At this point I like to use the file to ease back the corners of the blade so that the scraper's corners can't dig into the wood.

Honing the Edge

Remove the serrations left by the file, using a medium-to-fine stone. It is important to work the edge square to the stone. As shown in *Honing the Edge,* the blade can be attached with a hand clamp to a hardwood block with a square edge to help keep

FILING THE EDGE

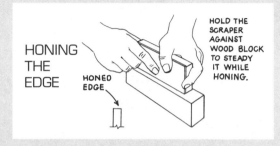

HONING THE EDGE

HONED EDGE

HOLD THE SCRAPER AGAINST WOOD BLOCK TO STEADY IT WHILE HONING.

blue (or black) line indicates you've overheated the tool, ruining the steel's "temper" and therefore its hardness. There are several things you can do to minimize the danger.

First, grind several tools during the same session. By grinding a little on one, then dunking it in a can of water as you grind the next, you keep from getting any one tool too hot.

Second, grind the cutting edge flat and 90 degrees to the back as shown.

Grind only far enough to remove the nick or create the shape you want. Then grind the bevel.

Finally, don't grind the bevel to a thin, sharp edge. The thinner the edge gets, the faster the heat builds up, increasing the risk of ruining the tool. Instead, grind the bevel close to where you want it, then finish it with a coarse sharpening stone.

Jeff Greef
Soquel, Calif.

it vertical. Move the scraper at a skew across the stone so you won't make a groove. The honing process is complete when a fingernail slides smoothly along the two sharp edges you have created.

Burnishing the Edge

If you lack a specially made burnisher, do not despair. I have never owned one myself. Any round, smooth, hard piece of steel will do, such as the shaft of a good screwdriver, a piece of drill rod, or the stem of an old engine valve. Clamp the scraper, and run the burnisher almost parallel to the face of the scraper, as shown in *Burnishing the Edge*.

Draw the burnisher toward you with two or three *firm* strokes, keeping it almost parallel to the scraper. You'll know when you're done by the shininess of the metal along the drawn edge.

Clamp the blade upright in the vise, and give the edge a few firm strokes with the burnisher at right angles to the blade. Now tip the burnisher 10 to 15 degrees from horizontal and pull it over the edge to draw the hook that will do the scraper's cutting, as shown in *Turning the Edge*. All of the burnishing strokes should be made smoothly

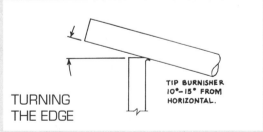

TURNING THE EDGE

TIP BURNISHER 10°–15° FROM HORIZONTAL.

and firmly. I like to draw a heavy hook on one side of the edge and a delicate one on the other.

—*RIC HANISCH*

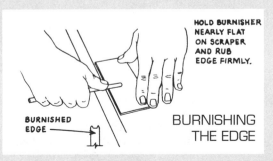

HOLD BURNISHER NEARLY FLAT ON SCRAPER AND RUB EDGE FIRMLY.

BURNISHED EDGE

BURNISHING THE EDGE

Sharpening a Cabinet Scraper

When you sharpen a cabinet scraper, your goal is to create a hooked edge. The process is different from sharpening an edge tool, and it requires a knack that comes with practice. Persevere and you'll soon be getting smooth, flat surfaces without first tearing the wood up with sandpaper.

Filing the Bevel

If your scraper is new, it probably came from the factory with a 45-degree bevel ground on one edge. A replacement blade may come without a bevel, so you'll have to grind one on a bench grinder.

If your scraper has been used before, the first sharpening step is to remove the old hooked edge. Lay the blade flat on an oilstone or waterstone, beveled-side up, and gently hone it. Continue until the burr is gone. Don't do this with a file or you will scratch the surface, making more work for yourself later.

Clamp the blade vertically in a vise, first padding the jaws with wood. Then pull a medium mill file along the bevel as shown in *Filing the Bevel,* maintaining the 45-degree angle. It is essential that the edge be dead straight—neither crowned nor hollow. Continue filing until you feel a distinct roughness when you run your finger along the edge.

Take the blade out of the vise, and remove the file marks with an 800-grit oilstone or waterstone. To do this, gently hone the edge at 45 degrees as shown in *Honing the Bevel.* Repeat with the blade flat on the stone, bevel-side up. Both edges must be smooth to the touch before you attempt to turn them: Any raggedness will show up as minute lines on the finished surface of the wood. A second honing using 1,200 grit, and a final one on a 6,000-grit waterstone, will be well worth the extra minute or two.

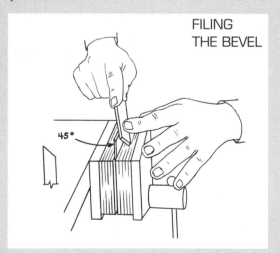

FILING
THE BEVEL

45°

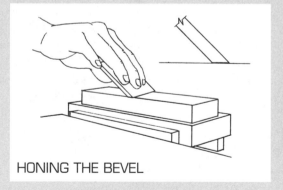

HONING THE BEVEL

Burnishing the Edge

Hold the blade firmly on the bench, bevel-side down. Add a few drops of oil,

BURNISHING
THE EDGE

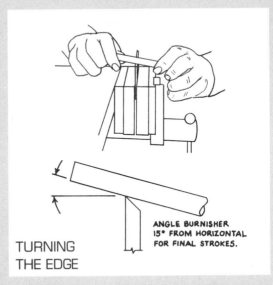

TURNING
THE EDGE

ANGLE BURNISHER
15° FROM HORIZONTAL
FOR FINAL STROKES.

and then, keeping the burnishing tool flat on the blade, briskly stroke back and forth to draw the edge, as shown in *Burnishing the Edge*. Do this about a dozen times, using moderate pressure.

Clamp the blade securely in a padded vise and put a drop of oil on the edge. Hold the hardened-steel burnishing tool at the same angle as the 45-degree factory bevel, and slide the tool back and forth, again using only moderate pressure. Continue the stroking motion, but gradually flatten the angle until you are holding the burnishing tool at about 15 degrees from horizontal, as shown in *Turning the Edge*. Test the burr with your finger, and stop when you can feel a distinct hook.

Place the cabinet scraper on a flat surface (such as a table saw, jointer, or piece of plate glass), slack off the two clamping screws, and slip a piece of newspaper under the front edge of the sole. Gently drop the blade in place, with the burr facing forward, and tighten the screws. Tighten the middle wing screw so the blade is sprung into a slight curve. The greater the pressure on this screw, the more curve and hence the greater the depth of cut.

Now you are ready to try the tool on a piece of hardwood scrap. If you find that you are getting dust rather than shavings, either the blade is in backward or you have not turned the edge properly. Perhaps you used too much pressure and turned the edge all the way over like a closed fist. The only remedy is to start over.

—*SIMON WATTS*
Watts is a professional woodworker and author in San Francisco, Calif.

BEVEL-GRINDING TEMPLATE

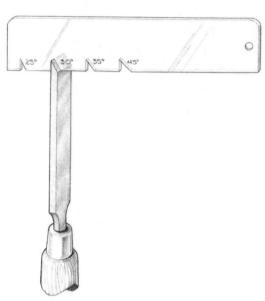

You can make a handy guide from acrylic plastic for testing the bevel of your edge tools. Carefully cut notches for the angles you want, and label them with an engraving tool or by scratching the plastic with a nail. A little black paint rubbed over the surface and wiped off will make the labels easier to see. Drill a hole in the template, and hang it up near your grinder so it will be handy when you need it.

John Roccanova
Ancramdale, N.Y.

BUFFING TO A RAZOR EDGE

When sharpening tools, I finish up by buffing the edge with a hard felt buffing wheel charged with emery. This leaves a long-lasting razor edge with a high polish. Such a smooth edge cuts down on drag, allowing the tool to glide through wood with little effort.

Rick Wright
Schnecksville, Pa.

GRINDING PLANER KNIVES

Here's a simple jig for sharpening planer and jointer knives on a belt sander. Move the block and knife back and forth across the sanding belt, concentrating pressure on the knife.

A. J. Tryba
Benton, Ill.

LIFE IN THE SLOW LANE

Most commercial electric grinders run too fast for me. So rather than

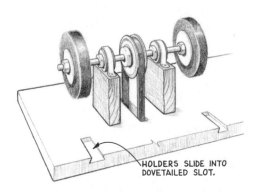

HOLDERS SLIDE INTO DOVETAILED SLOT.

spend a lot of money on one I didn't really like, I made my own. I mounted a suitable arbor in pillow blocks and connected it, through pulleys and a belt, to an old 1,725-rpm motor. The pulleys I chose reduce the speed to about 1,100 rpm, a speed I find comfortable for grinding.

In front of the wheels, I built an interchangable tool rest system. Different holders slip into the dovetailed groove to hold everything from long lathe gouges to delicate carving tools.

Bob Hawks
Tulsa, Okla.

BEWARE OF LOW-FLYING GRINDING WHEELS

Grinding wheels are quite brittle. A chance blow to one can easily fracture it, sending pieces flying the next time the grinder is used. Protect yourself by standing off to the side until a couple of seconds after the wheel has come up to full speed.

Jeff Greef
Soquel, Calif.

EASY-OFF EDGES

If a cutting edge seems dull, there simply may be a buildup of pitch on it. If so, spray the cutting edge with oven cleaner, let it stand a few moments, then wipe it off. There's

no need for heat. Cleaning a saw blade or plane iron is a lot less trouble than sharpening it.

Nick Engler
West Milton, Ohio

GRINDING WITH A BELT SANDER

If you don't need a bench grinder often enough to warrant buying one, use a belt sander—either a stationary one or a portable model held upside down. Grind toward the cutting edge, not away from it. Dip the tool in water frequently, as you would with any grinding operation on tempered steel.

Also, clean the sander thoroughly both before and after grinding. A blast of compressed air does nicely. Sparks and sanding dust can form an explosive combination. And stray metal dust may form rust spots under a water-based finish. It can also wreak havoc on ball bearings.

Jeff Greef
Soquel, Calif.

TESTING SHARPNESS

Perhaps the ultimate test for the sharpness of a chisel is to take a thin shaving off the end grain of a very soft wood. Only the sharpest of edges will do this without compressing the fibers somewhat.

Jeff Greef
Soquel, Calif.

A Look at Grinders

Chances are you are familiar with the standard bench grinder. It's a very simple tool, consisting of an induction motor with a grinding wheel on each end. For all its simplicity, the bench grinder is a versatile tool. Woodworkers use it to sharpen tools, metalworkers use it to shape metal. Fitted with a wire-brush wheel or a cotton buffing wheel, the grinder can also handle chores ranging from removing heavy rust scale to polishing jewelry.

The standard bench grinder will do a fine job of sharpening tools, but its high speed is a drawback when sharpening fine edge tools. This has led to the advent of the slow-speed water grinder, a tool designed specifically for sharpening edge tools. Let's take a look at these two types of grinders.

Bench Grinders

Grinders come with wheel diameters from 4½ inches to 10 inches, and with power ratings from ⅛ horsepower to more than 1 horsepower. All but the larger bench grinders spin at around 3,450 rpm. Models

with wheels larger than 10 inches usually spin at around 1,725 rpm.

Grinders have tool rests that are adjustable for a range of grinding bevels. Safety housings and plastic eye shields protect against sparks and possible injury from wheel breakage. Still, you should always wear safety goggles or a full face mask when grinding.

The 6-inch bench grinder is the most popular choice for small shops. Tool retailers usually carry a number of makes in this size, along with a selection of wheels and accessories. Prices can range greatly for grinders that may look similar and carry similar horsepower ratings, but the prices usually reflect significant differences in quality and performance.

In comparing name-brand grinders, the amperage rating is a better indicator of power than the quoted horsepower. One manufacturer's ⅓-horsepower, 3.8-amp grinder may be another's ⅓-horsepower, 2.5-amp model. Both may be high-quality tools, but the 3.8-amp grinder will accept a heavier feed pressure and will grind much faster.

Unfortunately, even amperage ratings don't tell the whole story. There are plenty of cheap "no-name" grinders for sale that were manufactured with very poor motor windings. Not only will these grinders fail to deliver on their power ratings, stalling even in light-duty use, but they may also soon burn out their windings and fail completely, usually in a cloud of smoke.

Comparing grinders by switching them on in the store is a good first test of quality.

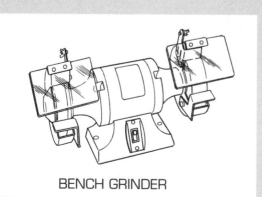

BENCH GRINDER

A worthy grinder gets up to speed quickly and without shudder, runs quietly, vibrates very little (vibration in a new grinder sometimes reflects an imbalance in the wheels, rather than a defect in the motor), and coasts without a shudder for a long time after it is switched off. These are signs of quality windings, good balance, and fine bearings.

Grinders usually come equipped with a coarse aluminum oxide wheel for aggressive stock removal plus a finer (commonly 60-grit) aluminum oxide wheel that can grind a relatively burr-free edge on near-square edged tools like drill and router bits, shears, and cold chisels.

For an even cleaner edge on tool steel, especially on acute-edged woodworking tools like chisels and plane irons, choose an aluminum oxide wheel of 100 grit or finer. For best results, select a soft-grade wheel; it sheds its cutting grains as they blunt, constantly exposing fresh grains that cut clean and cool. Wheel grades are designated by letter: A is softest, Z is hardest; the soft range is A to H.

Even with the softest and finest wheel, the bench grinder will not produce a finished edge on plane irons and chisels—these will still need honing, either on a bench stone or on a wet grinder. The bench grinder's function is to grind away nicks and restore the correct bevel prior to honing.

Choose a silicon carbide wheel for grinding very hard materials like carbide-tipped tools, glass, and ceramic. Silicon carbide is also the best choice for soft metals like aluminum, brass, and bronze.

You can't accurately grind freehand. So the first step in sharpening beveled edge tools with a bench grinder is to carefully adjust the tool rest to maintain the tool's original bevel. Position the tool rest so that the work will be at or slightly above the centerline of the wheel, with the gap between the tool rest and the wheel no greater than ⅛ inch. Test for the correct bevel setting by grinding just enough to produce a shiny spot as a reference.

Cutting edges die from heatstroke, not old age. The friction produced by a bench grinder's high speed will quickly draw the temper from the steel. You know this has happened when the edge turns blue. The discolored steel is now too weak to hold an edge; you've got to grind the discolored area away. To prevent overheating, keep the wheel clog-free by maintaining it with a star-wheel dresser or dressing stick; grind with light pressure, moving the workpiece back and forth across the wheel face; and quench the work in water every few seconds.

Water-Cooled Grinders

The water-cooled grinder is the ultimate tool for sharpening woodworking cutting edges. With its waterstone moving at slow speed, and constant cooling and lubrication with water, these grinders offer excellent control for precise sharpening and honing,

(continued)

A Look at Grinders—*Continued*

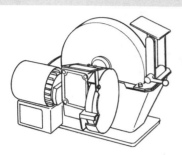

VERTICAL WATER-COOLED GRINDER

HORIZONTAL
WATER-COOLED
GRINDER

with no risk of overheating. While there is price overlap, water-cooled grinders generally cost more than bench grinders.

Vertical water-cooled grinders run a slow waterstone partly submerged in a trough. On some models the tool rest features a sliding miter gauge for greater control over both the bevel angle and the feed angle. The waterstone is usually driven through a reduction gear by a motor that also drives a standard 3,450-rpm grinding wheel.

Horizontal models cool their waterstones by trickling water from an overhead reservoir. The basic tool rest is a tilting bar that spans the face of the stone; some models mount an optional jig that clamps planer

and jointer blades in a sliding holder. With its flat grinding surface and horizontal orientation, this grinder is essentially a powered bench stone—if a tool has been ground to the correct bevel, and if you have a good touch for holding the tool at that bevel, honing operations can be done freehand.

Accessory waterstones in a range of grits are available for both the vertical and the horizontal grinder. One advantage of the horizontal grinder is that its design lets you change waterstones quickly.

—JIM MICHAUD
Michaud is a freelance writer and wood worker in Swampscott, Mass.

5

JOINERY

FLUTING DOWELS

I make my own fluted dowels without a special tool or jig. I simply crimp the dowel with the inner pipe-gripping teeth of ordinary pliers. I make a series of squeezes to cover the entire dowel. It takes about five seconds to flute a 2-inch length of dowel.

Robert Pauley
Decatur, Ga.

UNDERSIZED DOWELS FOR TEST ASSEMBLIES

I sometimes need dowels that are just slightly smaller than standard diameter. My most common use for these dowels is to test assemble a project for fit and alignment. Undersized dowels allow easy assembly and disassembly.

I use the sizing jig shown here to shave a tad off the dowels. To make the jig, I drill standard-sized holes in a piece of ¼-inch-thick steel. Then I use a heavy hammer to peen the perimeter of the holes on one face of the steel plate. This creates an inward burr. I then pass the dowels through the other side of the plate so that the burrs shave the dowels. Be sure to mark the downsized dowels so you don't accidentally use them in a glue-up.

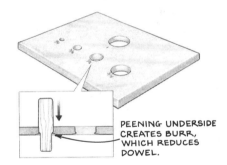

PEENING UNDERSIDE CREATES BURR, WHICH REDUCES DOWEL.

Sometimes dowels don't fit in holes because your drill bit is worn and this has reduced the hole diameter very slightly. In a pinch, you can use the jig to shave dowels for a glue-up, but for the strongest joint, you can't beat a good fit between a standard bit and standard dowels.

Jeff Greef
Soquel, Calif.

KERFED DOWELS FOR TEST ASSEMBLIES

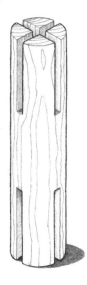

Have problems with dowels getting stuck in test assemblies? A couple of band-saw cuts will solve the problem. Rip the dowel down the center about one-third its length. Rotate the dowel 90 degrees and make another cut. Flip the dowel over and do the same thing on the other end. Use these dowels during test assemblies. They'll hold and still be easy to remove when you take the piece apart.

Charles DeMaine
Red Oak, Tex.

FOR DOWELS THAT STAY

When doweling pieces together, plane a small flat on one side of each dowel before inserting it. This allows any excess glue to escape when you clamp the joint. If you don't let the glue escape, the pressure can force the joint open again.

Nick Engler
West Milton, Ohio

QUICK DRILL PRESS

If you don't have a doweling jig, you can still drill a hole perpendicular to the surface of the wood. Guide the bit against a piece of wood, the end of which you've cut square.

David Page
Swarthmore, Pa.

DOWEL-CENTER REMOVER

I remove tight-fitting dowel centers by sharpening a V-notch in the end of a large, sturdy spoon and prying them out.

Richard Dorn
Oelwein, Iowa

SUREFIRE DOWEL DRYER

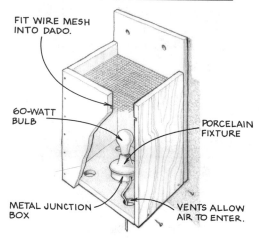

FIT WIRE MESH INTO DADO.

60-WATT BULB

PORCELAIN FIXTURE

METAL JUNCTION BOX

VENTS ALLOW AIR TO ENTER.

Have you ever driven a dowel into a hole and ended up splitting the board? Or maybe you've inserted a dowel for a test assembly only to find that you can't pull it out. If you live in a humid area, as I do, you've probably experienced these problems.

I made a simple dowel dryer that shrinks dowels slightly before using them. Put the dowels on the mesh, and then let them dry for about an hour. They should slip right into the hole.

One caution: Make sure everything fits before you glue up. Once glue hits these dry dowels, they will expand and make a very tight joint.

Brent Ewen
Hamilton, Ind.

HIGH-TECH DOWEL DRYER

Dowels too tight? Three or four minutes in a microwave oven will remove moisture and make the dowels easier to insert. This trick works great for joinery biscuits, too.

Royce W. Stafford
Jefferson City, Mo.

KEEPING BISCUITS DRY

Joinery biscuits are very prone to absorbing moisture from the air. This causes them to swell, sometimes to the point where they won't fit into their slots. The best way to avoid this is to keep the biscuits sealed in plastic. I buy quantities of biscuits in large bags and worry that some evening I'll forget to seal a bag and come back another day to a huge supply of unusable biscuits. Instead, I take a handful of biscuits at a time and store them in a small Ziploc resealable bag. This way, I only stand to spoil a few biscuits instead of several hundred.

Kenneth S. Burton, Jr.
Allentown, Pa.

CENTER FINDER

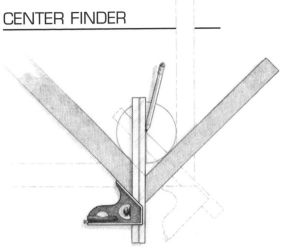

To find the center of a circle, I use a framing square together with a combination square, as shown in the drawing. Make sure the combination square's ruler bisects the framing square's right angle; draw two intersecting lines to locate the center of the circle.

John Roccanova
Ancramdale, N.Y.

FASTENING BREADBOARD ENDS

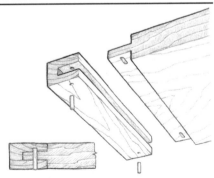

Breadboard ends are a traditional method of keeping tabletops flat while avoiding showing end grain. Unfortunately, breadboard ends create a new problem. Because their grain runs perpendicular to that of the table-top, the top can't expand and contract. The result—a split tabletop. I avoid this by attaching the breadboard ends with dowels in special holes.

First, put a breadboard end in place. Drill two ¼-inch holes through the bottom of the breadboard, through the tongue, and into the breadboard, as shown. Don't drill through to the top of the table. Remove the breadboard end and elongate the holes in the tongue with a rattail file. To attach the end, apply glue to only the middle 4 or 5 inches of the tongue. Put a dab of glue in the stopped holes in the top of the bread-

Routing Dadoes and Rabbets

Dadoes and rabbets are useful joints in furniture making, from the simplest bookcase to the most involved media center. They lend strength, stability, and ease of alignment to a project. Most craftsmen cut them with a router, table saw, or radial arm saw. It makes sense to use the router when the workpiece is large and difficult to maneuver, or when the cut must start or stop in the middle of a board.

Making the Guide

For dadoing, guide the router with a shop-made T-square for a fence. Make the T-square of 1 × 4s, as shown in *Router Dado Jig*. The bar is 6 to 12 inches longer than your workpiece is wide, and the head is between 12 and 24 inches long. Carefully mill the pieces, making sure their edges are straight and parallel. Glue and screw them together to form the square. Before the glue sets, check the alignment with an accurate framing square to make sure the bar is square to the head. Loosen the screws and adjust as necessary.

Once the glue sets, clamp the T-square to a piece of scrap and rout two shallow test dadoes across it and into the head, one on either side of the bar. The width of the router bit determines the width of the dado, so use the appropriately sized bit to rout these test dadoes. The dadoes on the head will guide you when you use the jig. The only drawback to this system is that you'll have to make a separate T-square for each width of dado you want to cut.

Cutting Dadoes

Cut your stock to size before dadoing it. Lay out the dadoes. Then align the T-square on the piece and clamp it in position as shown in *Cutting the Dadoes*. I like to use a wooden hand screw for this because the wooden jaws don't mar the work.

Make the cut in the direction that will cause the router to be pulled against the bar,

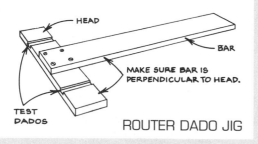

HEAD

BAR

MAKE SURE BAR IS PERPENDICULAR TO HEAD.

TEST DADOS

ROUTER DADO JIG

board. Don't apply glue to the elongated holes or to the hole in the bottom of the breadboard; it could squeeze out into the tongue, undoing all your hard work. Put the breadboard end in place and peg it with ¼-inch dowels.

David Page
Swarthmore, Pa.

QUICK DADOES WITH THE ROUTER

Rout evenly spaced dadoes without resetting a fence each time. If you have a series of dadoes to rout, such as grooves for small drawers in a cabinet, this system is accurate and quick. Rout the first dado with a straightedge or router fence attach-

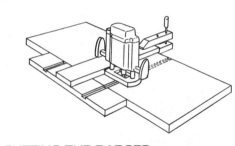

CUTTING THE DADOES

rather than wandering away from it. Standing on one end of the jig, always push the router away from you if it is on the right side of the square, and pull it toward you if it is on the left side of the square, as shown in *Routing Direction*.

If your router has a round base, keep the same point on the base pressed against the bar as you rout. Router motors tend not to be concentric with their bases. If you rotate

the router as you cut a dado, the dado may not be straight. In light of this, you might want to make a custom base for your router that has one flat side to ride along the bar.

If your project requires two pieces with matching dadoes, like the sides of a bookcase, you can rout both sides at once. Clamp the pieces together side by side as shown in *Routing Two Pieces*. Make sure their ends line up, then clamp the T-square so it spans both pieces. Rout the dadoes straight across. If you clamp the pieces together with their front edges touching, you'll eliminate any chance of tear-out that might show.

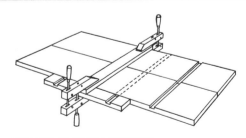

ROUTING TWO PIECES

—*Ben Erickson*
Erickson is a professional woodworker in Eutaw, Ala. He has contributed to many woodworking books and magazines.

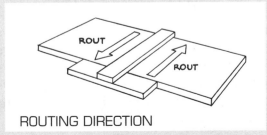

ROUTING DIRECTION

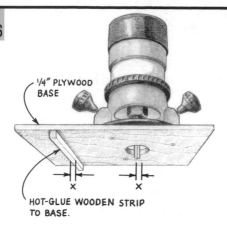

¼" PLYWOOD BASE

HOT-GLUE WOODEN STRIP TO BASE.

ment. Then rip a 6-inch-long wooden runner the same width as your dado. Make the runner slightly thinner than the dado depth. Use hot-melt glue to attach it to your router base, positioning it so that the distance between the bit and the strip equals the distance between dadoes. If the distance between dadoes is greater than the radius of your router base, replace the base with a rectangular sled of ¼-inch plywood and attach the strip to the sled base with hot-melt glue.

Put the runner in the first dado to make the second dado. Run it in the second dado to make the third, and so on.

David Page
Swarthmore, Pa.

TO CENTER A GROOVE

To truly center a groove in the edge of a frame, rip it twice on the table saw. First guide one face against the fence, and then the other. You may get a groove slightly wider than you want, so test it on scrap first, and then make any necessary adjustments.

M. S. Langley
Detroit, Mich.

HOT MORTISING BIT

If you rout mortises, use a machinist's end mill, available from most tool supply houses. End mills cut more smoothly than router bits. Unlike router bits, they are readily available in long lengths.

David Page
Swarthmore, Pa.

ANOTHER HOT BIT

Drill holes for mortises with a Forstner bit. A Forstner lets you drill overlapping holes, leaving less waste to chisel out. The holes are also flat-bottomed, which makes cleaning up the bottom of the mortise easier.

Jeff Day
Perkasie, Pa.

ALL'S WELL THAT ENDS WELL

When you rout a mortise, plunge-cut the ends first. Rout out the waste in between with a series of cuts, each slightly deeper than the previous cut. Cutting the ends first ensures they'll be straight.

Malden Rand
Huntington, W.Va.

CUT TENONS TO FIT THE MORTISES

When you rout your mortises, you don't have much control over the mortise's width—it's as wide as the router bit diameter. For a tight-fitting joint, rout your mortises first, then cut your tenons to fit.

M. S. Langley
Detroit, Mich.

PERFECT TENONS

You can cut tenons that are as precise as any routed mortise. Put two blades on your saw, separated by a spacer of the desired width. (They're a standard item in the Delta catalog.) Identical carbide rip blades work best. For a small saw, purchase thin-kerf rip blades. Cut the tenons with the help of a good tenoning jig.

> *Trebor Narom*
> *Onaled, N. Mex.*

MARKING TENON SHOULDERS

A sloppy shoulder makes for a sloppy-looking tenon. When I'm working by hand, I score the shoulder line about 1/16 inch deep. Then I chisel on the waste side of the line and angle a cut toward the scored line. The notch helps guide the saw.

If I'm cutting tenons on the table saw, I still score the shoulder line with a knife. It doesn't guide the cut, but if I screw up, it gives me a good line to trim to. If I have to trim, I usually undercut the shoulder, as shown.

> *Jeff Day*
> *Perkasie, Pa.*

MORTISE LAYOUT

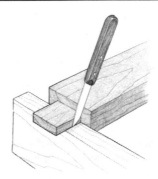

Lay out mortises from the tenons. Arrange the parts of a frame on the bench as they will be when assembled. Scribe the top and bottom of the mortise on the edge of the stiles by tracing along the tenons with a sharp knife. Lay out the sides of the mortise with a marking gauge.

> *M. S. Langley*
> *Detroit, Mich.*

LONG AND STRONG MORTISES

Cut mortises 1/16 inch deeper than the length of the tenons. The gap ensures that the tenon shoulder fits tightly, and it provides a place for excess glue.

> *Malden Rand*
> *Huntington, W.Va.*

LOOK BEFORE YOU LEAP

Mortise table legs before you taper or turn them. It's easier to measure and clamp square stock.

> *Jeff Day*
> *Perkasie, Pa.*

MAKING LAP JOINTS FLUSH

In cutting laps, the trick is getting the table saw's depth of cut just right, so that the joint fits precisely when assembled. Try this. Set the depth of

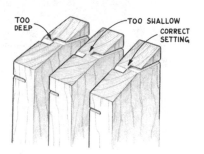

Cutting Tenons on the Table Saw

There are innumerable ways to assemble a frame, including dowels, biscuits, and even screws. But none of these joints is as strong as the mortise-and-tenon. The plunge router has taken the hassle out of chopping mortises, leaving cutting the tenon as the one time-consuming element of the joint. But making tenons need not be as involved as you might think. The fastest method I've found is to cut them on a table saw equipped with a dado cutter.

Preparing the Stock

Start by milling the stock to exact width and thickness. The thickness of the stock is of particular importance, because it determines the thickness of the tenon. Make sure all the pieces are the same thickness by running them through the planer at the same setting. Finally, cut the pieces to length. If you have two or more pieces to cut to the same length, use a stop block clamped along an auxiliary miter gauge fence to mark the measurement. You can use a handscrew as a stop, as shown in *Cutting Pieces to Length*.

Setting Up the Saw

Once the stock is dimensioned, install the dado cutter on the saw. Set it to cut as wide

CUTTING PIECES TO LENGTH

a kerf as possible, without exceeding the length of the tenon. Square the blade to the table, and square the miter gauge to the blade. Make a trial cut in a scrap and check the results with a square.

The best dado cutter to use for cutting tenons is a stack dado cutter because it cuts flat. A wobble dado cutter, with its tilted blade, makes a rounded cut. The higher-quality dado cutters will leave a smooth-faced tenon with a cleanly cut shoulder. If you have trouble getting a clean shoulder cut, you can score it first with a regular saw blade, then switch to the dado to finish the job.

cut roughly, using a measuring tape. Nip a corner of a scrap piece of the working stock. Roll the piece over and nip the opposite corner so the two cuts intersect. By looking at the end of the piece, where the cuts intersect, you'll be able to tell whether you need to adjust the depth of cut. Adjust the setting and try it on a new piece of scrap.

Bill Hylton
Emmaus, Pa.

Cutting the Tenon to Thickness

The length of the tenon is set with a stop. Here you have a choice, as shown in *Cutting Tenon Thickness*. You can use a stop on the auxiliary miter gauge fence; or you can use the rip fence for the stop. The thickness of the tenon is determined by the height of the blade. Take a piece of scrap stock the same width and thickness as your good stock and hold it against the miter gauge. Eyeball the blade height adjustment and cut both sides of the scrap. Check the piece in a mortise. If it is too loose, lower the blade a little. If it is too tight, raise the blade. Play with the adjustment until the tenon slides into the mortise with a slight drag. The saw is now set up to cut your tenons. Cut each tenon in several passes as necessary.

Cutting the Tenon to Width

Once all the tenons are cut to thickness, cut them to width, as shown. Take the test piece and stand it on edge against the miter gauge fence. Leave the stop in place and cut the tenon. You may have to adjust the blade up or down to trim the tenon to the necessary size. Once you get the saw set, cut all the tenons.

HANDSCREW AS A STOP

RIP FENCE AS A STOP

CUTTING TENON THICKNESS

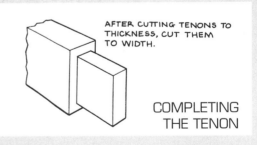

AFTER CUTTING TENONS TO THICKNESS, CUT THEM TO WIDTH.

COMPLETING THE TENON

—*Ben Erickson*

DEALING WITH BOWED DRAWER SIDES

If you've milled drawer sides and found that they bow front to back, orient them so the sides curve in. When you install the drawer bottom, it will push the sides back out.

David Page
Swarthmore, Pa.

DRAWERS, DRAWERS, DRAWERS

No matter how careful you are, no two drawer openings are identical. Fit each drawer separately, and then mark the drawers and their openings. I mark them by tapping the drawer back and drawer stile with a screwdriver to create Roman numerals. They don't damage the drawer, no one ever sees them, and they're pretty hard to erase by mistake.

M. S. Langley
Detroit, Mich.

CUTTING DRAWER BACKS TO WIDTH

Traditional drawers have backs that are narrower than the sides. This allows the drawer bottom to slide in from the back when you assemble the drawer. I start with a back the same size as the sides. When I rout the groove for the drawer bottom, I rout one in the back, too. The groove is a perfect guide for cutting the drawer back to width.

Ben Erickson
Eutaw, Ala.

ANGLE NAILS FOR BETTER HOLDING POWER

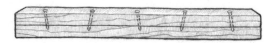

When nailing two pieces together, drive the nails at a slight angle, alternating angle direction with each nail as shown. This will make it difficult to pull the nailed joint apart.

Nick Engler
West Milton, Ohio

PRESCRIPTION FOR TIGHT CORNERS

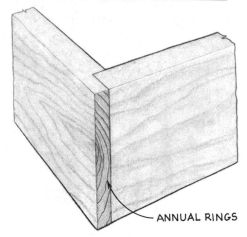

ANNUAL RINGS

To keep corners tight when assembling boxes, drawers, and chests, arrange the end grain of the parts so the annual rings curve out. Wood tends to cup in the direction opposite the rings. If the rings curve in, the corners may draw apart.

Nick Engler
West Milton, Ohio

Simple Drawer Joint

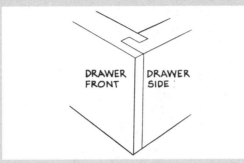

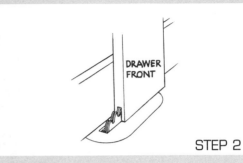

STEP 2

This drawer joint for ¾-inch stock won't match the strength of a dovetail. But it's stronger than a rabbet joint and just about as simple to make. Make the joint with a ¼-inch dado blade in the table saw. It's nearly foolproof because you use only one fence setting. First, put a high auxiliary fence against your regular table saw fence. Then follow these steps:

2. Now turn your attention to the *drawer front*. First raise the blade to ¾ inch. (Use a piece of the drawer stock as a depth guide.) Stand the drawer front on end, and guide it against the fence. Pass each end of the drawer front over the blade. Be sure to hold the workpiece firmly against the fence and down on the table.

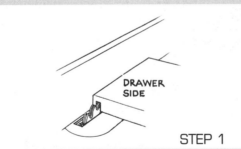

STEP 1

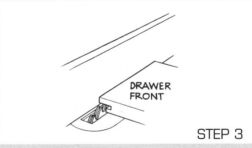

STEP 3

1. Set the blade to cut a ¼-inch dado. Position the fence ¼ inch from the cutter. Raise the cutter to ¼ inch. Put the inside of a *drawer side* down on the saw table and butt one end against the fence. Guide the piece with the miter gauge as you pass it over the blade. Make the same cut on all your drawer sides. Repeat the operation for the other end of the drawer sides if you are using this joint for the back of the drawers too.

3. Lower the cutter to about ⅜ inch. Put the inside of the drawer front down on the table. Butt one end of the drawer front against the fence. Guide the drawer front with the miter gauge as you pass the workpiece over the cutter. Repeat this operation for the other end of the drawer front.

—*JEFF GREEF*
   Greef is a woodworker in Soquel, Calif., who has written numerous articles about woodworking.

PREVENT RATTLING GLASS

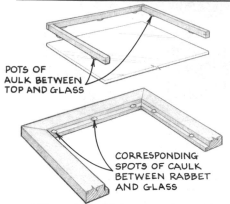

POTS OF
AULK BETWEEN
TOP AND GLASS

CORRESPONDING
SPOTS OF CAULK
BETWEEN RABBET
AND GLASS

When installing glass in cabinet doors, put spots of caulk in the corners and middle of the rabbet and between the glass and stops. This will prevent the glass from rattling when the stops eventually loosen.

Jeff Greef
Soquel, Calif.

FITTING DOOR PANELS

Always make a door panel long enough to fit snugly top to bottom, but slightly narrow to allow for expansion in humid weather. Here's the quickest way I've found to do this. Cut a panel that bottoms out in all the grooves. Then trim the panel to width by running it over the jointer a few times. Take off about ⅛ inch in the summer or ³⁄₁₆ inch in the winter.

Malden Rand
Huntington, W.Va.

CHEAP DOOR SHIMS

Here's a nickel's worth of free advice. When fitting flush doors to a cabinet, use nickels as shims. They're uniform in thickness, and you usually have a couple in your pocket. If you're feeling rich and want a closer fit, use dimes.

Bill Hylton
Emmaus, Pa.

DOUBLE COUNTERSINK TO ALLOW FOR WOOD MOVEMENT

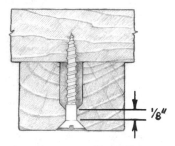

⅛"

Here's a way to allow for wood movement when you have to screw two pieces of wood together with their grains running perpendicular—when screwing a tabletop to drawer kickers, for example. Use a double countersink in the piece that gets the screw head. First countersink the side of the board that will be exposed, as you normally would. Then countersink the other side of the hole until you are within about ⅛ inch of the first countersink. This second countersink will give the screw room to tilt as it's dragged along by wood movement.

Jeff Greef
Soquel, Calif.

FIND THE SHINE

If you're assembling a joint and the pieces won't go together, take them apart and examine the mating surfaces. Any shiny areas indicate where the joint may be binding. Carefully pare these areas with a sharp chisel to relieve them.

Kenneth S. Burton, Jr.
Allentown, Pa.

DOVETAIL FILLER

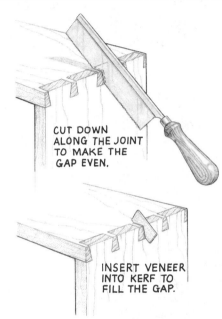

CUT DOWN ALONG THE JOINT TO MAKE THE GAP EVEN.

INSERT VENEER INTO KERF TO FILL THE GAP.

If, heaven forbid, you should happen to cut a dovetail joint that is less than perfect, don't panic. Glue up the joint. When the glue dries, cut down along the offending area with a dovetail saw as shown. This will create a consistent gap. Dab a little glue in the gap and slip in a piece of veneer as shown. Once the glue dries, you can trim and sand the veneer flush. Since the veneer will show as end grain on either side of the joint, it will be invisible.

Kenneth S. Burton, Jr.
Allentown, Pa.

USE A WRENCH TO DRIVE THREADED INSERTS

Threaded inserts have slots so that you can drive them with a screwdriver. But usually a screwdriver doesn't let you apply enough torque to do the job. A wrench works much better. With this method, thread a nut onto a bolt, then thread the insert onto the bolt until it hits the nut. Use the wrench to turn the nut, and drive the insert into place.

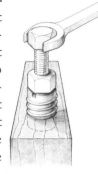

Kenneth S. Burton, Jr.
Allentown, Pa.

MAKING MOLDING FIT INTO CORNERS

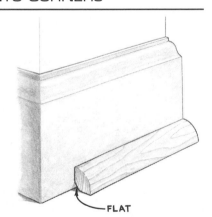

FLAT

When you're fitting molding into an inside corner, glue blobs or other slight obstructions will prevent a close fit. Often it is very difficult to get into the corner to clean it up. Plane a flat on the back of the molding instead. The molding will pop right into place.

Percy W. Blandford
Stratford-upon-Avon, England

Cutting Dadoes on the Table Saw

To many woodworkers, the term "dado" immediately brings to mind the table saw, with its accompanying dado cutter. This association is understandable, because the table saw is hard to beat at the task. It really shines in dadoing and grooving pieces that are easily moved and supported as they go through the saw.

Dado Cutters

You have your choice of two dado cutters on the market, stack and wobble, as shown in *Types of Dado Cutters*. The stack type consists of two saw blades that define the outside of the cut, and a set of chippers that remove the bulk of the waste in between.

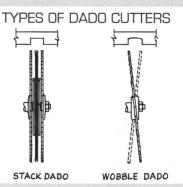

TYPES OF DADO CUTTERS

STACK DADO   WOBBLE DADO

Stack dadoes are generally more expensive than wobble dadoes but usually give superior results. They make a flat-bottomed dado, and they are easily reset to the same width by restacking the same components together. Their main disadvantage is that they don't readily cut in-between-sized grooves. This can be overcome by inserting thin shims between the blades as you install the dado cutter on the saw.

The other type of dado cutter, the wobble dado, consists of a single saw blade mounted between two tapered washers. These washers are twisted to cant the blade, so that its wobbling rotation cuts a wide kerf. The chief advantage of this system is that it is infinitely adjustable, provided you have the infinite patience to get it adjusted just right. The main drawback is that the blade's wobble produces an uneven bottom in the dado, as illustrated. This is more apparent on wide dadoes.

Cutting Dadoes

Dado cutters will produce both dadoes and grooves. The difference is slight. A dado is cut across the grain, and a groove is cut with the grain. This is fine if you work in solid wood, but when it comes to plywood and other "grainless" materials, the distinction is moot and the terms are virtually interchangeable.

Mount the cutter on your saw, set for the width of cut you're after. Make a cut in a scrap to test your setup. Adjust the cutter if necessary. Lay out the cuts on your stock. Then set either the rip fence or the miter gauge to guide the work through the cut.

Your choice between rip fence and miter

CUTTING GROOVES WITH
THE RIP FENCE

gauge as a guide depends on the shape of the workpiece. In general, if a piece's long edge is parallel to the cut, guide it along the rip fence, as shown in *Cutting Grooves with the Rip Fence*. If the long edge is perpendicular to the cut, use the miter gauge, as shown in *Cutting Dadoes with the Miter Gauge*. On large panels, you can use the rip fence to guide all cuts.

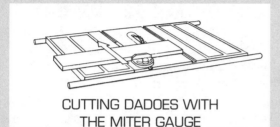

CUTTING DADOES WITH THE MITER GAUGE

If you have a number of duplicate pieces to cut, it helps to set up stops to locate the dadoes. This can be accomplished in several ways. You can clamp a stop block or handscrew to the miter gauge extension fence, as shown in *Miter Gauge Stop*. Or you can use the rip fence in conjunction with the miter gauge, as shown in *Rip Fence Stop*. (This is safe because you're not cutting off a piece that might get caught between the fence and the blade. Never use the fence as a stop when crosscutting.)

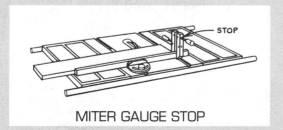

MITER GAUGE STOP

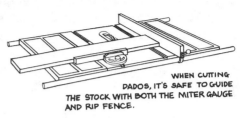

WHEN CUTTING DADOS, IT'S SAFE TO GUIDE THE STOCK WITH BOTH THE MITER GAUGE AND RIP FENCE.

RIP FENCE STOP

If you're cutting multiple dadoes in a number of pieces, you can insert spacers between the end of the pieces and the stop to position each dado, as shown in *Using Spacers*. This will save you from having to reset the stop between cuts.

As you're cutting, be sure to push the stock down flat on the saw table. If the piece rises above the table, the dado won't be a consistent depth, which can affect the way things fit together. Also, keep the feed rate slow and be alert for kickback. A wide dado blade exerts a lot of force on a board and can throw a piece backward with startling speed.

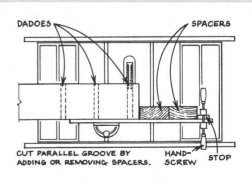

DADOES   SPACERS

CUT PARALLEL GROOVE BY ADDING OR REMOVING SPACERS.   HAND-SCREW   STOP

USING SPACERS

—*BEN ERICKSON*

Cutting Dovetails by Hand

Beyond a few basic hand tools, you'll need only two things to cut dovetails: patience and practice. If you're patient enough, your first dovetails will be surprisingly good. With a little practice, even the worst dovetails get better.

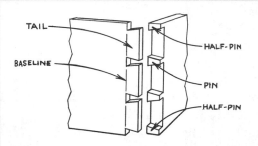

DOVETAIL JOINT, EXPLODED VIEW

The first step in laying out the joint is to scribe the baseline of the pins and tails. This line, shown in *Scribing the Baseline,* determines the length of the tails and pins. To draw the baseline, set a marking gauge to approximately 1/32 inch more than the thickness of the stock. The resulting baseline makes the tails and pins slightly longer than needed—you'll have to sand them flush when you're finished. Think of it as a safety margin. If the pins and tails could were too *short,* you'd have to sand down the entire

SCRIBING THE BASELINE

side of the project. Once you've set the gauge, scribe a line across the ends of the board, as shown in *Scribing the Baseline.* Mark the outside surface with an X.

Cutting the Pins

I start by laying out the pins. On 1/2- to 3/4-inch stock, the centers of the pins should be 1 1/2 to 2 1/2 inches apart. Space the pins equally, and orient them so the narrow side of each pin is on the outside surface. On your first few tries, make the narrow side of the pins at least 1/4 inch wide. A narrower tail looks—and is—more delicate. Wait until you've had some practice.

The pins slope about 80 degrees, and you lay them out with a sliding T-bevel. Since an 80-degree slope rises 1 inch over a run of 6 inches, I set the T-bevel by drawing a 6-inch and a 1-inch line on the bench, as shown in *Setting the Slope.*

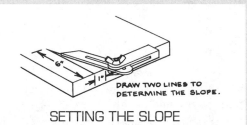

SETTING THE SLOPE

Lay out the slope of the pins on the end grain, as shown in *Laying Out the Pins.* Use a knife for this: It leaves a finer line than a pencil. As you lay out the pins, note that the outside edges of the board have what are called half-pins, shown in the *Dovetail Joint, Exploded View.* Half-pins *are the same width as other pins* but are so named because they slope only on one edge. Once you've drawn

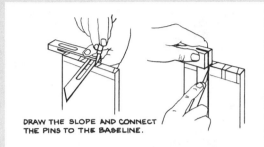

DRAW THE SLOPE AND CONNECT THE PINS TO THE BASELINE.

LAYING OUT THE PINS

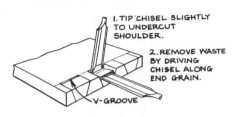

1. TIP CHISEL SLIGHTLY TO UNDERCUT SHOULDER.

2. REMOVE WASTE BY DRIVING CHISEL ALONG END GRAIN.

V-GROOVE

CHOPPING OUT THE WASTE

the pins on the end grain, connect them to the baselines with a square, as shown.

It's time to begin cutting the joint. Put the pin board in the vise, and cut along the lines as shown in *Cutting the Pins*. Cut along the edge of all the pins, staying on the waste side of the lines. Don't cut below the baseline—if you do, it will show in the finished joint.

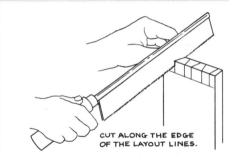

CUT ALONG THE EDGE OF THE LAYOUT LINES.

CUTTING THE PINS

Switch to the chisel to remove the waste between the pins. Start with a wide chisel, using it like a knife to deepen the baseline. Then gently push the chisel in from the waste side to create a small V-groove. This groove creates a very clean line along the baseline, which is crucial to crisp-looking dovetails. It also hides the undercutting you'll do next.

Tap the chisel lightly with a mallet to remove more waste. Angle the chisel slightly as shown in *Chopping Out the Waste*, undercutting the pins in the process. Undercutting gives you a little clearance when you put the joint together. You'll appreciate it: Even the slightest protrusion would keep the joint from coming together tightly. After making the undercut, drive the chisel from the end grain toward the baseline, removing a thin piece of waste. Repeat the process until you're halfway through the board; turn the board over, and remove the rest of the waste the same way. Clean out stray fibers with a chisel or knife.

Cutting the Tails

Use the pins as a template to lay out the tails. Begin with the tail piece on the bench, outside-face down. Put the pin board on the tail piece, outside-face out. Align the edges of the boards, and trace around the pins to

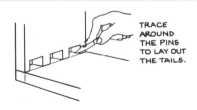

TRACE AROUND THE PINS TO LAY OUT THE TAILS.

LAYING OUT THE TAILS

(continued)

Cutting Dovetails by Hand—*Continued*

lay out the tails, as shown in *Laying Out the Tails*. Trace from the inside corner of the joint so that you can make sure the face of the pins remains on the baseline. Remove the pin board, and mark the waste portions with Xs. With a square, draw pencil lines across the end grain from the ends of the traced line.

Saw and chisel out the waste between the tails the same way you did the pin piece. Try to split the line with the saw.

Saw away the waste on the outside edges of the board. Undercutting with a chisel here would be visible in the finished joint.

Test fit the joint, and trim with a chisel as necessary. Eventually, you'll get good enough that they'll fit on first fit. Until you do, trim any binding surfaces carefully.

—*WALKER T. WEED III*
Weed is a professional woodworker in Dummerston, Vt., and is a juried member of the League of New Hampshire Craftsmen.

FITTING SHELVES IN GROOVES

If you're housing a shelf in a dado or groove, cut the groove—if only in a sample—before you plane the shelves. When you plane the shelf to thickness, plane it to fit snugly in the groove. Cut the groove with a router, by the way; it's the best method for getting a consistent groove.

Jeff Day
Perkasie, Pa.

FITTING MORE SHELVES IN GROOVES

If you're using preplaned stock, you'll find it often varies in thickness. This can be a real problem when you want a shelf to fit snugly in a dado. For best results, rout a dado narrower than the shelf. Then cut a tongue on the shelf that fits in the dado.

M. S. Langley
Detroit, Mich.

FITTING INLAY

If you have difficulty getting inlay to flex into a curved groove, bend it around a hot soldering iron.

Fred Matlack
Emmaus, Pa.

HAND-CUT DOVETAIL GAUGE

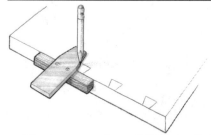

If you cut a lot of dovetails by hand, make your own layout gauge. Use hardwood for the fence and plexiglass, phenolic, aluminum, brass, hardwood, or even hardwood plywood for the blade. On one end, cut the blade to the angle you prefer for your dovetails. Leave the other end

(continued on page 92)

Cutting Dovetails on the Table Saw

When cutting dovetails, I like to cut the tails on a table saw and then mark out and saw the pins in the usual way. I find this method takes only half the time, and I end up with clean, accurate surfaces that need minimal fitting.

If there is a choice, I always cut the tails in the shorter piece of wood. Holding a long board vertically and passing it over the saw blade is awkward if not downright dangerous. It is essential to use a quality saw blade—I much prefer the carbide-tipped variety for its clean, uniform cut.

When cutting very fine tails—those in small drawers, for example—you may not be able to use a regular ⅛-inch-thick carbide blade. In such a case I use a steel planer blade. It has no set to the teeth.

The first step is to cut each piece to length, making sure that the cuts are dead square. Then set a cutting gauge to just a hair over the thickness of the stock you are using, and mark a line across both sides and the two edges of each piece to be joined. Now lay out the tails, with a chisel-pointed pencil, on one end of one board only. Square the lines across the edge and mark the other side. Mark the waste so you won't saw on the wrong side of the line.

Set the blade of the table saw to the dovetail angle, which is usually about 15 degrees. Place the marked board vertically on the table. Raise the blade until it is ¹⁄₁₆ inch below the gauged line. Make a new wooden fence for the miter gauge, 2 or 3 inches high, so it supports the stock and won't be cut in half by the saw blade. This fence will also help prevent tear-out.

Hold the board vertically, with the blade on the waste side of one of the pencil lines. Put a stop block against the side of the board and clamp it to the miter gauge fence, as shown. Make the cut, then turn the board around and make a second cut with the same stop setting. If both ends of the board are to be dovetailed, turn it end to end, and make the same two cuts.

Now, without changing any settings, make the same cuts in each of the remaining boards. Then move the stop block and make another series of cuts. Continue until you cut all the tails.

You'll find that the saw blade has removed most of the waste. Chisel away the rest. From here on you continue in the usual way—marking the pins from the tails with a knife, sawing them out, and chiseling the waste.

—SIMON WATTS
Watts is a professional woodworker and author in San Francisco, Calif.

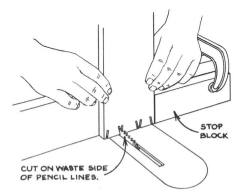

CUT ON WASTE SIDE OF PENCIL LINES.

STOP BLOCK

CUTTING TAILS ON THE TABLE SAW

Cutting Half-Blind Dovetails

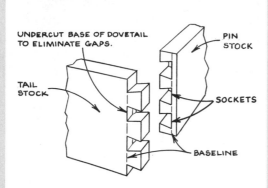

CUTTING HALF-BLIND DOVETAILS, EXPLODED VIEW

Half-blind dovetails—commonly used to join drawer sides to drawer fronts—are easier than they look. With half-blind dovetails, you see only one side of the joint, so small inaccuracies aren't as noticeable as on through dovetails. In fact, if you're just learning to cut dovetails, half-blind tails are a good place to start.

Begin, as with through dovetails, by laying out the baselines. The rules for positioning the baseline aren't hard-and-fast. If you're doing something like a drawer, the sides of the piece may be thinner than the front. And no matter what you're dovetailing, the length of the tails is somewhat variable. *Scribing the Baselines* will help you make the right decisions.

When I cut the dovetails, my method differs slightly from that described in "Cutting Dovetails by Hand" on page 86. I begin the joint with the tails. Since I often build multiples of a piece, I like to use sheet-metal templates to make layout a bit quicker and more accurate. If you'd like, however, you can lay them out with a sliding T-bevel as explained in "Cutting Dovetails by Hand."

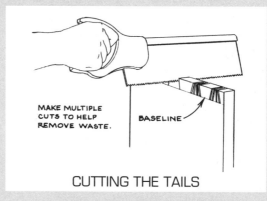

CUTTING THE TAILS

Once I've cut out the tail, I make a few extra cuts within the waste area, as shown in *Cutting the Tails*. This makes it easier to clean out the waste. I then clamp the stock to my bench and position the chisel about $\frac{1}{16}$ inch in front of the baseline. I strike it with a mallet to make a cut about $\frac{1}{8}$ inch deep, turn it over, and then chop out the waste. The initial $\frac{1}{8}$-inch-deep cut prevents chip-out. Undercut slightly as you work.

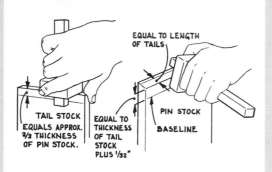

SCRIBING THE BASELINES

Cutting the Pins

I trace around the pins with a chip-carving knife to lay out the tails. That way, if I've made a slight error on the tails, the pins account for it, giving me a gap-free joint. Once I've laid out the pins on the end grain, as shown in *Laying Out the Pins,* I extend the lines down the inner face, using a square and a knife.

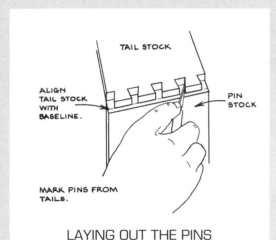

LAYING OUT THE PINS

As you cut the pins, you'll have to hold the saw diagonally, as shown in *Cutting the Pins.* This time saw about 1/32 inch on the waste side of the line. Once again, make additional cuts between the pins to ease waste removal. You can't cut into either the baseline or depth line without ruining the appearance of the joint. As a result, you won't be able to cut into the back corner of the sockets. In a minute, you'll clean up the corners with a chisel.

Chop out the pins much as you chopped out the tails. Clamp the stock to the bench,

and make a downward cut across the grain and about 1/16 inch above the baseline. Chop about 1/8 inch deep at each pass, working with care. After each cross-grain cut, clean out the waste by paring from the end grain. Do this in thin layers rather than large chips—the pins are delicate. As mentioned, you'll find that the saw cuts don't define the entire edge of the pin. Carefully guide a chisel along the sawed surfaces to clean into the corners of the sockets.

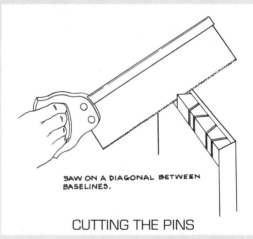

CUTTING THE PINS

When you're done, tap the tail stock into the pin stock. As you tap, feel for stiff resistance and check the back of your tails for crushed fibers. Either is a sign that you'll have to have to pare the joint for a better fit. If so, pare the waste of the pins. Working into the end grain is easier and gives you better control.

—*Mario Rodriguez*
Rodriguez is a professional woodworker in Warwick, N.Y.

straight for use as a square. Glue and/or screw the fence to the blade, and make it all as precise and square as you can.

Frank Wright
Holland, Mich.

UNDERCUT DOVETAILS

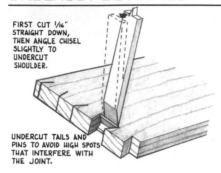

FIRST CUT 1/16" STRAIGHT DOWN, THEN ANGLE CHISEL SLIGHTLY TO UNDERCUT SHOULDER.

UNDERCUT TAILS AND PINS TO AVOID HIGH SPOTS THAT INTERFERE WITH THE JOINT.

When you're cutting dovetails, cut just on the waste side of the line. To avoid fitting problems, undercut the pins and tails as shown.

Jeff Day
Perkasie, Pa.

PUTTING YOUR TAILS TOGETHER

When you assemble dovetails, start the pins and tails together without glue. When the pins are no more than 1/16 inch into the sockets between the tails, apply glue to all of the exposed mating surfaces. Pull the dovetails tightly together with clamps.

David Page
Swarthmore, Pa.

CLAMPING DOVETAILS

For supertight dovetails, clamp them between glue blocks that are notched around the pins. The

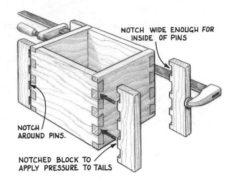

NOTCH WIDE ENOUGH FOR INSIDE OF PINS

NOTCH AROUND PINS.

NOTCHED BLOCK TO APPLY PRESSURE TO TAILS

notched glue blocks apply pressure directly to the tails and push them against the pins.

Malden Rand
Huntington, W.Va.

MASS-PRODUCTION DOVETAILS

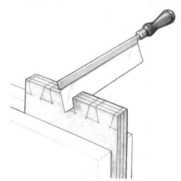

When I'm cutting a series of dovetails, I perform similar operations at the same time. I lay out the dovetails on all the side pieces, for example, stack them in the vise, and cut them all at once. (Get yourself a good stout dovetail saw to do this, one of the expensive ones with a brass back.) I chop out the waste between them all at once and then cut the pins to match.

Jeff Day
Perkasie, Pa.

6 WORKBENCHES, MATERIALS HANDLING, AND STORAGE

BENCH HOOK

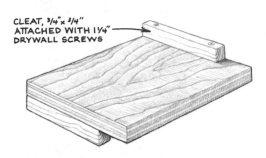

CLEAT, 3/4" x 3/4"
ATTACHED WITH 1¼"
DRYWALL SCREWS

A bench hook is one of the most basic and versatile additions to any workbench. It's a flat board with cleats on opposing sides and ends. Hook one cleat on the edge of the bench in front of you. Use the other end as a stop to support your work.

When you're crosscutting with a handsaw, the bench hook keeps the stock off the bench and firmly positioned square to the saw. When you're hand planing with a bench hook, work pushes against the top cleat as you push the plane.

Supporting work on a bench hook is better than clamping it between a vise and a bench dog. Clamping the wood between two points may cause it to bow upward so you can't plane it truly flat.

You can make your bench hook of solid wood. Plywood is even better, especially for the base, because it is flat and stable.

Roy Moss
Rio Rancho, N. Mex.

PLYWOOD CARRIER

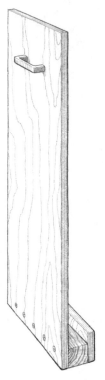

It's not the weight so much as the shape that makes it difficult to carry sheets of plywood. With one hand hooked under the sheet and one on top, you end up twisting yourself into an awkward, tilted position that can't be good for the old vertebrae. Slipping your fingers out from under the sheet without pinching them is tricky, too. This plywood carrier eliminates both problems. It has a conveniently placed handle so you can stand up straight as you carry the sheet. And your fingers are not underneath when you put the sheet down.

Jeff Greef
Soquel, Calif.

MAGAZINE OR PLAN HOLDER

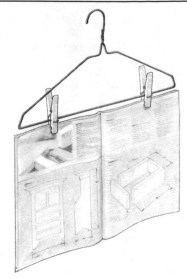

Here's a convenient way to keep your plans off the workbench yet conveniently on hand during a project. Put two spring clothespins over the bar of a wire clothes hanger. Open to the page you want and clip the magazine or plan to the hanger. Hang it on the shop wall.

Ralph S. Wilkes
Branchport, N.Y.

BENCH STOP FOR JOINTING

This simple wedged bench stop holds stock firmly for edge-jointing with a hand plane, and it won't mar the workpiece. Forward pressure while planing tightens the stop. To release it, just tap on the narrow end of the movable wedge with a mallet. I put a bevel of about 10 degrees on the mating edges of the wedges so the movable wedge can't pop up. I attach

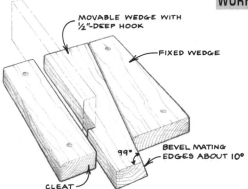

MOVABLE WEDGE WITH
½"-DEEP HOOK

FIXED WEDGE

BEVEL MATING
EDGES ABOUT 10°

99°

CLEAT

my stop directly to my bench with #8 × 1½-inch flathead wood screws. If you don't want to screw into your bench, mount the stop on a piece of plywood. Secure the plywood to the bench with vise dogs or clamps.

Ralph S. Wilkes
Branchport, N.Y.

QUICK WORK SURFACE SUPPORT

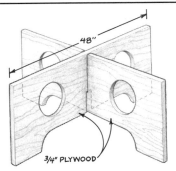

48"

3/4" PLYWOOD

This work surface support turns a sheet of plywood into a temporary workbench. It's quick, is easy to make, and disassembles to store flat. Cut a notch halfway through two pieces of plywood so they will interlock as shown. Cut holes to lighten the legs without reducing strength. The curves cut into the bottom create four feet so the supports will be less

likely to rock. Make the support whatever height suits your work—about 18 inches is handy for assembling cabinets. I make mine the full 48-inch width of a sheet of plywood. This way, I don't have to cut the stock to width and I can throw a full sheet of plywood on top to make a temporary work surface.

Jim Tolpin
Port Townsend, Wash.

PANEL-CUTTING BENCH

Cutting plywood, laminates, panels, or anything else big and cumbersome is tough without using a panel saw. I built a panel-cutting bench that screws to the top of two wooden sawhorses. The bench consists of four 8-foot 2 × 4s and also a couple of 30-inch 1 × 6s. Space the 2 × 4s evenly and screw them to the 1 × 6s. Then screw both of the 1 × 6s to the sawhorses.

Tom Groller
Palmerton, Pa.

VISE-MOUNTING ADVICE

Mount your vise ¹⁄₁₆ inch below your bench top, out of the way of parts sliding along the work surface. This margin also allows you to sand or plane the bench top a few times before reaching the level of your vise.

Jeff Greef
Soquel, Calif.

VISE HELPER

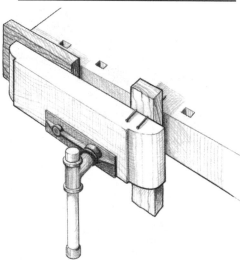

It's hard to grip a piece of wood at one end of many woodworking vises because the jaws won't stay parallel. To solve this problem, drop a block of the same thickness as the stock you want to grip in the other end of the vise. The vise jaws will stay parallel, resulting in a better grip. Add nails at one end of the block to keep it from slipping through the vise jaws and dropping to the floor.

William Guthrie
Pontiac, Mich.

PINCH PREVENTERS

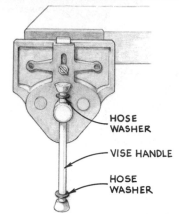

HOSE WASHER

VISE HANDLE

HOSE WASHER

Have you ever pinched your finger between the handle and shaft of your metal vise? I have. Once too often. To solve the problem, I slipped a rubber washer onto both ends of the handle as shown. Be sure to purchase washers with a hole diameter equal to the handle's shank diameter.

Gordon Krupp
Northbrook, Ill.

SPACE-SAVING SAW SETUP

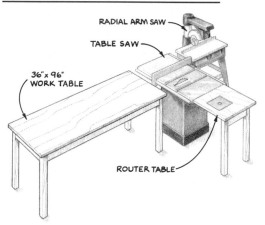

RADIAL ARM SAW

TABLE SAW

36" x 96" WORK TABLE

ROUTER TABLE

Here's how I arrange my stationary saws to conserve space in my tight shop. This arrangement makes it easy to crosscut long pieces on the radial arm saw, and it provides plenty of support for cutting large panels on the table saw. Adding the router table to the side of the table saw lets me use the rip fence to handle wide stock on the router table. It also increases the width of the saw table to 78 inches.

Bob Hawks
Tulsa, Okla.

BUILDING WORK SURFACES TO THE SAME HEIGHT

When building workbenches and tool cabinets for your shop, make all the bench tops and work surfaces the same height whenever possible. This will make it easier to handle materials in your shop. For example, when cutting long boards on your table saw, you can use your workbench as an extension to help support the boards as they come off the saw. However, you may want to position the work surfaces of some tools *below* the norm. If you keep a jointer beside your table saw, for instance, the top of the jointer fence should be below the saw table. This way, it won't interfere when crosscutting long boards.

Nick Engler
West Milton, Ohio

SHHH! I'M WORKING

My downstairs neighbors used to complain about the noise when I was making something on my workbench in the evening or on weekends. (I live on the top floor of an apartment building.) After talking with them I tried putting several layers of rubber-backed carpeting under each leg of my bench. Now it's their television that bothers me!

Simon Watts
San Francisco, Calif.

WORKBENCH TOP REBORN

There are lots of ways to create a good workbench top, but every top should have two qualities: It must be strong, and it must be flat. My bench top is a worn and knife-hacked 2½-inch-thick maple slab that had been discarded from a restaurant kitchen. I turned it over and attached it to my bench frame. After a little sanding, it looked like new.

Ralph S. Wilkes
Branchport, N.Y.

HOLES IN THE WALL

Maneuvering long stock can be a real hassle in a small shop. Whenever you want to pass long boards through a machine, there always seems to be a wall in the way. To solve the problem, I cut a hole in the wall next to my radial arm saw and let the board hang outside during a cut. I installed a door in the hole to keep the weather out. The same idea could be used to make room for outfeed from a planer, jointer, or table saw.

Jeff Greef
Soquel, Calif.

WASTE NOT

Epoxy resins and hardeners are thick stuff—and expensive. To empty the last bit into another container, I connect the two containers, one above the other, with their caps glued together and a hole drilled through the caps. I let the upper one drain into the other container for as long as it takes. Hot-melt glue works for joining the caps.

Allen L. Riggs
Hill City, Kans.

PREVENT GLAZING COMPOUND FROM HARDENING

It happens every time. You use half a can of glazing compound, put the top back on, and the stuff goes hard. The problem is, enough air was trapped in the can to cure the compound. To prevent this, cut a disc of waxed paper, sheet plastic, or aluminum foil to the same diameter as the can, and press it down on the compound before replacing the cover.

Ralph S. Wilkes
Branchport, N.Y.

PLYWOOD CUBBIES

Use all those small plywood scraps you've accumulated to make cubbies. Screw the cubbies to the wall or stack them to hold tools and other items.

Jeff Greef
Soquel, Calif.

DRAWER COMPARTMENTS

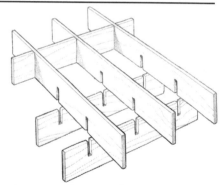

Arrange drawers for small boxes of screws, nails, and hardware by dividing the space with slotted, interlocking pieces of ¼-inch plywood.

Jeff Greef
Soquel, Calif.

BAG THOSE OLD JEANS

When your spouse won't let you be seen in your old jeans anymore, you *still* have a good excuse for not throwing them away. Cut off the legs below the knee, turn them inside out, sew the cut ends closed, then turn them right-side out. You've got a sturdy bag for carrying planes, chisels, or anything else that needs protection in your tool box.

Ric Hanisch
Quakertown, Pa.

LUMBER RACKS

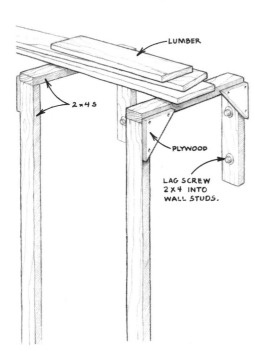

Get that lumber up off the floor with 2 × 4 racks built against the wall. Brace the joints with triangular pieces of plywood as shown.

Jeff Greef
Soquel, Calif.

HOMEMADE BRACKETS

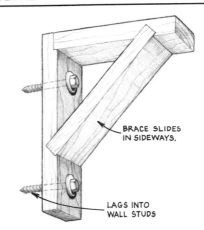

Tired of trotting down to the hardware store every time I needed a bracket or shelf support, I began turning out my own. I make them of scrap softwood and cut the diagonal brace and saw slots to fit. I screw the bracket to the wall and then slide the brace in. There's no need for glue, because friction holds the brace in place. Most often, ¾ × 2-inch stock is sufficient, but I use 2 × 4s when making brackets to support lumber.

Simon Watts
San Francisco, Calif.

AIRTIGHT DOWEL STORAGE

Grooved dowels are a lot cheaper if you buy them in bulk. The problem is that once you open the package, the dowels tend to swell when the weather gets humid. To prevent this, store the dowels in old margarine tubs. If they do swell, stick them in the microwave for 15 seconds or so to cook the moisture out.

Tom Groller
Palmerton, Pa.

STORING DOWELS AND MOLDING

I store all my dowels and thin molding upright in one big garbage can. To keep the materials sorted, I tuck them in cardboard tubing from rolled carpets.

Ralph S. Wilkes
Branchport, N.Y.

PORTABLE BENCH LIGHT

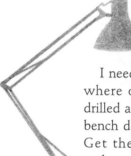

I needed a light I could place anywhere on my bench. To do this, I drilled a hole in the top of a wooden bench dog to fit a flexible-arm lamp. Get the lamp before you drill to make sure that the hole size is right.

Yeung Chan
Millbrae, Calif.

LAMP ON A CLAMP

This simple arm lets me use a pipe clamp to position light where I need it on my bench. I use it with a cheap clamp-on light fixture. The arm is easily removed from the clamp when I need the clamp for its usual duties.

The arm is made from a scrap of 2 × 6 or 2 × 8. Make the arm whatever length suits your work. Use a band saw to cut a slot and curve as shown in the drawing, and drill a hole for the pipe. Drill a ¼-inch hole for a carriage bolt as shown. Tighten the bar clamp to the bench, slide the

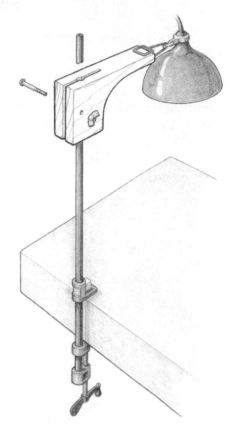

arm down the pipe, and tighten a washer and wing nut onto the carriage bolt to secure the arm. Clamp the lamp to the arm and you are ready to work.

Joseph Doczy
Fayetteville, Ark.

PORTABLE SHOP LIGHT

It's always handy to have extra light wherever you need it around the shop. A mechanic's drop light is great for this purpose, especially one that is attached to a retractable reel. Hang it from the ceiling, and grab it when you need it.

David Page
Swarthmore, Pa.

GOOSENECK SHOP LAMP

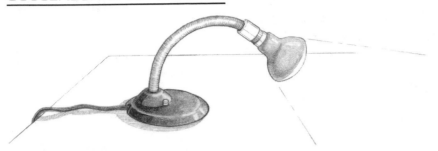

An old gooseneck desk lamp is a handy item to have around the workshop. Discard the original shade, and screw a reflector bulb into the socket. It's just the thing for close work on the bench, since it can be easily adjusted to any position.

Ralph S. Wilkes
Branchport, N.Y.

PORTABLE DISC STORAGE

Storage or file boxes for computer disks make great organizers for sanding discs. These boxes come in a variety of capacities, with and without dividers. A 6-inch-diameter sanding disc fits nicely in file boxes intended for 5¼-inch computer disks.

Andrew Lenhart
Royal Oak, Mich.

FILE SANDPAPER UNDER "S"

I've found that manila file folders make a great place to store sheets of sandpaper. Before, I always had to hunt through a stack of odds and ends. Now I put sandpaper in a folder labeled for the grit number and store the folders in the filing cabinet with my woodworking magazines and papers.

Robert Pauley
Decatur, Ga.

NEW USE FOR OLD COMPUTER CABINETS

IBM punch cards are obsolete, and so are the filing cabinets designed for their storage. These heavily constructed cabinets are ideal for storing hand tools such as planes and chisels. Used office furniture companies are a possible source.

Ric Hanisch
Quakertown, Pa.

ORGANIZING SMALL BLADES

I store and organize small blades (for the coping saw, scroll saw, saber saw, and hack saw) in short lengths of plastic pipe. I put the blades inside the pipes and cork one or both ends. To keep these homemade containers convenient, I store them in slightly larger pieces of plastic pipe. I fasten the pipe sections to the wall with a screw at the top and a long screw or nail at the bottom as shown in the drawing.

Bill Houghton
Sebastopol, Calif.

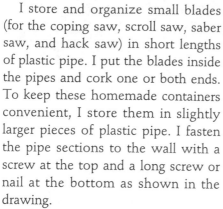

ROUTER BIT STORAGE

To keep router bits organized and protected from nicks, store them in a block of wood with holes drilled to match your bit shanks. Drill only enough holes for the bits you now own. Add more holes as you acquire bits. This way you can space the holes according to bit size.

Jeff Greef
Soquel, Calif.

STYROFOAM TOOL HOLDER

To organize chisels, screwdrivers, and drill bits, simply stick them in a

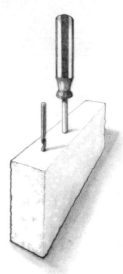

block of Styrofoam. For your large-diameter tools, it's helpful to predrill a small hole before you press the tool into the Styrofoam.

The foam is rigid enough to stand on its own, it protects the cutting edges of sharp tools, and the tool holder is handy to carry in the shop.

Lee Maughan
Panaca, Nev.

HANG THAT SQUARE

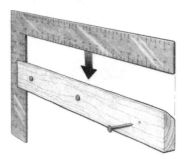

The accuracy of framing squares is not improved by dropping them. To protect my squares and to store them conveniently, I devised a holder. I cut a piece of 1 × 3 the same length as the inside of the blade (longer leg) of the square and sawed a 45-degree bevel along one edge. I then nailed the strip to the wall within easy reach of my bench.

Jim Allder
Pearland, Tex.

MAGNETIC TOOL HOLDERS

Magnetic kitchen-knife holders work well in the shop for holding chisels, screwdrivers, and other small metal tools.

Jeff Greef
Soquel, Calif.

MAGNETIC SAW HOLDERS

I have a number of Japanese saws that I use frequently. They are elegant tools and I enjoy seeing them. I used to put them away each time in their cardboard sleeves, but now I have a better idea. I put magnetic door latches above my bench so I can just lean over and . . . *click*—they're in place.

Simon Watts
San Francisco, Calif.

CALCULATING MOISTURE CONTENT OF WOOD

If you dry your own lumber, the rule of thumb is to let the wood dry for one year per inch of thickness. However, it can take anywhere from several months to several years for the moisture to evaporate from green lumber, depending on not only the thickness but also the species of the wood. To accurately gauge the mois-ture content of the wood as it dries, test it from time to time. Cut a small block from the *middle* of a green board and weigh it. Let it dry for several hours in a slow oven (275 to 300 degrees Fahrenheit) and weigh it again. To find the moisture content, plug the two different weights into this formula:

Moisture content
= [(weight wet − weight dry)
÷ weight dry] × 100

For example, if the sample weighs 4 ounces when green and 3 ounces when dry, the moisture content is 33 percent:

[(4 − 3) ÷ 3] × 100 = 33

Air-dried wood never gets as dry as kiln-dried, so don't expect the moisture content to fall below 10 percent unless you live in a very dry climate. In most locations, air-dried lumber is ready to use when the moisture content is between 10 and 12 percent.

Nick Engler
West Milton, Ohio

LONG ENOUGH?

Before you put lumber on the rack, use a black felt-tipped marker to write the length of each board on its end. Then you won't fool yourself into thinking you have a nice long board up there only to pull out a 3-footer. Also, it's not always easy to tell the species from the end of the board, so write this information on the end as well, using your own code.

David Page
Swarthmore, Pa.

NEW LIFE FOR SCRAP

Imagine all the wood scraps you throw out each year. I've started gluing everything into blocks, regardless of species, and then resawing for turning stock or to make any off-the-wall little box or other little project I can invent.

Bill Parrish
Norris, Tenn.

CHECKMATING THE CHECKS

Anyone who works with green wood knows how rapidly it can dry out, checking along the way. My solution is to put the freshly cut chunks in plastic garbage bags along with wet sawdust. I seal the bag with the ties provided and set it in a cool place. In hot weather, you might add a couple of handfuls of salt to discourage mold.

Boles Derenda
West Seneca, N.Y.

ACCLIMATE YOUR LUMBER

Even though I work with only kiln-dried lumber, I don't have enough room to store it indoors. As a result, I store it outside, under cover. Because the air in my shop is drier than the outside air, (especially in winter), I always bring stock into the shop at least one week before I work it. This prevents the wood from shrinking, cracking, or twisting in the middle of a project.

Tom Groller
Palmerton, Pa.

FLATTENING VENEERS

When veneers get badly warped or wavy before you use them, spray them with a plant mister, put them under weight, and let them dry.

Tom Groller
Palmerton, Pa.

PICKING UP SPILLED NAILS

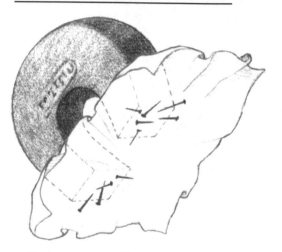

Picking up spilled nails with a magnet seemed silly to me because picking the nails off the magnet was as much work as picking them off the floor. That was before it occurred to me that I could pull all the nails off the magnet at once by wrapping it in a handkerchief first.

Doug Parker
Appling, Ga.

DOUBLE-DUTY DUMPSTERS

To make handling trash in the shop easier, I've purchased several rubber garbage cans with five-wheel dollies. Their stability makes them suited for uses besides handling waste. Recently, they've doubled as turntables in the spray booth. The 32-inch height makes them ideal for elevating work to be sprayed. I also use them for wheeling furniture pieces from one machine to another. The added ballast of trash makes them even less prone to tip.

Lee Maughan
Panaca, Nev.

EGG CARTON SORTER

Most workshops have a can of assorted nails, screws, washers, bolts, and other small items that didn't get put back away the last time they were used. When you finally get inspired to sort this stuff out, use an egg carton to speed the job. It takes up a lot less space than a dozen containers. When you are done sorting, just scoop the hardware into its proper containers.

Ralph S. Wilkes
Branchport, N.Y.

SHOP-BUILT DOLLY

I made a dolly for my workshop by attaching four flat-plate furniture casters to a ¾ × 18 × 26-inch piece of plywood. I use it to move heavy furniture and shop machinery.

Ralph S. Wilkes
Branchport, N.Y.

HANDSCREW STORAGE

Suspend your handscrews from the ceiling with this arrangement of common pipe fittings. Use three 2- or 3-foot

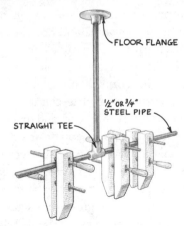

FLOOR FLANGE

½" OR ¾" STEEL PIPE

STRAIGHT TEE

lengths of steel pipe, a floor flange, and a straight T with female threads.

Jeff Greef
Soquel, Calif.

ROLLING CLAMP CART

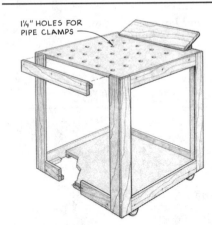

1¼" HOLES FOR PIPE CLAMPS

No longer do I test my sprinting skills by dashing across the shop to get one more clamp during a glue-up. The clamps are always right on hand and organized since I built this rolling clamp cart. The cart is essentially a 3-foot cube constructed of ¾ × 3½-inch boards. The top and bottom are ¾-inch plywood, and the top is drilled with holes for my pipe clamps. The angled board on one side holds C-clamps and doubles as a push handle. Spring clamps get stored on the legs. I put a hook on one side for corner clamps.

Construction of the clamp cart is down and dirty. I glued and screwed ¾-inch-wide cleats to the inside of the rails, running the cleats over the stiles to form a lap joint. The cleats support the plywood top and bottom. The rails are glued and screwed to the plywood. The C-clamp board is held at an angle by a 29-inch-long piece of 2 X 4 that I ripped with a cut angled from opposing corners. This assembly also is glued and screwed to the cart. The cart rolls on furniture casters.

Bill Parrish
Norris, Tenn.

SAWING STANDS

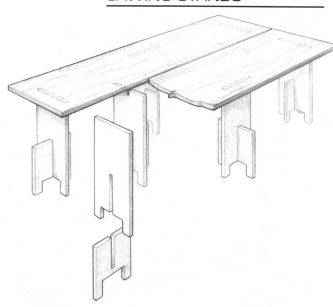

I use several easily made and easily disassembled particleboard stands to support plywood when sawing it with a portable saw. I get by with a minimum number of stands by positioning them directly along the path of the saw. Then I saw right through the stands, which continue to support both sides of the cut.

Ron Pavelka
Orange, Calif.

BENCH-TOP MACHINES

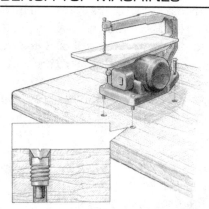

I have a small workshop, so I have to double up tools in the available space. One of my space-saving moves was to equip my workbench with four threaded-insert nuts that let me easily attach or remove my scroll saw. I set them a fraction below the surface of the bench so I can install flathead machine screws to keep dust and chips from filling holes when the scroll saw is not in use.

This idea works equally well for any bench-top machine that isn't used frequently, such as a grinder or mortising machine.

Robert Heil
Rockford, Ill.

MACHINE CASTERS

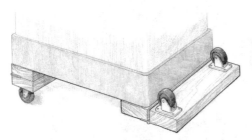

I often need to move my stationary machines around my small shop to make room for projects. To simplify the process, I've fitted them with casters mounted on hinged 2 × 4s that can be flipped under the base by lifting one end of the machine at a time. I used ordinary door hinges, and casters that each have a load rating of at least a quarter of the weight of the machine.

David R. Johnson
Apple Valley, Minn.

LOCKING CASTERS

I mount my stationary machines on casters with a locking lever on each wheel. With the wheels locked there is no chance that the machine will move, ruining a cut. My planer, however, is mounted on ball casters rather than wheel casters. These casters turn easily enough to let you move the machine but not so freely that the machine will wander across the floor while you use it. The ball casters are more convenient than the wheel casters, and it does no harm if the planer shifts a bit while I'm feeding a board. In fact, I've occasionally given the planer a shove when it became evident that an outfeeding board was about to hit something in the shop.

Jeff Greef
Soquel, Calif.

PROTECT GLASS-PANEL EDGES

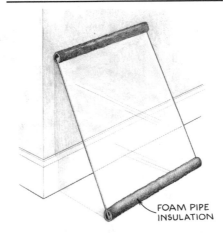

FOAM PIPE
INSULATION

It doesn't take much to crack or chip the edges of a sheet of glass or mirror plate while it's stored against a wall of the shop awaiting use in a project. If the panel is accidentally rested on a small piece of grit, the panel's weight can easily cause a chip to occur. To protect the panel until I need it, I slip foam pipe insulation over the edges that will contact the floor and wall.

Walter J. Morrison
Northport, N.Y.

7 DESIGNING AND BUILDING YOUR OWN WORKBENCH

DESIGN CONSIDERATIONS

Think of a woodworker's bench. Most likely the image in your mind is a stout, narrow maple table. It's hip-high, and it has vises at both ends. When most people think of woodworking, they think of Gepetto hard at work at this classic European workbench.

This classic bench is a superb tool that has evolved for hundreds of years. It came out of preindustrial European joinery shops, where it was used to hold flat boards for hand planing surfaces and edges and for cutting end joints: traditional cabinet-making techniques.

Purchasing such a bench can be expensive. A top-of-the-line tradi-

tional joiner's bench can cost more than a table saw, jointer, and planer combined. Even a cheap traditional bench can cost several hundred dollars. And once you've spent that money, a traditional joiner's bench may not be what you need. If you are building large plywood cabinets, for example, you'll want a wider bench. If you're carving, you'll want something smaller. And if you want a bench for home-maintenance chores as well as woodworking, the joiner's bench will be too specialized for much of what you do.

Your best bet: Design and build your own bench. You'll get exactly what you need, and you'll save money. But what exactly do you need? Let's take a look at the big questions first. Then, at the end of the chapter, you'll find some actual plans: One for a simple bench, the other for a more rigorous bench, likely to meet any demand you place on it.

HOW HIGH?

The height of a bench varies depending on its intended use. For hand-tool work, set the top surface of the bench to a height just below your hip bone, or to about where your wrist hangs with your arm held limp at your side. If you are between 5 feet 6 inches and 6 feet tall, this will likely come to between 34 and 36 inches from the floor. If the bench will serve as an outfeed table for your table saw or other stationary tools, build it to match the tool table height. If you do a lot of work with routers and other portable power tools, you may want to increase the height to about elbow level.

HOW WIDE?

Width varies, too. For stability, a freestanding bench should be at least 24 inches wide. A narrow bench like this is very handy for most joinery work because you can clamp something in the vise and then work on at least three sides of it. A narrow bench can be convenient for planing or sanding panels because you can secure panels to the bench and work on the entire surface without repositioning the panel or reaching over an expanse of bench. Also, a narrow bench discourages clutter. Even if it does get cluttered, it's quicker to clear 12 square feet than 18 square feet.

On the other hand, if most of your work is large and you use a lot of plywood or other sheet goods, a narrow bench isn't what you need. Maybe you don't even need a "bench" at all. Perhaps you would be better served by a wide outfeed table that wraps around the sides of your table saw to support sheet goods as you cut them.

If you are a homeowner with a woodworking hobby, you might be looking for a bench that's narrow enough for woodworking but wide enough for other chores—refinishing or painting furniture, for example. A bench width of about 33 inches would be a good compromise.

HOW LONG?

If your bench is 6 feet long, you'll be able to easily work on pieces that are 10 or even 12 feet long. You'll probably never work on anything longer than that. After all, you want to be able to get around your bench without buying a bus ticket.

Often, the space in your shop will limit the length (and perhaps the width) of your bench. If your bench will be freestanding, you'll want at least 3 feet of elbow room on all sides.

TRADITIONAL JOINER'S BENCH

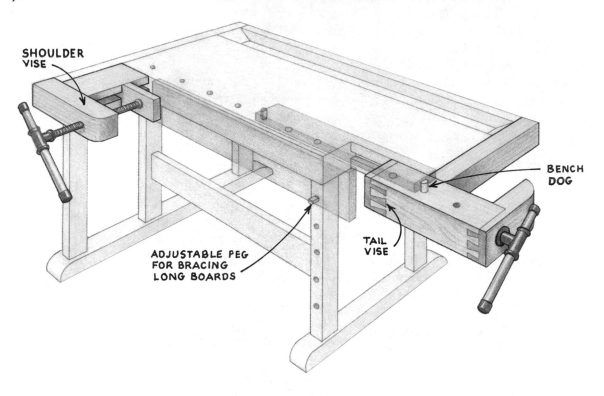

SHOULDER VISE

BENCH DOG

ADJUSTABLE PEG FOR BRACING LONG BOARDS

TAIL VISE

CARVER'S BENCH

A 6-foot-long bench isn't a liability for most kinds of work. The one notable exception is carving. Carvers need a heavy, sturdy bench that will stay put during handwork. They don't usually work on long, straight boards. They need lots of clamping options and they need access to all sides of their work. The *Carver's Bench* shown on the opposite page has a 24 × 36-inch top. It has drawers to store a carver's myriad of hand tools. The tools and drawers make the bench heavier and less likely to move under the pressure of carving.

DO I WANT STORAGE?

The space under the bench top can provide lots of handy storage space in the form of drawers or shelves. As with the carver's bench, the tools stored there will add weight and stability to your bench. But many woodworkers want their workbench to be just a workbench. They have plenty of storage nearby, and they like the idea of a bench that's dedicated to nothing but the task at hand. And perhaps you want your bench to be easy to knock down and move around the shop. A bench full of tools isn't going anywhere on short notice.

If you add a bank of drawers or a cupboard for hand tools, they're likely to catch a lot of dust, unless you also put in a dust shelf. A dust shelf is simply a shelf that runs the full length and width of the drawers or cupboard. Make it 6 or 8 inches below the bench top. This makes a handy shelf for the tools you are using for the current job. Also, it gives you the option of running clamps under the bench top.

Another traditional kind of storage is the tool well, like the one shown in *Traditional Joiner's Bench* on the opposite page. This is where you can put tools without knocking them off the bench as you work. Some woodworkers think tool wells store more dust than tools.

THE DOG DECISION

When it comes to bench dogs, you have two main decisions to make: Do you want round dog holes or rectangular dog holes? And do you want to use steel dogs or wooden dogs?

Round holes are easy to make; just drill them. For a rectangular hole, you'll either have to chop a square mortise or rout grooves in pieces before the bench top is glued up. Round dogs can twist in their holes. This can be annoying. But it can also be handy for clamping odd shapes. One real advantage of rectangular dogs is that it's easy to design them with a head that will recess just below the surface of the bench. This means you'll never have to go hunting for the dog: It will always be in one of the holes. Also, you can easily incorporate a simple spring so that dog height is adjustable. "The Advanced Bench" on page 121 uses rectangular dogs with these features opposing the end vise. It uses round dogs opposing the face vise.

Some woodworkers like steel dogs because they are stronger than wooden dogs. You can, however, design around the problem. A ½-inch-diameter steel dog will be strong enough for any job, but the same work will require ¾-inch wooden-dowel dogs. Before deciding on the extra strength of metal, consider this, as well. Metal may damage either your tools or the wood. Wooden dogs, on the other hand, won't leave marks on your stock and won't damage a plane on an errant pass. One more note about bench dogs: They'll grip better if you slant the holes a couple of degrees so that the dogs lean in toward the vise.

CONSTRUCTION TIPS

Whether you are building a full-blown cabinetmaker's bench or a simple all-purpose work table, you want it to be heavy and rigid. The bench must not rack or slide along the floor under your work movements. The time-honored method of gaining this mass is to equip the bench with a thick, solid wood top. But there are other ways to gain mass, as described in "Bench-Top Options" on page 114.

Whatever top you choose must be solidly connected to a sturdy base. To eliminate wobble, the joinery of the legs to the aprons and stretchers must be made as rigid as possible. You can make an extremely rigid base with the screw and glue con-

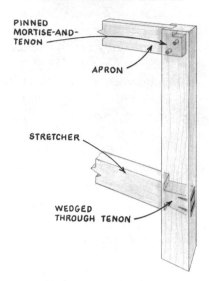

BASE JOINERY DETAIL

PINNED MORTISE-AND-TENON

APRON

STRETCHER

WEDGED THROUGH TENON

struction of the "The Basic Bench" on page 118. Another way to gain tremendous strength and stability is to fasten the bench to wall studs. The traditional solution is the somewhat more elegant (and more time-consuming) mortise and tenon. You can glue the base together and use either pinned mortise-and-tenon joints or wedged through tenons for extra strength. Most people, however, simply bolt the tenons in their mortises, as in "The Advanced Bench" on page 121. This allows them to disassemble the bench if they need to move it.

A solid wood top will expand and contract with humidity changes. You need to allow for this movement when you attach the top to the base. On a narrow bench, such as "The Advanced Bench" on page 121, you can accomplish this by using bolts in slotted or oversized holes. On that

ATTACHMENT CLEATS

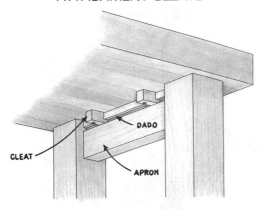

CLEAT

DADO

APRON

bench, the bolts are only 12 inches apart—the oversized holes allow enough movement.

For a wider bench, use cleats that travel in grooved aprons. This allows the top to freely expand and contract with seasonal changes in moisture content. Never fix the stock rigidly to the apron—its compulsion to move could easily twist the base, making the bench rock. Even worse, the table could split.

SOME ADVICE ON VISES

Size and shape are only half the battle when it comes to designing your workbench. Choosing vises and deciding how to incorporate them into your bench is a crucial part of designing a bench that will serve your needs. There are several types of woodworking vises to choose from and various ways to position them around the bench. Here are some things to think about in choosing vises for your bench.

The simplest approach is to buy a metal-jawed vise with a pop-up dog like the one shown in *Metal Woodworking Vise* on page 114. Cover the vise faces with wood to protect your work. If you are right-handed, mount the vise on the right end of your bench, with the side of the vise flush with the front edge of the bench as shown. If you are left-handed, mount the vise on the left end.

Drill a series of holes opposing the vise's dog, and make or buy a round bench dog.

Metal vises are popular because they are easy to mount. And most of them have a quick-release mechanism that lets you squeeze a lever to slide the jaw in and out. One drawback is that the screw is centered on the bottom of the vise, where it sometimes gets in the way. Another drawback is price: You can take a couple of friends to the fanciest restaurant in town for the price of a good metal vise.

A more elegant, and usually cheaper, approach is to buy metal screw hardware and use it to build wooden vises into your bench.

The simplest hardware to use is designed to construct a face vise, like that shown on the *Carver's Bench* on page 110. It has a screw

METAL WOODWORKING VISE

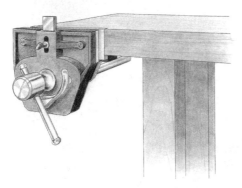

FACE VISE

FACE-VISE BENCH SCREW

flanked by two guide bars, just like a metal vise. It functions like a metal vise, too, except it doesn't have a quick-release feature.

A recent innovation is twin-screw hardware to make a vise that spans one entire end of the bench. This end-vise hardware, which is used on "The Advanced Bench" shown on page 121, employs two screws linked by a chain drive. End vises give you a lot of clamping surface for holding large work. Also,

they can be used with two sets of opposing dog holes for securing large panels. You can make a very good end vise with face-vise hardware. The only problem is that when you put pressure on one side of the vise, as you often will, you may strain, and eventually strip, the one central screw.

BENCH-TOP OPTIONS

If you prefer to build your own bench top, four options are given below. Any of these will work well on the *Basic Bench Base* on page 119.

Never paint or stain a workbench top since the color can be rubbed off onto your projects. For protection, brush on two or three coats of penetrating furniture oil such as tung oil or Danish oil. Linseed oil, sometimes mixed with turpentine to speed dry-

ing, is a good choice. Finish the composition bench tops just as you would a solid wood top. Surface coatings, such as lacquer, varnish, and shellac, are not good choices.

SOLID WOOD WITH TONGUE AND GROOVE

If any bench top could be considered standard, it is this one. It consists of solid wood edge-glued with a ½ × ½-inch tongue and groove. Use a durable, stable hardwood such as hard maple or beech. The joint adds strength and aligns the boards.

When you mill your stock, make sure it is perfectly square. Leave it slightly longer than final length. Cut the groove in one edge of each board with a ½-inch dado cutter on the table saw. Rout the tongue with a 1-inch straight bit in a heavy-duty router. Glue the boards together, alternating clamps over and under. A good strategy is to glue up sections narrow enough to go through your thickness planer and then plane the sections to final thickness before gluing them together. After the glue cures, crosscut the ends square to length.

SOLID WOOD WITH SPLINES

This is a strong, attractive bench top, but it's a challenge to make it flat. The first step toward ensuring a flat bench is to be very careful to mill your stock square.

Cut the pieces to length on the table saw or radial arm saw. Make certain they are accurate by cutting them against a stop.

To get the top surfaces to line up flush when you glue the top together, rout grooves in each block with a router and wing cutter. Cut plywood or solid wood splines to fit in the grooves, and glue them in place as you glue up the top. Again, you can glue up in sections and plane the sections to final dimensions before gluing them together.

BENCH-TOP OPTIONS

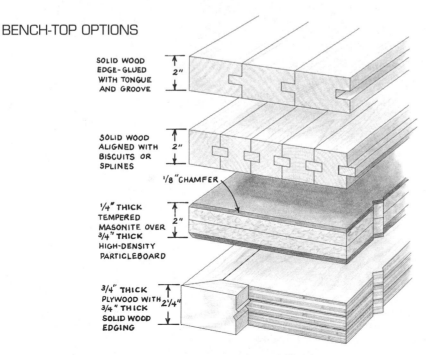

SOLID WOOD EDGE-GLUED WITH TONGUE AND GROOVE — 2"

SOLID WOOD ALIGNED WITH BISCUITS OR SPLINES — 2"

⅛" CHAMFER

¼" THICK TEMPERED MASONITE OVER ¾" THICK HIGH-DENSITY PARTICLEBOARD — 2"

¾" THICK PLYWOOD WITH ¾" THICK SOLID WOOD EDGING — 2¼"

MASONITE OVER PARTICLEBOARD

This top consists of two layers of ¾-inch high-density particleboard with a layer of ¼-inch tempered Masonite on top and bottom. It's strong, durable, and cheap. Just make sure you get a good glue bond between the layers of the sandwich. The best way to get this is to use sturdy cauls clamped across the glued-up pieces. Short lengths of 2 X 4s work well. Joint a high point in the middle of one edge of each caul. Put that edge down against the top as you clamp it, and you get clamping pressure in the center of the bench top spreading out to the edges.

Cut and glue together the particleboard core pieces first. Nail several 1-inch brads through the bottom to keep the pieces from sliding around during glue-up. After that glue cures, glue the tempered Masonite skins on the top and bottom. Make certain that the Masonite is tempered; if it isn't, it will be too soft and coarse. Use brads to position the Masonite, leaving the heads exposed so you can pull them out. Rout the edges flush, if necessary, then rout a ⅛-inch chamfer around the edges of the top and bottom. The chamfer keeps the Masonite, which is slightly brittle, from crumbling with use. You could also apply a solid wood edge to the top, as described next.

PLYWOOD WITH SOLID WOOD EDGING

Make this top with hardwood plywood, not construction-grade plywood. Birch or maple plywood is standard, although you can choose walnut or cherry plywood for the top layer for a more distinctive look.

Cut and glue three plywood layers accurately so the edges will be flush and the solid wood edging will fit tightly. Although the edging can match or contrast with the top plywood veneer layer, it should be hardwood. Glue the plywood layers together with the cauls as described in "Masonite over Particleboard." Align them carefully after you have applied the glue, and hold them with small brads. Glue two layers, let them dry, then glue on the third. If the edges don't align, trim them with a flush trim bit in a router, or trim the top slightly on the table saw. Trimming the top on the saw is the best way to make sure the top remains square.

Miter the edging pieces around the top. Cut them and hold them in place with clamps until you are satisfied with the fit of the miters. Then remove two opposite edging pieces, and glue and reclamp them to the edges of the top. Fit the edging flush or just proud of the plywood top. When the glue has cured, remove the remaining two edging pieces, and glue and reclamp them to the top. When the glue has cured, hand plane the edging flush with the top.

THE ASSEMBLY TABLE

Unless your projects are very small, the bench height that is ideal for making parts is too high and often too narrow for assembling those parts. So you may want to make a separate assembly table. Most people find a platform set to about knee height is ideal for assembly work. The assembly table's surface should be 36 to 48 inches wide and at least 4 feet long. Make the bench stable, and shim it flat and level—it can then serve as a reference surface for aligning parts. If you intend to glue up parts on this table, make cleanup easy by surfacing it with a sheet of plastic laminate, like Formica. Choose a matte finish to reduce its slipperiness. To prevent uneven moisture absorption from warping the top, laminate the bottom of the table also. Position the assembly table in the shop such that there is access from all four sides.

If space is a problem, consider a knock-down assembly table.

A solid-core door leveled with shims and secured with screws to a pair of low sawhorses serves quite well, yet it breaks down for storage in minutes. If it sounds a bit lightweight, don't worry. You won't be planing or pounding on an assembly table: The saw horse solution is plenty strong enough.

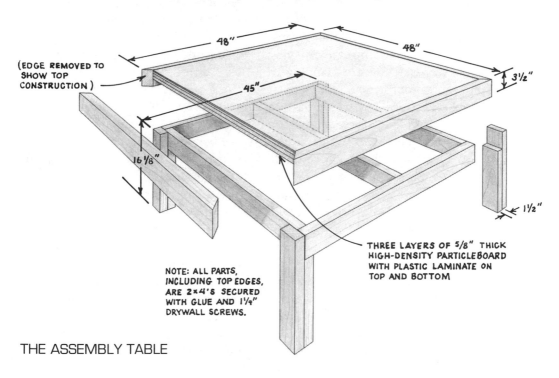

(EDGE REMOVED TO SHOW TOP CONSTRUCTION)

48"

48"

3½"

45"

16⅛"

1½"

NOTE: ALL PARTS, INCLUDING TOP EDGES, ARE 2×4'S SECURED WITH GLUE AND 1¼" DRYWALL SCREWS.

THREE LAYERS OF 5/8" THICK HIGH-DENSITY PARTICLEBOARD WITH PLASTIC LAMINATE ON TOP AND BOTTOM

THE ASSEMBLY TABLE

ASSEMBLY STOOL

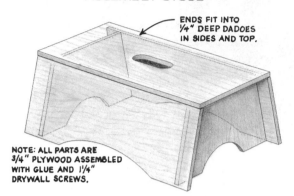

ENDS FIT INTO
1/4" DEEP DADOES
IN SIDES AND TOP.

NOTE: ALL PARTS ARE
3/4" PLYWOOD ASSEMBLED
WITH GLUE AND 1 1/4"
DRYWALL SCREWS.

If you don't have the floor space for even a knock-down assembly table, there is yet another solution, provided your shop ceiling is at least 8 feet high. Make a wide bench of convenient height for joinery work, and then make an assembly step stool to stand on, like the one shown. This plywood stool is light enough to move easily but big enough to let you move around a bit during assembly.

THE BASIC BENCH

A traditional European woodworking bench calls for a solid wood top, but there are lots of ways to get there. The only rules are that the top must be flat, stable, sturdy, and durable and that it must be able to accommodate any dog holes or vises you are planning to build into your bench. One popular bench-top option is to purchase a piece of butcher-block countertop from your lumberyard. This is perhaps the easiest, although certainly not the least expensive, way to guarantee a flat, well-glued, extremely durable bench top. A store-bought butcher block is incorporated into "The Advanced Bench" on page 121. A piece of butcher block atop the base described here will provide you with a fine bench you can assemble in less than a day. Not every bench needs to be an altar to your skills. All you really need is a bench that's flat and sturdy. This simple base, combined with any of the tops discussed in "Bench-Top Options" on page 114, fits the bill. It's inexpensive to make and the joinery is simple crosscuts, glue, and drywall screws. You don't even need clamps. Just use a power drill to drive the drywall screws. No need to predrill. If and when the time comes to build the bench of your dreams, the basic bench will continue to serve as an auxiliary assembly table.

All the lumber in this bench is dimensional 2 × 4s. Use fir—it's straight and stable. With a 2-inch-thick top, this bench will be 34 inches high—perfect for an average-sized male. Since it's the same height as most table saws, it also makes a great outfeed table. To customize the height, see "Design Considerations" on page 108.

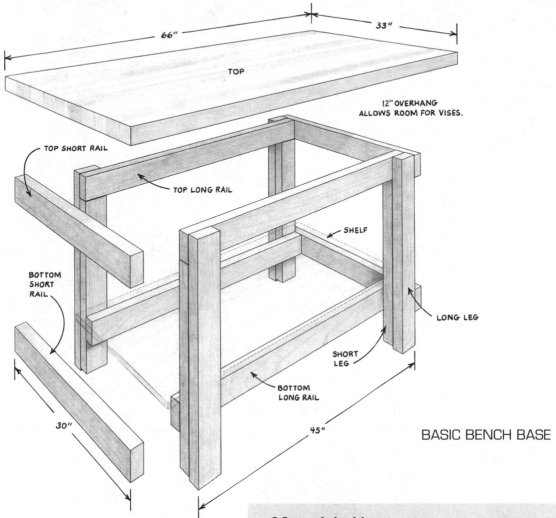

66"

33"

TOP

12" OVERHANG
ALLOWS ROOM FOR VISES.

TOP SHORT RAIL

TOP LONG RAIL

SHELF

BOTTOM
SHORT
RAIL

LONG LEG

SHORT
LEG

BOTTOM
LONG RAIL

30"

45"

BASIC BENCH BASE

BUILDING
THE SIMPLE BASE

1. Cut all the parts to size.
None of the lengths in the Materials
Lists are crucial; you can change
them to suit your needs. What is
important is that all like parts be
exactly the same length. You can cut
the parts on a motorized miter saw, a

Materials List

Part	Quantity	Dimensions
Long legs	4	1½" × 3½" × 32"
Short legs	4	1½" × 3½" × 28"
Long rails	4	1½" × 3½" × 45"
Short rails	4	1½" × 3½" × 30"
Plywood shelf	1	¾" × 24" × 45"

Hardware
2½" drywall screws, as needed
1¼" drywall screws, as needed

GANG CUTTING

radial arm saw, or a table saw with a long miter-gauge extension. Whatever tool you use, set up a stop to ensure uniform lengths. Or, you can do an excellent job with a portable circular saw as shown in *Gang Cutting* above. Line up all the stock for the long legs with one end perfectly flush. Screw or clamp a straight rip of plywood or other straightedge squarely across the stock, and gang-cut the long legs. Repeat this process for all other like parts.

2. Attach the long legs to the top long rails. Glue and screw a long leg to each end of a top long rail as shown in *Basic Bench Base* on page 119. Make sure the leg is square to the rail. Use four 2½-inch screws in each joint. Repeat this procedure for the other top rail and remaining long legs. Use the 2½-inch screws for all 2 × 4 assemblies.

3. Attach the short legs to the long legs. Put glue along the inside of a long leg. Put a short leg in place, making sure the pieces are flush along the sides. Screw the short legs in place. Repeat this procedure for each leg. The short legs will be ½ inch short of the bottom of the long legs. Without compromising strength or stability, this makes it less likely that your bench will rock because of irregularities in the floor.

4. Attach the bottom long rails to the legs. Strike a line across the inside of each leg 7½ inches from the bottom of each short leg (8 inches from the floor). Glue and screw the bottom long rails to the legs, with the bottom of the rails along the lines. Make sure the ends of the rails are square to the legs and flush with the outside of the legs.

5. Attach the bottom short rails to the legs. Glue and screw the bottom short rails to the legs. Make sure the tops of all rails are flush and the ends of the short rails are flush with the outside of the legs. Again, use four screws at each joint.

6. Install the shelf. The shelf is more than a storage place; it helps to stiffen the bench. Storing heavy items on the shelf will make the bench even more stable. Cut the plywood shelf to the dimensions in the Materials List on page 119. Put glue along the tops of the bottom rails, and screw the shelf into place with 1¼-inch drywall screws spaced about 12 inches apart.

THE ADVANCED BENCH

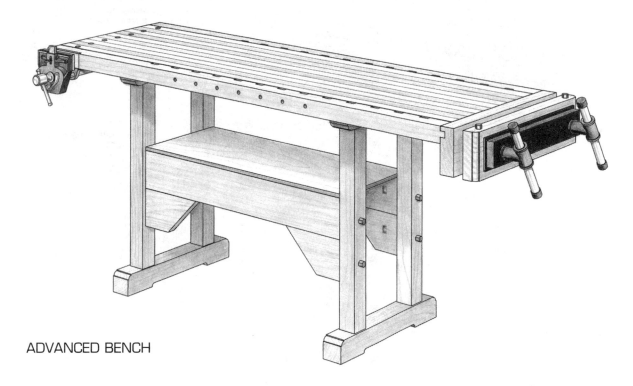

ADVANCED BENCH

This bench is designed to be the last bench you'll ever need, without being the last you'd ever want to build.

One of the hardest parts of creating a fine workbench is getting the top perfectly flat. A store-bought maple butcher-block countertop makes it easy on this bench. Make the other parts from a strong, well-seasoned wood, such as hard maple, beech, or birch. All the wood should be clear and free of knots.

The bench has both square and round dog holes. Round holes in the shoulder vise jaw and across the bench are easy to drill and allow the dogs to twist to hold odd-shaped pieces. Half-inch-diameter bolts work well as round dogs. Square holes in the dog rails are easy to rout and give you dogs that won't twist during those heavy-duty applications.

The bench uses two commercially available vises. On the left front edge is a quick-release woodworking vise with a pop-up dog like the one shown in *Metal Woodworking Vise* on page 114. The other is a twin-screw vise that spans the right end of the bench. This vise has two screws that are connected with a

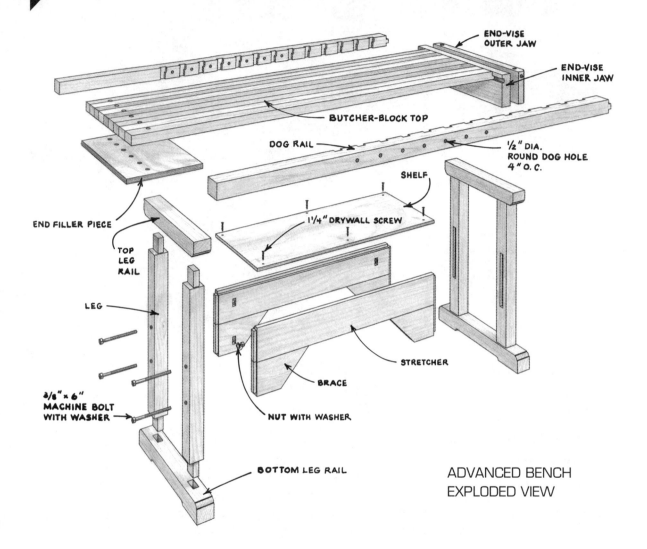

END-VISE
OUTER JAW

END-VISE
INNER JAW

BUTCHER-BLOCK TOP

DOG RAIL

½" DIA.
ROUND DOG HOLE
4" O. C.

SHELF

1¼" DRYWALL SCREW

END FILLER PIECE

TOP
LEG
RAIL

LEG

3/8" x 6"
MACHINE BOLT
WITH WASHER

NUT WITH WASHER

BRACE

STRETCHER

BOTTOM LEG RAIL

ADVANCED BENCH
EXPLODED VIEW

chain drive. It has two handles so you can move the vise jaw by turning either handle. The twin-screw vise is made by Veritas. You can get one from The Woodworkers' Store, 21801 Industrial Boulevard, Rogers, MN 55374-9514 (612-428-3200). The item number is 88725. The twin-screw vise comes with installa-tion instructions. Buy both your vises before you build the bench so you can make sure you build the bench to fit.

The bench base is simple and tradi-tional. Mortises in the leg rails receive tenons on the legs. The stretchers include braces to eliminate any chance that the bench will rack when you go to work with your biggest hand plane. Shallow mortises in the legs receive stretcher tenons. The stretchers are machine-bolted to the legs for knock-down convenience. A plywood shelf provides storage while increasing the bench's stability.

BUILDING THE ADVANCED BENCH

1. Cut the top to size. You can buy a 6-foot length of butcher block in a standard countertop width of 25 inches. This means you'll have to rip the butcher block to 19 inches wide, but you won't have to crosscut it. Before ripping to length, joint one edge of the piece. Run that edge against the table saw's rip fence. This way, both edges will be finish-free, so you'll get a good glue bond with the dog rails.

2. Make the dog rails. When attaching the dog rails to the butcher block, it is difficult to get top surfaces perfectly flush. To solve this problem, make the rails slightly thicker than they'll need to be and then plane or rout them flush after they are installed.

Make your dog rail thick enough so that the top edges of the metal vise jaws will be flush with the bench top. To get this thickness, measure the distance from the top of the vise's rear jaw to the mounting plate. Plane your stock 1/16 inch thicker than this. Joint, rip, and crosscut the stock to the width and length in the Materials List at right. Now use a marking gauge to scribe a line along the inside edge of each rail. Make the line 1/16 inch from the top surface of each rail.

3. Rout the square dog holes and drill the round holes. Use a 1/2-inch-diameter straight bit and a 5/8-inch-diameter guide bushing to rout the square dog holes. Make a template like the one shown in *Guide Bushing Template for Routing Dog Holes* on page 124. Attach the cleat to the template so that the dog holes will lean 2 degrees toward the end vise. This will help the dogs grip better.

Lay out centerlines for 13 square holes on each rail, spacing the centerlines 4 inches apart. Rout the holes 1/2 inch deep.

Drill seven 1/2-inch-diameter holes

Materials List

Part	Quantity	Dimensions
Butcher block	1	1½" × 19" × 72"
Dog rails	2	*To fit* × 2½" × 72"
Vise jaws	2	2" × 6" × 24"
End filler piece	1	*To fit* × 12¾" × 19"
Legs	2	2½" × 2½" × 32"
Top leg rails	2	2½" × 3" × 19"
Bottom leg rails	2	3" × 3" × 22"
Stretchers	2	1¼" × 5½" × 38"
Braces	2	1¼" × 5½" × 10"
Plywood shelf	1	½" × 13¾" × 37"

Hardware

Four ⅜" dia. × 6" machine bolts with washers and nuts
Four ⅜" dia. × 3½" lag bolts with washers
4 machine bolts to fit metal vise
Six 1¼" drywall screws
Two #4 × ½" flathead wood screws

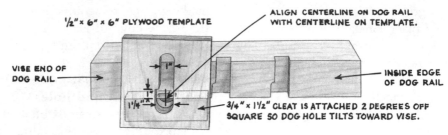

ALIGN CENTERLINE ON DOG RAIL WITH CENTERLINE ON TEMPLATE.

½" x 6" x 6" PLYWOOD TEMPLATE

VISE END OF DOG RAIL

INSIDE EDGE OF DOG RAIL

1"

1"

1¼"

¾" x 1½" CLEAT IS ATTACHED 2 DEGREES OFF SQUARE SO DOG HOLE TILTS TOWARD VISE.

ROUT ½" DEEP WITH A ½" DIA. BIT AND A ⅝" DIA. GUIDE BUSHING.

GUIDE BUSHING TEMPLATE FOR ROUTING DOG HOLES

in the sides of the rails, positioning the holes on 4-inch centers between the square holes as shown in the *Advanced Bench Exploded View* on page 122.

4. Glue the dog rails to the butcher block. For better control, glue and clamp one rail to the butcher block, let the glue cure, and then glue and clamp the other rail in place. Using your scribe marks as a guide, make the top of the rails ⅛ inch proud of the butcher block.

You can make the rails flush with the butcher block by careful work with a sharp jointer plane. Or you can use your router with your largest-diameter straight bit. Mount the router to a piece of plywood as shown in *Routing the Dog Rails Flush*.

5. Rabbet the butcher block and make a tongue on the dog rails. The end of the butcher block is rabbeted to fit a groove in the end-vise inner jaw. Tongues in the dog rails also fit this groove. These details are shown in *End-Vise Joinery Detail* on the opposite page. Put a ½-inch straight bit in your router and set the depth to ¾ inch. Clamp a

straightedge over the bench top as a guide to rout the rabbet in the butcher block and the top of the tongue in the dog rails. Flip the bench top over. Set the router on a dog rail, and drop the bit down to touch the underside of the butcher block. Set the straightedge fence again, and rout the bottom of the tongues flush with the bottom of the butcher block.

6. Make the end-vise jaws and join the inner jaw to the bench. Cut the end-vise jaws to the dimen-

ROUTING THE DOG RAILS FLUSH

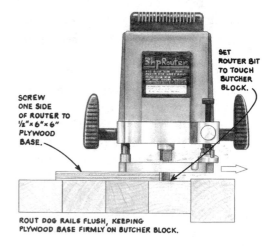

SET ROUTER BIT TO TOUCH BUTCHER BLOCK.

SCREW ONE SIDE OF ROUTER TO ½" x 6" x 6" PLYWOOD BASE.

ROUT DOG RAILS FLUSH, KEEPING PLYWOOD BASE FIRMLY ON BUTCHER BLOCK.

sions that are given in the Materials List on page 123. Then plane a ³⁄₃₂-inch taper on the inside face of the outer jaw as shown in *End-Vise Joinery Detail*. This taper will make the top of the vise grab first, improving the grip. If you like, you can rout a ¼-inch chamfer on the outside edges of the outer jaw as shown in the drawing.

Drill two ½-inch-diameter, 1-inch-deep holes in the top of the outer jaw to oppose the square holes. Drill a hole of the same size and depth in each side of the outer jaw to oppose the holes in the sides of the dog rails.

Rout or saw the groove in the inner jaw as shown in the drawing. The twin-screw vise comes with bolts and threaded metal dowel for attaching the outer jaw. Follow the instructions that come with the vise. Do not glue the inner jaw to the bench.

7. Make and attach the end filler piece. Cut the end filler piece to the length and width in the Materials List on page 123. Make the piece thick enough to be flush with the bottom of the dog rails. Glue the piece under the butcher block, flush with the end of the bench. Make sure the grain in the filler piece runs in the same direction as the grain in the bench top.

8. Make the leg assemblies. Dimension stock for the legs and leg rails to the dimensions in the Materials List on page 123. Cut tenons on the ends of the legs and

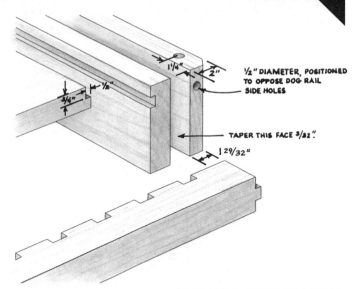

END-VISE JOINERY DETAIL

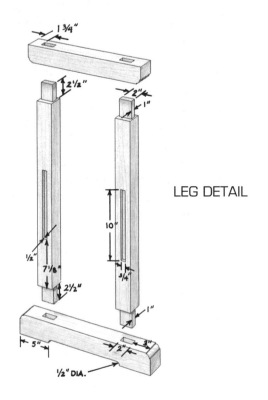

LEG DETAIL

STRETCHER AND BRACE DETAIL

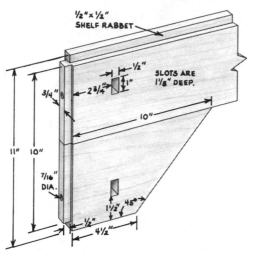

½" × ½" SHELF RABBET

½"

SLOTS ARE 1⅛" DEEP.

2¾"

1"

¾"

10"

11"

10"

7/16" DIA.

1½"

45°

½"

4½"

corresponding mortises in the rails. Note that all these tenons are the same size. This means they go through the 2½-inch-thick top rails but not through the 3-inch-thick bottom rails. Also cut the shallow mortises in the legs to receive the stretcher/brace tenons. Dimensions for all these joints are given in *Leg Detail* on page 125.

Now cut the ½-inch-deep recess that makes the feet in the bottom rails. If you like, rout a ¼-inch roundover with a ⅛-inch shoulder on the top of the bottom rails and the bottom of the top rails.

Glue and clamp the leg assemblies.

9. Make the stretchers and braces. Cut the stretchers and braces to the dimensions in the Materials List on page 123. Cut a 45-degree angle on one end of each brace. Make the tenons on the stretcher and braces as shown in *Stretcher and Brace Detail* above. Run the pieces flat on

the table saw to make the side shoulders. Use a chisel to chop the shoulders at the top of the stetchers and bottom of the braces.

Make a ½ × ½-inch rabbet along the top inside edge of each stretcher to receive the shelf. Drill and chisel the nut slots in the stretcher and braces as shown in the drawing. Glue the braces to the stretchers.

10. Assemble the base and cut the shelf. Insert the stretcher/brace tenons into their mortises. Drill 7/16-inch-diameter holes for the ⅜-inch-diameter machine bolts. Drill these holes through the legs and into the stretchers and braces. Position the holes so that they will be 1½ inches from the top of the stretchers and the bottom of the braces. Remove the legs and continue the bolt holes through to the slots.

Cut the shelf to the dimensions in the Materials List on page 123. Attach the shelf to the stretcher with six 1¼-inch drywall screws.

11. Attach the metal vise. Bolt the metal vise to the bench top with machine bolts through the top of the bench. Use machine bolts that fit the vise.

12. Attach the bench top to the base. Position the top on the base with the end filler piece against a top leg rail. Drill four 9/32-inch pilot holes through the top leg rails and 1 inch deep into the bench top. Drill the holes 1½ inches in from each leg. Remove the top, and enlarge the holes in the rails to ⅜ inch. Rock the drill from side to side along the length of the rails to enlarge the holes into slots. Reassemble the bench with four ⅜-inch-diameter ✕ 3½-inch-long lag bolts with washers. Finish assembling the end vise according to the directions that are provided by the manufacturer.

13. Make the bench dogs. Plane straight-grained hardwood stock to ¹¹⁄₁₆ inch thick. Cut two bench dogs on the band saw to the dimensions shown in *Bench Dog Dimensions* at left. Note that one corner of each dog is rounded to fit the inside corner you made when routing the dog holes. Cut the spring strip separately. Attach the strip to the dogs with #4 ✕ ½-inch flathead wood screws in countersunk holes.

BENCH DOG DIMENSIONS

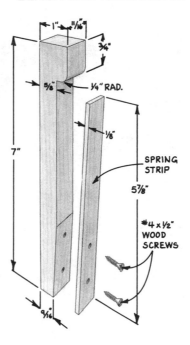

8 BENDING

QUICK RELEASE

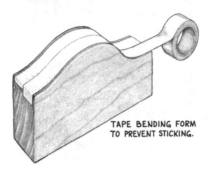

TAPE BENDING FORM
TO PREVENT STICKING.

When gluing up bent laminations, it is quite possible to accidently glue your work right to the form. To prevent this from happening, cover the form with a layer of plastic packing tape. Glue won't stick to the tape, so the bent piece will pop right out of the form. And, unlike wax, tape doesn't present the danger of contaminating the surface of your work.

Kenneth S. Burton, Jr.
Allentown, Pa.

EVERY FORM SHOULD HAVE A CORK LINING

Line bent lamination forms with a thin layer of cork. This resilient material is sold in sheets at most home centers as a wall covering. It helps smooth out any irregularities in the form, and it keeps the form from marring the work.

M. S. McIntosh
Middletown, Ohio

A FEW EXTRA STRIPS NEVER HURT ANYTHING

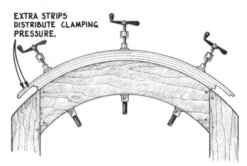

EXTRA STRIPS
DISTRIBUTE CLAMPING
PRESSURE.

The next time you do a bent lamination over a one-sided form, cut two or three extra laminates as you are preparing the stock. Then include these extra strips on the outside of the glue-up. Just don't put any glue on these pieces. The extra strips will help distribute the clamping pressure, preventing the clamps from marring the work.

But what if you don't have enough stock to cut extra strips, or the material you're working with is too expensive to use that way? There is an alternative. Cut several strips of tempered hardboard (Masonite) the same size as your regular strips. Then do the glue-up with these strips on the outside of the bend. The hardboard will protect your stock and distribute the clamping pressure just as well.

Kenneth S. Burton, Jr.
Allentown, Pa.

PARTIAL LAMINATIONS

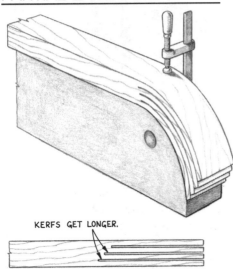

KERFS GET LONGER.

There are situations where you want a piece of wood to run straight for a distance then break into a curve. A good example of this would be a sled runner. While you could steam such a piece, I find it easier to make what I call a partial lamination.

I cut a series of kerfs in one end of the piece as shown. This can be done on either the table saw or the band saw. The table saw produces

straighter cuts but removes a lot of wood. The band saw removes much less wood but can be difficult to control. Experiment to see which gives you better results.

The bend will be stronger if you graduate the cuts in length. Also, if you choose to make them on the table saw, flip the wood over between each cut. This will alternate the sloping ends of the cuts, making for a more uniform bend.

Spread glue in the kerfs, then glue the piece up over a form. The bent part will be thinner than the straight section, but with the cuts graduated, the reduction in thickness will seem like a taper and may actually improve the look of your design.

Percy W. Blandford
Stratford-upon-Avon, England

SPREADING GLUE MADE EASY

A printer's ink roller, or "brayer," does an excellent job of spreading glue for bent lamination glue-ups and similar tasks. It is fast and spreads an even coat. Because the brayer doesn't absorb glue, it is very easy to clean up. You should be able to find one at an art supply store.

> *Kenneth S. Burton, Jr.*
> *Allentown, Pa.*

GLUE ON THE ROCKS

Plastic resin glue is the best choice for most bent laminations because it doesn't creep under tension as yellow glue sometimes can. On a warm day, however, it may set up faster than you'd like it to. To increase the working time, add an ice cube or two to the mix. Keeping the glue cold will give you more time to work with it.

> *Custis Babcock*
> *Monterey, Pa.*

FOR THE SAKE OF APPEARANCES

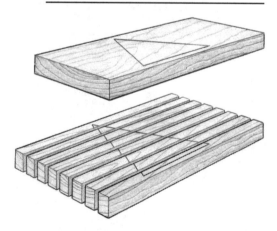

If you keep the strips for a bent lamination in the same order they were cut, the resulting bend will look like a solid piece of wood, because the glue lines will get lost in the grain pattern. To make it easy to keep the pieces in order, draw a triangle on one side of the board before you rip it into strips. The marks will then serve as a guide when you're ready to glue up.

> *Kenneth S. Burton, Jr.*
> *Allentown, Pa.*

MAKING CURVED MOLDINGS

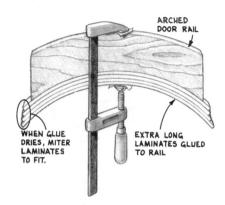

ARCHED DOOR RAIL

WHEN GLUE DRIES, MITER LAMINATES TO FIT.

EXTRA LONG LAMINATES GLUED TO RAIL

To make a molding that conforms to the curve of an arched cabinet door, use the door itself as your form. Glue up a bent lamination in place along the curve you wish to match. Be sure to use clamp pads to prevent damaging both the door and the molding.

> *Jeff Greef*
> *Soquel, Calif.*

LAYING OUT CURVES

Generating large, smooth curves in the shop can be tough. This simple, shop-made tool will make the task easier. I call it a spline. It consists of a long, straight-grained strip of wood about 1½ inches wide and ¼ inch thick (for tighter curves, use a thinner

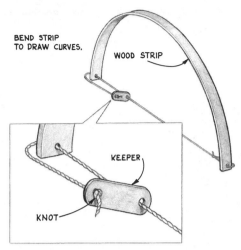

BEND STRIP TO DRAW CURVES.

WOOD STRIP

KEEPER

KNOT

SHAPING FORMS

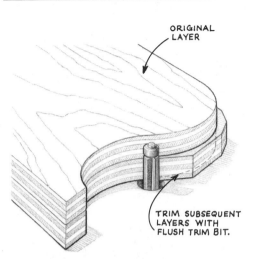

ORIGINAL LAYER

TRIM SUBSEQUENT LAYERS WITH FLUSH TRIM BIT.

strip). Drill a ⅛-inch hole through each end of the strip. Tie a string through the hole at one end. Then loop the other end through the other hole and tie it to a keeper as shown.

To use the spline, tighten the string until the strip forms the curve you want. The keeper will hold the curve as you trace it onto your stock. If the wood is of even thickness and straight-grained, it will bend smoothly and symmetrically. You might want to experiment with a tapered strip to form asymmetrical curves.

Gnarly Strop
Worley's Corner, Pa.

CHECKING SYMMETRY

If you want to check a curved piece to see whether it is symmetrical, trace the curve on a piece of paper, then flip the piece over and trace it again, right on top of the first line. Any discrepancies between the two will be obvious.

Sam Gribbly
Catskill, N.Y.

A piece of bent wood is often only as good as the form it was bent over. So it is very important that the form be as accurate as possible. But it's not easy to shape a form that's 3 or more inches thick. Instead of shaping the whole thickness at once, build the form up in layers, shaping them as you go.

Start with a single thickness of plywood. Cut and sand it to shape. Then use it as a pattern to lay out the shape on the other layers. Cut the other layers roughly to shape, keeping to the outside of the line. Once all the pieces are cut out, screw the original to one of the subsequent layers. Trim the oversized piece to shape with a flush-trim bit in a table-mounted router. Then add another piece to the stack and trim it as well. Keep adding layers and trimming until the form is thick enough.

Kenneth S. Burton, Jr.
Allentown, Pa.

Making a Bent Lamination

Most machines are designed to cut in straight lines, so it's easiest to produce cabinets, furniture, and millwork with flat wood and square joints. But adding a simple curve to a piece of furniture can enhance its visual appeal.

A bent lamination is often the most efficient method for obtaining a curved part for a furniture project. It's not tough to do, as long as you follow a logical procedure, have everything you need at hand, and make a dry run before gluing up your lamination.

The drawing *Table with Curved Apron* shows a three-legged corner table I built. The table is simple, with a gradual curve, so it was the perfect project for my first try at bent lamination.

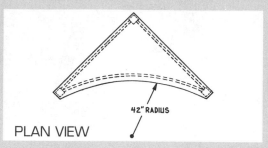

PLAN VIEW

42" RADIUS

consists of two curved plates separated by ribs and faced on one side, as shown in *Bending Form*. You can bend on either the concave or convex side of a form, but I usually prefer the concave side for two reasons. First, it takes just one clamp in the center to get everything in place. And second, a concave bend will spring back less after bending.

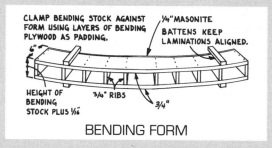

CLAMP BENDING STOCK AGAINST FORM USING LAYERS OF BENDING PLYWOOD AS PADDING.
¼" MASONITE
BATTENS KEEP LAMINATIONS ALIGNED.
HEIGHT OF BENDING STOCK PLUS ¹⁄₁₆
¾" RIBS
¾"

BENDING FORM

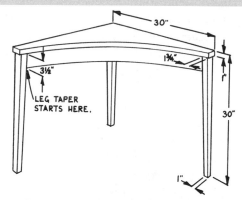

30"
1¾"
3½"
LEG TAPER STARTS HERE.
30"
1"

TABLE WITH CURVED APRON

I started by drawing a plan view of the table. From the plan view, I drew a full-scale layout of the curved apron. To make the layout more durable than paper, I did it on ¼-inch plywood.

Next I made the bending form. The form

I made the concave radius of the plates 1 inch less than the radius of the concave outside face of the apron. This allowed for the ¼-inch-thick facing plus the ¾-inch-thick apron, as shown in *Gluing Up the Lamination*. The height of the form equals the width of the bending stock plus about ¹⁄₁₆ inch. I bent my apron stock at 4 inches wide and then jointed and ripped it to a final width of 3½ inches. I faced the form with ¼-inch-thick Masonite. I cut two more pieces of

Masonite to the same size as the face piece for use as pads to distribute the clamping pressure. Masonite is thin enough to conform to a gentle curve while rigid enough to provide a uniform surface. For more-severe bends, use bending plywood, available from many plywood suppliers. Use staples or countersunk screws, and glue, to attach the facing. To complete my form, I added battens on top and bottom to keep the laminations aligned. The extra 1/16 inch of form height let the stock slide in easily.

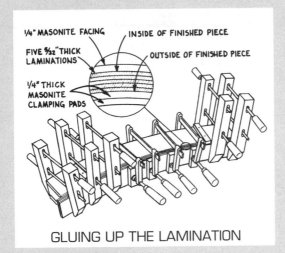

1/4" MASONITE FACING   INSIDE OF FINISHED PIECE

FIVE 5/32" THICK LAMINATIONS   OUTSIDE OF FINISHED PIECE

1/4" THICK MASONITE CLAMPING PADS

GLUING UP THE LAMINATION

Next I milled my apron stock, leaving it a couple of inches longer and 1/2 inch wider than the finished dimensions. I resawed the stock into five strips, then planed each to 5/32 inch thick. More-severe bends require thinner laminations. As a rule of thumb, you should be able to bend a single strip into the form with only moderate hand pressure.

When planing thin wood, cover your planer bed with an auxiliary table that's topped with plastic laminate. Otherwise, the thin stock gets deformed by the roller under the cutters, causing severe tear-out. Attach a cleat to the bottom of the infeed side of the board so it won't feed into the planer.

Now you are ready for a dry run. This will ensure that you have everything you need at hand, especially enough clamps. It will also give you an idea of how long the glue-up will take, helping you decide which glue to use. Yellow glue sets in about 15 minutes, while plastic resin glue gives you about 30 minutes. Spread glue on both faces of each layer—except, of course, the two faces that will be the inside and outside of the finished piece.

The key to a successful bent lamination is equal distribution of clamping pressure. To accomplish this, I added two layers of Masonite between my clamps and the outside layer. Wooden handscrews are ideal, as long as the jaws reach across the entire face of the form. My second choice is quick-action clamps with wood blocks. Work from the center out to the ends. Tighten each clamp moderately at first, then go back and fully tighten them all. Wipe off excess glue, and allow the glue-up to cure overnight.

The completed lamination must be jointed before ripping to final width. Scrape or sand off any remaining glue; dried glue will chip jointer knives. Jointing a curved piece is a little tricky the first couple of times, so proceed cautiously. Ripping also requires extra caution; do it with the convex side down. It's useful to have a helper to receive the piece as it comes off the saw.

(continued)

Making a Bent Lamination—*Continued*

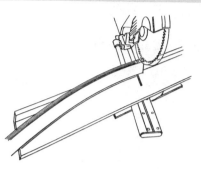

CROSSCUTTING THE APRON

I used a chop saw to crosscut the apron to final width, as shown in *Crosscutting the Apron*. I transferred the lines from my full-scale layout and then placed the apron on edge to make the cuts. I made trial cuts to be sure the angle was correct.

So go ahead, throw your next project a curve. It just might turn into a home run.

—*Tony O'Malley*
O'Malley is a professional woodworker in Philadelphia, Pa.

THE PERFECT MATCH

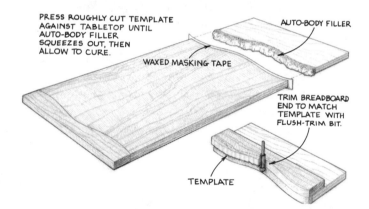

PRESS ROUGHLY CUT TEMPLATE AGAINST TABLETOP UNTIL AUTO-BODY FILLER SQUEEZES OUT, THEN ALLOW TO CURE.

WAXED MASKING TAPE

AUTO-BODY FILLER

TRIM BREADBOARD END TO MATCH TEMPLATE WITH FLUSH-TRIM BIT.

TEMPLATE

I needed a perfect fit between breadboard ends and the curved end of a fancy tabletop. I cut a plywood template to approximate shape, spread auto-body filler on the roughly cut edge, and pressed it against the curved end of the tabletop. Masking tape on the table edge and an application of paste wax over the tape prevented the filler from bonding to the tabletop. When the filler cured, I cleaned up the surfaces of the template and used a flush-trim bit in the router to shape the breadboard end to match the template.

Ed Stuckey
Detroit, Mich.

HOLEY FORMS, BATMAN!

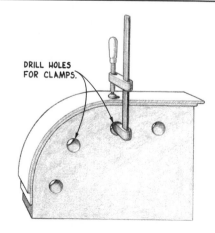

DRILL HOLES FOR CLAMPS.

If you have trouble with your clamps slipping on a bending form, here's an answer. Drill 2-inch-diameter holes through the form as shown. The holes will accept one jaw of each clamp for a slip-proof glue-up.

Kenneth S. Burton, Jr.
Allentown, Pa.

FORM SANDWICHES

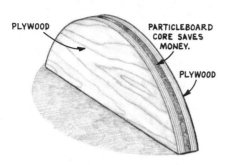

Plywood is the best material to use for bending forms because it is strong. But it can be expensive if you have to make many forms. One way to cut costs without sacrificing much strength is to alternate layers of plywood and particleboard as shown.

Morgan Ingalls
Walnut Grove, Mo.

BENDING FORM HOLDS WORK DURING MACHINING

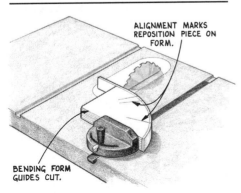

Bent wood pieces are, at best, awkward to hold as you machine them. Sometimes this can be helped by placing the bent piece back on the form and then using the form itself as a holder. To facilitate this, make a mark on the face of the form and a corresponding one on the bent piece before you originally unclamp the bend. Then use these marks as guides when you go to reposition the bend on the form.

Kenneth S. Burton, Jr.
Allentown, Pa.

STEAM DUCT

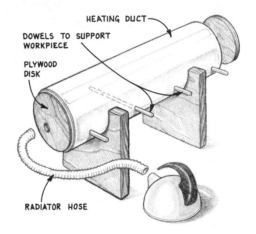

You can make an excellent steamer from a length of galvanized heating duct, to use for bending wood. I've used a length of 10-inch-diameter stove pipe, left over from a repair job on my house. You can also purchase almost any length of duct from an HVAC supplier. It comes in both round and rectangular sections.

I drilled a series of holes along the length of the duct and stuck dowels through them to form a rack for the steaming pieces to rest on. I plugged one end with a plywood disk and sealed the seam with caulk. The plug in the other end is loose and acts as a door. I connect the steamer to a tea kettle on my stove with a length of radiator hose. When in use, I tip the sealed end of the duct up so any condensation runs out the door end.

David Page
Swarthmore, Pa.

TWIN PARTS

If you're making bent parts that must be identical, consistency should be your watchword. Cut the pieces from the same board. Steam them for equal amounts of time. And in the case of bent laminations, cut all the strips to the same thickness. Finally,

leave them on the form for the same amount of time, preferably under the same weather conditions. The more consistent you can be, the better your chances are for making identical parts.

Kenneth S. Burton, Jr.
Allentown, Pa.

AMNESIA PREVENTION

If you intend to use your bending forms over again, write notes directly on them about how they work. Include information such as the length and thickness of the laminates, the amount of spring back, exactly what the radius of the curve is, and so on. It is amazing what you can forget once you put something away in storage.

Hack Blodger
Loafer's Glory, N.C.

SANDING

SANDPAPER ORIGAMI

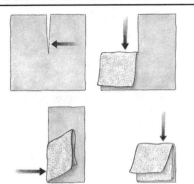

Here's a way to fold up sandpaper for hand sanding that a local boat builder showed me. You cut the sandpaper halfway through and then fold it as shown. It makes a nice, thick pad, and nowhere is the grit rubbing against itself.

Madeleine Johnson
Halifax, Nova Scotia

MORE SANDPAPER ORIGAMI

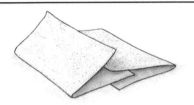

When sanding by hand, I use two quarter-sheets of sandpaper folded in half and interlocked. I can then flip the paper over for a finer or coarser grit. When the abrasive gets worn, I reverse the interlock. I also find that sandpaper folded this way stays in my hand better than a single piece folded in half.

David Hurd
Madison, Wis.

SANDPAPER CUTTER

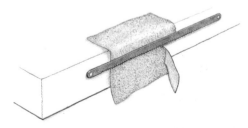

To tear sandpaper to size, loosely tack or screw a hacksaw blade to the edge of your workbench, teeth down. Slip the paper behind the hacksaw blade with the desired amount below the teeth, and tear it toward you.

Brian A. Green
Foam Lake, Saskatchewan

PLYWOOD SANDING BLOCK

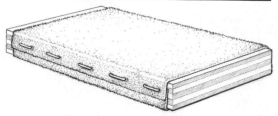

I make my sanding blocks from 3 × 5-inch pieces of ½-inch plywood. I cover each block with five pieces of 5 × 7-inch sandpaper that I cut from standard-sized sheets. (I use the leftover scraps when sanding turnings on my lathe.) To attach the paper to the block, I staple it as shown. As the abrasive wears out, I cut the paper free from the block and continue sanding with the next piece in the stack.

Tony Kosykoski
Belle Vernon, Pa.

CUSTOM-CONTOURED SANDING BLOCKS

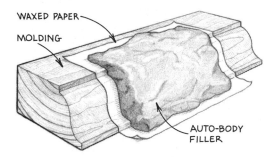

WAXED PAPER

MOLDING

AUTO-BODY FILLER

Sanding complex moldings or the bevels on raised panels can be a nuisance. These tasks can be made easier with custom sanding blocks that match the contours of the workpiece. You can easily make these blocks with auto-body filler. Put a piece of waxed paper over a section of the shape to be sanded. Then put a big glob of filler on the paper. When the filler hardens, pop it off the paper and trim the edges to a comfortable grip.

Jeff Greef
Soquel, Calif.

CUSTOM-CONTOURED SANDING BLOCKS, THE SEQUEL

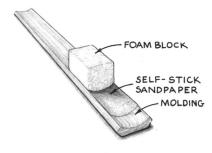

FOAM BLOCK

SELF-STICK SANDPAPER

MOLDING

You can also make a custom-contoured sanding block from a piece of foam insulation board. To shape the block, carefully adhere 80-grit, self-stick sandpaper to several inches of the molding you want to sand. Rub a block of foam insulation over the abrasive molding until the foam block matches the contours of the molding. Then line the inside of the sanding block with sandpaper and you're ready to go.

Trebor Narom
Onaled, N. Mex.

CURVED SANDING BLOCKS

Curved surfaces are easier to sand when using sanding blocks that match the curve. Trace the curve from the workpiece onto a sanding

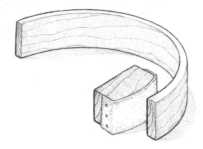

block. Cut the curve on the block with a band saw and sand it to shape. Wrap sandpaper over the block, and sand away.

Jeff Greef
Soquel, Calif.

OGEE SANDING BLOCKS

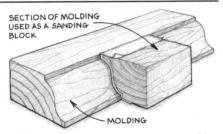

SECTION OF MOLDING USED AS A SANDING BLOCK

MOLDING

The curves on some ogee profiles are such that a scrap of the profile can be used as a ready-made sanding block.

Jeff Greef
Soquel, Calif.

SANDING YOUR WAY INTO A CORNER

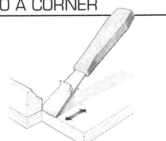

Occasionally we all run into the same problem—trying to finish sand an inside corner. You can only get so close with most orbital sanders. This leaves a small area that must be finished by hand. The easiest way I've found to do this is to wrap a piece of sandpaper around the blade of a putty knife. The flat end of the blade goes right into the corner, and the spring action of the blade ensures that the sandpaper is in contact with the surface.

Walter J. Morrison
Northport, N.Y.

SHOP-MADE BOW SANDER

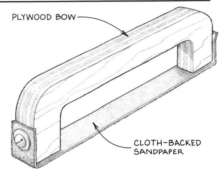

PLYWOOD BOW

CLOTH-BACKED SANDPAPER

A bow sander is just the thing for sanding rounded carvings and other convex surfaces. Make the bow from a piece of ¾-inch plywood. Cut a piece of cloth-backed sandpaper to fit, and attach it to the bow with panhead screws and washers as shown.

Charles Holroyd
Arcadia, Calif.

COPING SANDER

To sand small, inside holes on a project, I epoxy the broken ends of a coping saw blade to a strip of cloth-backed abrasive. When the glue dries,

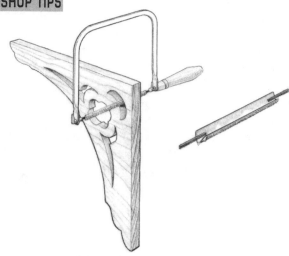

I insert the strip through the project and mount it in a coping saw.

John Teehee
Hilo, Hawaii

SHOP-MADE, ABRASIVE RIFFLERS

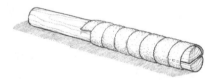

Carvers use small files, called rifflers, to smooth out small radii in their work. You can easily make your own different-diameter sanding rifflers from dowels. Cut a ½-inch-long notch in the end of the dowel as shown. Coat 3 to 4 inches of the dowel with glue. Place the end of a ½-inch-wide strip of sandpaper in the notch and wrap the tail around the dowel. Use a rubber band to clamp the paper in place while the glue dries.

Roy Moss
Rio Rancho, N. Mex.

SHOP-MADE WOOD "FILES"

Files come in handy for certain woodworking jobs, but files meant for metal will clog quickly if you use them on wood. I make my own woodworking "files" by gluing sandpaper to wooden paint-stirring paddles with yellow glue. The longest-lasting abrasives I've found are those for drum floor sanders.

Using a wooden file has a number of advantages. If the abrasive gets worn at the end, you can saw the end off to reach better abrasive. You can thin down an edge of the stick to sand in narrow grooves. And you can cut the stick to any shape necessary to reach hard-to-get-at places.

Nelson H. Rittenhouse
Wayne, N.J.

ANOTHER USE FOR EMERY BOARDS

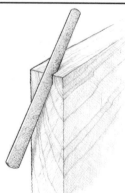

An ordinary emery board can handle a lot of fine sanding jobs, particularly on thin stock. There's a coarse and a fine side, and for tight spots, you can cut one end to a point with a pair of scissors.

R. J. Rhodes
Lincoln, Nebr.

SANDPAPER STASH

Store your sandpaper in a multi-compartment file folder, each grit in a separate compartment.

Jeff Greef
Soquel, Calif.

A QUICK-RESPONSE SANDING STATION

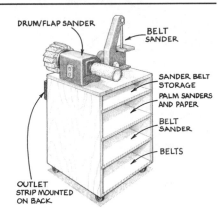

I built this sanding station to house all my sanding equipment. There is room for two bench machines on top, with storage for other tools and supplies underneath. It is mounted on casters, so I can wheel it close to the project at hand and then stash it out of the way when I don't need it. There is an outlet strip mounted on the back to provide power for the various tools. This way I only have to run one cord to the wall.

Bill Parrish
Norris, Tenn.

PARKING A SANDER

When using an orbital finishing sander, I find it helpful to have a 12-inch-square piece of carpet close by. The power can be turned off and the sander can be placed on the carpet to safely come to a complete stop.

John Hisey
Bainbridge Island, Wash.

LOADING A SANDER FOR EFFICIENCY

When sanding with an orbital sander, clip three pieces of sandpaper to it, one on top of the other. Then when one piece wears out, simply rip it off and continue sanding with the next.

Tom Groller
Palmerton, Pa.

SANDING FLAT

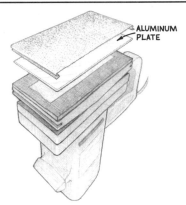

When sanding a large, flat surface with an electric pad sander, excessive pressure can result in a wavy surface. This happens because the soft rubber pad allows the sandpaper to dip down into softer areas and remove more material. (continued on page 146)

Choosing Power Sanders

You face many choices when shopping for sanding equipment. Manufacturers are always coming up with something new, both in specialized sanders and in tools with a broad performance range that can handle both fast stock removal and very fine smoothing. Here's a rundown of what's available to help you choose the sanding equipment that fits your shop and your budget.

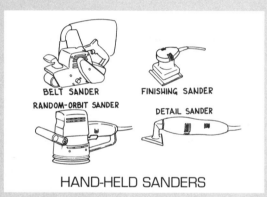

HAND-HELD SANDERS

Belt Sanders

The belt sander is an old workhorse that's hard to beat for leveling and smoothing large surfaces. The common sizes, determined by belt width and length, are 3 × 21-inch, 3 × 24-inch, and 4 × 24-inch. Even the smaller models can sand very aggressively.

Because they remove stock so quickly, belt sanders must be carefully controlled, especially the powerful heavyweights that exceed 15 pounds. Belt sanders can easily dig in and gouge your work. To prevent gouging, always start the belt sander before putting it on the work, and raise it before turning the machine off. Newer models feature electronic speed regulation. A new accessory for belt sanders is a clamp-on perimeter frame; it supports the tool on all sides to keep the platen parallel with the work and also controls depth of cut. Optional bench-mounting stands are available for many models, but woodworkers often make their own mounts and tilt tables. Mounting the sander in a stand makes it easier to sand small parts. A tilt table lets you sand edges square or beveled. Most belt sanders can be fitted with a dust collector.

Disc Sanders

The standard disc sander is so powerful and aggressive, you won't want it near most fine woodworking projects. You can't use it for finish sanding, because the rotating motion means you'll always be sanding across the grain. The exception is for shaping: These sanders remove stock so fast that you can use them to rough out shapes or trim end grain. Other than that, disc sanders are best used with a coarse disc for removing paint and rust and for work on hard surfaces such as metal.

Some disc sanders consist of a sanding head fitted to an angle grinder. Others are designed specifically for sanding. Common disc diameters are 5-inch, 6-inch, and 7-inch. All can be fitted with a buffing pad. Choose a two-speed or variable-speed tool for work on plastics or for paint removal; discs clog quickly with melted plastic or paint if spun too fast.

Finishing Sanders

Finishing sanders are also called pad sanders or orbital sanders. They are available in a wide range of sizes, from light and compact ⅙-sheet and ¼-sheet palm sanders to heavy ½-sheet models. The most common are the ⅙-sheet tool with two handles and the ¼-sheet palm model. Most are single-speed units that drive a soft pad through a minute orbit at a very high speed (over 10,000 orbits per minute). Nearly all are designed to spring-clamp standard sandpaper front and rear. However, some models also accept a conversion pad to mount pressure-sensitive adhesive paper (available either precut or in bulk rolls), and you can buy palm sanders designed strictly for pressure-sensitive adhesive discs.

There are two drawbacks to the orbital design. One is that the small orbits don't throw sanding dust away like the motion of belt and disc sanders. And since the orbit is always the same, orbital sanders can leave whorls on the work. To solve both problems, keep the sander in constant motion as you use it. Some models also can be switched to a straight back-and-forth motion for very fine whorl-free sanding with the grain.

For leveling and smoothing between finish coats, any finishing sander that clamps regular sandpaper can also clamp wet/dry paper. Not all models are equipped or adaptable for dust pickup; those equipped with a surround shroud for dust pickup have a restricted ability to edge into inside corners.

Random-Orbit Sanders

Random-orbit sanders are one of those innovations that made woodworkers say, "Now why didn't they think of this before?" These sanders employ a rotating disc, like a disc sander, but the arbor oscillates on an eccentric gear. This creates a random orbit—the sandpaper spins in an ever-changing path. The result really is the best of two worlds. You get the fast stock removal of a light-duty disc sander; and the random orbit eliminates cross-grain scratches, so that you are spared the whorls you can get with a finishing sander.

The random-orbit sander doesn't remove stock quite as quickly as a good belt sander, which remains the better tool for leveling large surfaces. For finish sanding, the random model is a better choice than the orbital sander, with one exception—the disc doesn't fit into inside corners. But if I could have only one sander in my shop, I'd make it a random-orbit.

One of the trickiest sanding situations is joints where two pieces meet with their grain running perpendicular—for example, when a rail meets a stile. This is no problem with a random-orbit sander. Just run the sander over the joint and you'll have a level, smooth, scratch-free joint.

The random-orbit sander is unsurpassed for smoothing end grain. On tight-grained woods such as cherry and maple, it produces a glass-smooth end-grain surface.

(continued)

Choosing Power Sanders—*Continued*

Some random-orbit models don't engage the eccentric gear unless there is pressure on the disc. This means if you turn the machine on and then lower it to the work, it may hit the work like a straight disc sander, perhaps gouging or burning. This can be a problem if you have developed the habit of starting sanders before putting them on the work.

Random-orbit sanders are available with fixed or adjustable speed, and disc diameters that include 4½-inch, 5-inch, and 6-inch. Some models use pressure-sensitive adhesive discs, while others use a Velcro hook-and-loop attachment. Velcro discs cost more than pressure-sensitive adhesive discs, but you can reuse them. They make sense if you do small projects in which you progress through finer grits without using up each disc. Also, you have to remember to remove adhesive discs at the end of the day, even if they aren't used up yet. If you leave them overnight, you'll need solvent to get them off in the morning.

Most random-orbit sanders have a good dust collection system, but some models take dust collection a step further by drawing dust through holes in the disc and pad. Constant dust extraction eliminates under-pad scoring and improves the sanding performance. Accessories include sanding pads of different densities for flat or contour sanding, buffing pads, and sponge pads to hold polishing compounds.

Detail Sanders

Detail sanders are another recent innovation. Powerful for their size, they oscillate a small triangular sanding pad at up to 20,000 orbits per minute. They are compact both as a unit and at the business end, and they reach into awkward places where other power sanders can't. The extremely high orbit speed allows the sanding pad to edge into inside corners without bouncing around. Accessories include soft contour pads, wax/buffing pads, and even scraper blades to remove glue and paint.

Stationary Sanders

The most common type of stationary sander runs a disc and a belt from the same motor. These sanders come in floor models and as bench tools. They are fast and versatile, and they're especially useful for shaping, squaring, and smoothing small stock. A tilting table supports the work as you put it against the disc.

The belt drive is designed to tilt and lock at

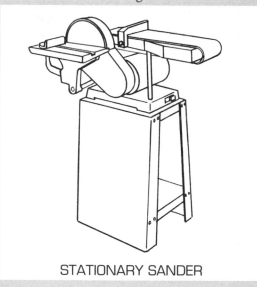

STATIONARY SANDER

any angle from horizontal to 90 degrees, allowing good access to both the flat platen and the area where the belt goes around the rollers. The disc sander, with its locking tilt table, is the ideal tool for precision-sanding angles and bevels. Some models feature a tilt table that can also be mounted against the belt. Variations on the standard tool include models with either a belt sander or disc sander on one end of a standard bench grinder.

Models with 1-inch-wide belts are especially handy for sanding contours because you can remove the platen, allowing the belt to follow curves. The 1-inch sanders are also efficient tools for grinding and polishing metal and other hard materials. Belts are available in a wide choice of grits, and the tool can also mount buffing belts. Some models feature a flexible shaft attachment to power rotary cutting and grinding tools and drum sanders.

Contour Sanders, Flap Sanders, and Sanding Drums

Air-filled contour sanders, flap sanders, and sanding drums can be drill-chucked and used as portable tools. They also can be operated as stationary tools when powered by a lathe or drill press or by a dedicated horizontal or vertical drum sander often found in production shops.

Air-filled contour sanders and flap sanders flex and conform to the shape of the work to allow the power sanding of pieces that otherwise could be sanded only by hand. A sanding drum chucked in a drill press is a simple and effective tool for shaping, squaring, and finish sanding both straight and curved work. Some professional shops have stationary vertical drum sanders that oscillate the drum up and down, so the paper wears evenly. Drums are available in a wide range of sizes and with a wide selection of sanding sleeves, including carbide. Chucked in a fast drill motor or flexible shaft, a sanding drum is a especially useful in opening up and smoothing holes and cutouts.

Thickness Sanders

Thickness sanders are stationary production tools that make quick work of sanding panels and boards to close tolerances. Commercial belt and drum models look and operate like planers: They have self-feeding, variable-speed rollers or conveyor belts, fine thickness adjustment, and impressive capacity. Small-shop drum models share most of the features of commercial models. A different kind of small-shop thickness sander is a 44-inch-wide horizontal sanding drum mechanism sold as an accessory for radial arm saws, with additional kits to convert the tool to freestanding operation and power feed.

The edge-sander is a stationary tool that is basically a belt sanding drive mounted against a tilt table. Production shops use it to edge-sand panels and boards. Some models oscillate the entire belt drive up and down to expose fresh belt surface as the work is fed through.

—*Jim Michaud*
Michaud is a freelance writer and woodworker in Swampscott, Mass.

If this plagues your work, install a ⅟₁₆-inch-thick aluminum plate between the rubber pad and the sandpaper. Make sure that the aluminum plate is flat and that its edges and corners are smooth and generously rounded to prevent it from accidentally marring your work. Fasten the plate to the rubber pad with double-sided carpet tape.

Walter J. Morrison
Northport, N.Y.

UPDATE YOUR SANDER

If the pad on your orbital sander wasn't made for adhesive-backed sandpaper, cover its pad with duct tape. The sandpaper will adhere to the tape and will peel off without tearing up the pad.

Walter J. Martin
Buffalo, N.Y.

SANDING SMALL PIECES

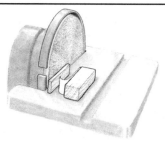

When sanding very thin stock on a belt or disc sander, you can easily trim your fingernails along with the wood if you aren't careful. To avoid such a manicure, I attach the work to a larger block with double-sided carpet tape.

H. R. McDermid
Vernon, British Columbia

A SAFER WAY TO SAND SMALL PARTS

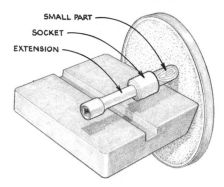

SMALL PART
SOCKET
EXTENSION

Small parts such as dowels or knobs can be safely sanded on a disc or belt sander using a holder made from a socket-wrench socket and extension shaft. Wrap one end of the piece with masking tape and force-fit it into an appropriately sized socket. Then make a handle by snapping the socket onto the extension shaft. This will give you a secure grip and will keep your fingers out of harm's way. With the wide variety of standard and metric sockets available, you should be able to find the size you need to hold almost any diameter part. For pieces of very small diameter, you might try holding them in a nut driver instead.

Walter J. Morrison
Northport, N.Y.

SANDING THE ENDS OF SPINDLE TURNINGS

Sanding the very end of a piece that has been turned between centers on the lathe can be tough. I have found, however, that I can chuck such a piece in a drill and sand its end on my disc sander with the drill running.

David R. Johnson
Apple Valley, Minn.

A SANDING BELT CLEANER WITH SOLE

Get an extra mile from an old pair of crepe-soled shoes or boots. Cut off the heels and use them as you would use a gum-rubber cleaning stick to clean sanding belts.

G. M. Gauger
Austin, Tex.

SPIN-POLISH

You can sand, wire-brush, or buff small round objects like knobs or wheels by mounting them on a slightly loose-fitting dowel or rod and letting the tool spin them as it does its sanding. Adjust the angle between the rod and the tool to get the amount of spin and abrasion that you want. A piece of tubing over the rod will help keep the workpiece from running off the end.

Russell Field
Federal Valley, Wash.

DUST-FREE DRUM SANDING

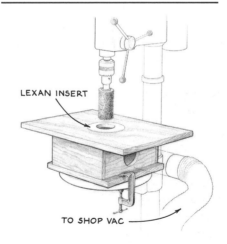

LEXAN INSERT

TO SHOP VAC

For dust-free drum sanding on your drill press, build a sanding table to clamp to your drill-press table as shown in the drawing. The ⅜-inch-thick Lexan inserts allow you to use different-diameter drums and maintain a ⅛-inch maximum clearance between the drum and the insert.

Jeff Chancey
St. Joseph, Mich.

Choosing the Right Abrasive

Most woodworkers are familiar with sandpaper and steel wool, but, let's face it, knowing which to use when is no simple matter. Open coat or closed coat? Stearated or not? Which grit should you use, and when? Basically speaking, you'll find yourself reaching for sandpaper when you're preparing wood for finishing. Steel wool is best for stripping a finish. The newer synthetic steel wools are excellent for polishing a finish.

Sandpaper

"Sandpaper Grades and Their Uses" on the opposite page will help you select the right degree of grit fineness for the job on hand. But there's more to choosing sandpaper than selecting the grade. Grit materials and backings make a difference in the performance, longevity, and cost of sheet-coated abrasives, as sandpapers are technically called. For example, sanding a finish coat with the same grade of closed-coat aluminum oxide paper or stearated silicon carbide paper will achieve the same degree of finish. But in this application the clog-resistant stearated paper will outlast many sheets of gummed-up aluminum oxide paper.

Sheet-coated abrasives are usually backed with paper of various weights. Some ultra-fine sheets are backed with polyester film. Belts are cloth-backed. Discs are backed with paper, cloth, or a rigid fiber.

Grit materials commonly used in woodworking are garnet, aluminum oxide, and silicon carbide. Garnet is a sharp, fast-cutting natural grit excellent for wood sanding. It's available in sheets and discs. Aluminum oxide is a hard and durable synthetic grit. It's not as sharp as garnet but lasts longer. Aluminum oxide is available in sheets, discs, and belts. Silicon carbide is sharp and hard. This is the most common abrasive in wet/dry and stearated (self-lubricating) papers. Stearated papers are preloaded with a dry, soapy lubricant to eliminate clogging. They are easily recognized by their gray color.

The grit is glued to backings in closed-coat or open-coat patterns. In closed-coat the backing is completely covered with grit; in open-coat the backing is only partly covered. Open-coat is less prone to clogging and overheating when you sand finishes or resinous wood.

Finishing and Stripping Pads

Steel wool is the most common type of pad used for finishing and refinishing. You'll also find copper wool and bronze. Newer on the market are synthetic fiber pads such as 3M Scotch-Brite pads, which are similar to household scouring pads. These synthetic pads are sometimes sold as synthetic steel wool. They have become popular because they don't shred or rust and will not embed steel slivers in the wood grain. Steel slivers can cause rust stains.

The metal wools come in seven grades ranging from coarse to finest. These grades are given numbers, ranging from 3 for coarse to 0000 for finest. Synthetic pads are graded on the same scale but don't come in medium, very fine, and finest. Here's a synopsis of the grades and some of their uses.

• Coarse (3) is used to remove finishes and rust.

• Medium Coarse (2) is used to remove old wax and clean old surfaces.

• Medium (1) is used to smooth raised grain, prepare wood for a first coat of finish, and smooth sealer or primer.

• Fine (0) is used to clean metal and is used with finish remover to strip finish from furniture.

• Very Fine (00) is used to apply stain and buff painted finishes and to cut gloss to semi-gloss.

• Extra Fine (000) is used to buff between coats, buff new wax finishes, and polish metal.

• Finest (0000) is used with wax or oil to buff shellac or lacquer.

—*Jim Michaud*

SANDPAPER GRADES AND THEIR USES

Material	Use	Garnet				Aluminum Oxide					Wet/Dry Silicon Carbide				Stearated Silicon Carbide		Drywall Sheets Silicon Carbide		Sanding Screen	Emery Cloth		
		VF	F	M	C	VF	F	M	C	EC	UF	SF	EF	VF	EF	VF	F	M	M	F	M	C
Wood	Stripping								●	●												
	Heavy sanding				●				●	●												
	Moderate sanding			●				●											●	●			
	Finish sanding		●			●									●		●					
Paint and clear finishes	Sanding sealer/primer	●				●								●		●						
	Between coats												●	●	●							
Metal	Rust removal								●	●												●
	Grinding/sanding							●	●												●	
	Cleaning/deburring							●	●									●	●		●	
	Finishing/polishing					●					●	●	●	●			●			●		
Plastics	Shaping								●	●												
	Light sanding							●										●	●			
	Finishing					●	●									●						
Drywall	Initial sanding																	●	●			
	Finish sanding																●					

GRADES: **UF** Ultra Fine (600-500)   **EF** Extra Fine (320-280)   **F** Fine (180-150)   **C** Coarse (60-50)
              SF Super Fine (400-360)   **VF** Very Fine (240-220)   **M** Medium (120-80)   **EC** Extra Coarse (40-36)

MULTILAYERED DRUM SANDER

My slickest trick for sanding inside curves on scrollwork is to wrap multiple layers of adhesive-backed sandpaper around a steel rod chucked in a drill or lathe. As the paper wears, I peel off a layer and continue sanding. Be sure to wrap the sandpaper *opposite* the direction of rotation.

Stephen Blaisdell
Naugatuck, Conn.

IMPROMPTU DRUM SANDERS

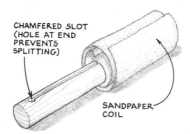

CHAMFERED SLOT (HOLE AT END PREVENTS SPLITTING)

SANDPAPER COIL

I often make impromptu drum sanders from short lengths of dowel. Cut a slot partway through the dowel as shown. Drill a hole at the end of the slot to prevent the dowel from splitting. Chamfer one side of the slot as shown to help the sandpaper coil around the dowel. Cut a strip of sandpaper the same width as the slot is long. Slip one end in the slot and coil the tail around the dowel. Wrap the paper in the direction opposite the rotation. Secure the paper with a small rubber band at the top or bottom, whichever is more appropriate.

Walter J. Morrison
Northport, N.Y.

THE STRONG-ARM OSCILLATING SPINDLE SANDER

Sanding with a drum sander on a drill press usually leaves score marks on the workpiece. You can prevent the scoring by moving the drum up and down during the final sanding. The combined vertical and circular motion is similar to the action of an expensive oscillating spindle sander.

Stephen Blaisdell
Naugatuck, Conn.

SHOP-MADE LATHE SANDING DRUM

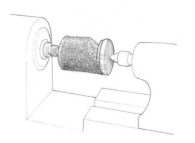

You can make your own sanding drum for your lathe. Turn two wooden plugs with a rabbet sized to fit standard sanding-drum sleeves, as shown in the drawing. Slip a sleeve on one plug and pack it full of sawdust and/or shavings. Cap the sleeve with the second plug and mount it between centers on the lathe. Turn on the lathe and go to it. You can adjust the firmness of the drum by the amount of dust and shavings you pack into it.

Lyle Terrell
New Orleans, La.

SMOOTHER LATHE TURNINGS

When sanding a spindle turning on a lathe, first sand it down to the finest grit you plan to use. Remove the spindle from the lathe, flip it end for end, and remount it. Sand with the finest grit again. Flipping the spindle reverses the direction of rotation. When you sand the spindle a second time with a fine abrasive, you knock off most of the "whiskers"—loose wood fibers—that you couldn't remove when the spindle was turning in the other direction.

Nick Engler
West Milton, Ohio

PRESANDING—A STITCH IN TIME

Even though it breaks the work flow, I presand anything I can before assembling it. The inside of drawers will never be as easy to reach as they are before they are assembled. The same goes for shelves housed in dadoes and table legs and aprons. Sand to about 180 grit, and assemble. Give it a light once-over again with 180 or 220 just before you apply finish. One tip: Don't sand surfaces that will be parts of a joint—stop sanding before you reach the dovetails, the finger joints, the tenons, or the housed part of a shelf. Sanding these surfaces creates gaps in the finished project.

M. S. Langley
Detroit, Mich.

10 HARDWARE AND FASTENERS

DRIVING WOOD SCREWS EASILY

Lubricating wood screws makes them go in much easier, increasing your efficiency. On brass screws, it can make the difference between ruining the slot and not. Or it can mean driving a drywall screw all the way home versus snapping its head off. But using the wrong lubricant can also lead to some real headaches. Soap, for example, is a popular choice, but it can cause the screws to rust severely. Try wax or grease instead.

Ernie Conover
Parkman, Ohio

JIFFY LUBE

The best stuff I've found for lubricating screws is automobile door hinge lubricant (such as Door Ease). I keep a tube of it in the corner of my tool box so it is always ready when I need it.

Myron S. Levy
Gold Hill, Oreg.

THE CASE FOR BUTCHER'S WAX

My preference for a screw lubricant is Butcher's Wax. I keep a can handy on my bench and poke the screws directly into the wax before driving them.

Ric Hanisch
Quakertown, Pa.

GETTING DOWN TO BRASS SCREWS

Brass screws look great on a finished project, but driving them can be a nightmare. At best, the heads strip. On a really bad day, the screw will break off inside the wood. So do all your fitting and fussing with steel screws the same size and thread as the brass screws you'll be using. The steel is tough, and it's unlikely to break. It also taps a thread in the wood. After you've applied the finish, take out the steel screws and replace them with brass. They'll drive like a dream. It doesn't hurt to wax all the screws—steel and brass—before driving them.

Jeff Day
Perkasie, Pa.

OR TRY SOME HELP FROM THE PLUMBER

It seems everyone's got a different system for lubricating screws. Well, so do I. My choice is to use a toilet bowl wax ring. The rings are made from a soft sticky wax that clings well to screws, they're cheap, and they seem to last practically forever. Smash one into a margarine tub and keep it near your screw gun for convenience.

David Page
Swarthmore, Pa.

THE SAME HOLDS TRUE FOR NAILS

Nails, too, benefit from a touch of lubrication. They go in easier and are much less likely to curl up and die if they are sporting a coat of wax. To this end, I drilled a hole in end of my hammer handle and filled it with

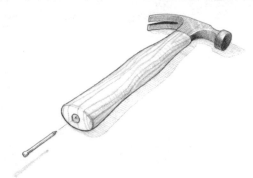

melted paraffin. Now, before I drive a nail, I slip it in and out of the hole to lube it perfectly.

Bradley Hankins
Arlington, Tex.

GOODBYE TO BENT NAILS

When you're driving small nails (or brads) into hardwood, nine times out of ten they'll bend, damaging a nearly finished project. Don't get a bigger hammer. Instead, predrill holes for the nails, using a nail as a drill bit. Grind or clip off the head from the same size nail you'll be using. Put the nail in your electric hand drill and drill the holes. Nails drive easily into the holes, and they don't lose any of their holding power.

Jeff Day
Perkasie, Pa.

SCREW REMOVAL

A stubborn wood screw can be removed fairly easily if you first heat its head with a soldering iron.

Ernie Conover
Parkman, Ohio

Power Fastening Systems

Tool makers offer a dizzying array of specialized power tools that have automated virtually every fastening operation. Carpenters still sling a trusty hammer in their tool belt and keep a screwdriver handy, but on most construction sites they don't draw these tools too often—air nailers and power drivers have taken over.

Few of the very specialized tools for construction and production furniture manufacturing will be of interest to the home woodworker and small-shop owner (who may draw the line somewhere before stapling drawers together). But many of the commonly available power fasteners—notably drill/drivers—should already be in most small shops, while others are worth considering for purchase or rental.

Power Screw Driving

The first woodworker ever to buy an electric drill probably chucked a screwdriver blade in it and tried to drive a slotted screw. The experiment couldn't have been a great success—the speed of the drill would have caused the bit to slip out of the slot and gouge the work.

Power screw driving has come a long way since then. Today most electric drills have variable speed and are reversible, and they provide control when driving and removing screws. Both corded and cordless models are available.

One specialized version is the drywall screw gun, a professional tool that will fasten drywall faster than you can say "drywall screw." Another is the cordless electric

screwdriver, a slower, high-torque tool. Both of these hybrids are dedicated screwdrivers; neither is designed to drill holes.

Phillips screws, with two slots crossing at right angles, are less likely to be stripped. The same is true of Robertson screws, which feature a square recess that virtually eliminates stripping the screw head.

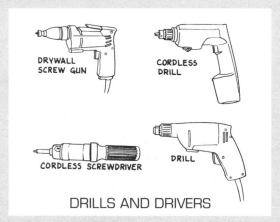

DRILLS AND DRIVERS

Variable-Speed Reversible Drills

If you are going to have only one tool for drilling and driving, get a variable-speed reversible (VSR) drill. Look for a model geared for 1,200 or fewer rpm. VSRs geared for higher rpm are hard to control when driving screws, even if they feature smooth speed control. Also, lower speeds mean more torque. Most VSR drills have chucks that will take bits up to ⅜ inch diameter. These ⅜-inch drills are a good choice for most drilling and driving jobs you'll encounter in woodworking, but you also have the choice of heavier-duty drills with ½-inch chucks. Some VSR drills come with a keyless chuck. An auxiliary side handle is available for some models.

Cordless drills have evolved greatly in recent years. Once a substitute for corded drills only when cords couldn't reach, cordless drills are now feature-packed, versatile, and powerful tools that have relegated many of their corded forebears to occasional use. Powered by removable battery packs that typically recharge in one hour, they range greatly in performance and price.

For driving screws, the tool should have variable speed control in two ranges and in reverse, an adjustable torque-control clutch, and an electric brake. Although spare battery packs are expensive, they let you continue driving all day long.

A great new drill accessory called a Chuck Mate lets you alternate quickly from drilling pilot holes to driving screws. This is a quick-change, adapter-held drill/countersink that slips over the screwdriver bit. Another inexpensive accessory is a clutch mechanism that automatically controls countersink depth and allows a VSR to function as a drywall screw gun. A simple accessory often overlooked is a long bit. You'll find that using a bit that's up to 6 inches long will give you more control than a stubby bit, especially when driving screws at an angle.

Cordless Screwdrivers

Cordless screwdrivers, both in-line models and pistol-grip models, don't have chucks. Instead, they hold ¼-inch hex-shank bits in a collet. Some are cheap enough to replace the screwdriver in the kitchen tool drawer. Although these screwdrivers cannot match the power and stamina of the larger cordless drills, they deliver surprising torque and, on one charge, do work that would numb most forearms in a contest using a manual screwdriver.

Some models have integral batteries, which means the tool must be retired to the charging stand when the battery is discharged. Others have removable battery packs. Especially useful for assembly and disassembly jobs involving many fasteners, these compact workhorses are great tools for home and shop use.

Drywall Screw Guns

Drywall screw guns hold a Phillips screw magnetically, drive it to a regulated countersink depth, then release it by the action of a clutch. This allows screws to be driven below the surface without breaking the paper of the drywall, making the screws easy to cover with joint compound. Most models feature trigger-controlled variable speed but are typically used at full throttle by drywall hangers.

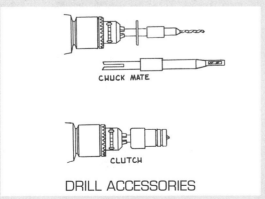

CHUCK MATE

CLUTCH

DRILL ACCESSORIES

(continued)

Power Fastening Systems—*Continued*

Air-Powered Nailers

Air nailers operate with a piston-driven blade that punches the nail down to a regulated depth. They are now used in all major phases of house building, from framing to trim. Cabinet shops also use them extensively. However, air nailers are still priced out of the range of the occasional carpenter or home woodworker. Also, these guns use collated nails that cost significantly more than loose nails. However, you can rent a nailer and compressor, something to consider for a big job.

A safety feature common to all nailers is that they operate only when in contact with the work. Sequential-trip models require squeezing the trigger after the tool's nosepiece is set down on the work. Contact-trip models allow even faster operation: With the trigger held down, the tool will bounce-fire nails wherever the nosepiece is brought into contact with the work.

Framing nailers are heavy-duty tools designed to drive common nails for framing, decking, and sheathing. Linear-magazine

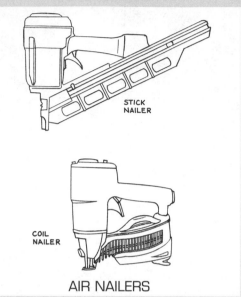

STICK NAILER

COIL NAILER

AIR NAILERS

models, called "stick nailers," feed collated strips of nails down an angled channel. Circular-magazine models, called "coil nailers," feed rolled belts of nails from a drum.

Nails of various kinds are available in sticks and coils, including spiral and ring shank, galvanized, and stainless steel. Shank diameters are usually smaller than common

PLUG PULLER

Here's a sure-fire way to remove a wooden plug that covers a screw head. Drill a ⅛-inch pilot hole through the center of the plug. Then drive a drywall screw through the center. The hardened drywall screw bottoms on the hidden screw head and forces the plug up out of the hole.

Kent A. Johnson
Evansville, Ind.

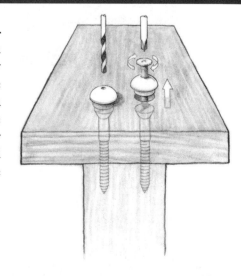

AIR PALM NAILER

Finish nailers work the same way as framing nailers, but they are lighter and are designed to drive and countersink finish nails for interior and exterior trim, paneling, furniture, and cabinetmaking. Manufacturers offer nails of various types for the finish nailers, including square shank with L- or T-head, ring shank, screw shank, painted, galvanized, aluminum, and even solid plastic.

Brad nailers drive small-gauge brads and headless pins. Useful for light trim work and cabinetmaking, brad drivers are now available in electric models for the shop without a compressor. Brads are either plain steel or color-coated.

Power Staplers

Power staplers come in air-powered, electric, and cordless electric models. They speed up upholstering, installation of insulation and ceiling tile, and other light fastening applications.

nails, as the one-stroke punch of the nailer drives the nail without much risk of bending. Power-driven nails have a plastic coating that is instantly liquefied by the driving friction. This lubricates the nail for easier penetration. When the coating cools, it coats the wood fibers and glues the nail in place.

An adjunct to the framing nailer is the air palm nailer, a compact air-powered impact hammer useful for driving common nails and spikes in places too tight for the framing nailer or for swinging a hammer.

—Jim Michaud
Michaud is a freelance writer and wood worker in Swampscott, Mass.

HIGH-CLASS FURNITURE LEVELERS

Elegant leveling feet can be an integral part of your furniture design. Epoxy a carriage bolt into a turning blank, then spin it into a hole in some wood mounted on the faceplate. Turn it to suit your taste. A threaded insert in the bottom of the furniture leg completes the arrangement.

Gordon Krupp
Northbrook, Ill.

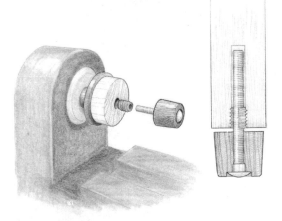

SHOP-MADE KNOBS FOR JIGS

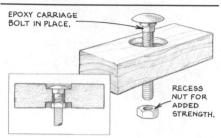

EPOXY CARRIAGE BOLT IN PLACE.

RECESS NUT FOR ADDED STRENGTH.

When working with jigs or fixtures, reaching for a wrench to make adjustments can become a pain. Instead, epoxy a carriage bolt to a block of wood to make adjustment knobs that you can easily tighten by hand.

Jeff Greef
Soquel, Calif.

SORTING PAN FOR FASTENERS

Everyone's got a can of oddball screws and hardware someplace. You know, that's where you threw those extra screws and nails that you thought might be useful someday. But it's a pain in the neck to pour the whole mess out onto your workbench, sort through it to find the one screw you want, and then try to put it all back into the container again. To simplify this task, make a sorting pan by cutting an inch or so of metal from the corner of a rectangular baking pan. Pour the parts out into the pan to sort through them, then use the open corner as a funnel to pour the parts back into their container.

Nick Engler
West Milton, Ohio

AGING HARDWARE

When making reproductions of antiques, authentic-looking hardware can be hard to come by. Instead you can make your own "old" hardware by aging new pieces.

For iron or steel hardware, start by soaking it in a 10 percent solution of nitric acid for 10 to 20 minutes. This strips off the rust-inhibiting coating. Rinse the hardware in water, then dip it in gun bluing (available at gun stores) and let it dry. The joints will show streaks of rust, while the flat areas will turn black like hand-forged iron implements.

To age brass hardware, let it soak in paint stripper for an hour or so to strip off the lacquer coating. Rinse it in tap water and dip it in salt water. Then suspend it for several days in a closed container above a small quantity of household ammonia. The salt and the ammonia fumes will tarnish the brass, giving it an antique appearance.

Nick Engler
West Milton, Ohio

AVOID THREAD DAMAGE WHEN CUTTING A BOLT

If you have to cut through a threaded rod, or through the threads on a bolt, turn a nut onto the threads first. Then make the cut. After cutting, file or grind the end to round it slightly, then back the nut off. This will smooth the cut threads so it is possible to start the nut next time.

Ralph S. Wilkes
Branchport, N.Y.

NO-ROUT SCREW SLOTS

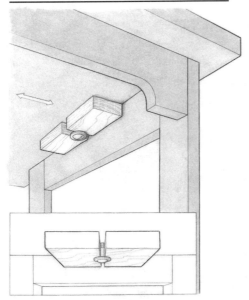

Here's an easy way to attach tabletops or cabinet tops. Like the screw-in-slotted-hole method, it

allows the top to move with the seasons; but it doesn't require any routing to produce the slot. The screw slot is formed by the gap between two ¾ × 1½ × 2-inch wooden blocks glued to the table aprons or cabinet sides. Use the intended screw as a spacer to separate the blocks. A buttonhead screw with a washer works best. When the screw is installed, it can slide between the blocks as the top expands and contracts.

Patrick Warner
Escondido, Calif.

THESE KNOBS ARE NOT FOR TURNING

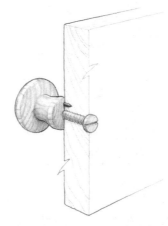

Wooden knobs—the kind with a single screw—often become loose and twist in the hand. To cure this, I drill a pilot hole in the back of the knob and insert a small brad or nail with the point protruding ⅛ inch or so. When this nail bites into the drawer front, the knob will never turn again. If your bits aren't small

(continued on page 164)

Knockdown Fittings

Knockdown fittings make it easy to assemble and disassemble a piece without degrading the holding power of the fasteners. Most woodworkers are familiar with common types of knockdown fittings such as bed hardware, table-leg hanger bolts, and shelf supports. Spawned by the popularity of Scandinavian-designed furniture and the use of veneered and plastic-laminated particleboard in furniture making, there are now hundreds of knockdown fittings available for a wide range of applications. These fasteners provide secure joints in particleboard and end grain that could not be achieved with traditional fasteners. They also allow furniture pieces of all kinds to be shipped as compact kits for assembly after purchase.

Knockdown fittings fall into two categories. One uses bolts or screws that thread into threaded inserts or metal cross-dowels, or into surface-mounted blocks. The other category of fitting has parts that interlock by wedge, cam, or spring action. Some fittings, especially those designed to be recessed completely into the work, require boring precise blind holes with a jig, drill press, or both. Most require a metric bit. For joining major pieces, test-fitted guide dowels or biscuits are often used between knockdown fittings to locate the pieces securely and cut down on the number of fittings required. Here is a small sampling of the knockdown fittings available today.

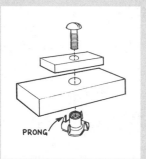

PRONG

T-Nut

The T-nut has prongs that anchor it into the work. You drill a hole for the nut and then tap it into place with a hammer to sink the prongs into the wood. The nut receives an ordinary machine screw or bolt. When countersunk, the T-nut can be used on the exposed side of panels that will be covered with plastic laminate.

SCREWDRIVER SLOT

Threaded Insert

Available in steel, brass, and zinc, threaded inserts have deep threads that self-tap into blind holes in wood, plywood, or particleboard. Metric sizes are also available. Wallboard anchors, designed to self-tap into drywall and accept a standard drywall screw, can also serve as threaded inserts when driven into a pilot hole in plywood or particleboard.

Glue-In Bushing

Glue-in bushings are ridged plastic sleeves that go into a predrilled hole. As the name implies, they rely on glue to secure them in the hole. Some have internal threads to accept bolts, or connector-bolt components of recessed knockdown fittings. Others have no internal threads; they are used with wood screws that self-tap into the plastic.

Expanding Bushing

Expanding bushings are either plastic or metal. They have tapered internal threads that spread the bushing as the bolt is driven in. This expansion secures the bushing.

Mortised Hooked Cam Latch

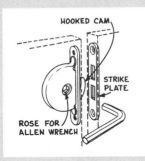

These fittings are commonly used for securing large movable partitions and screens. Both the hooked cam and the strike plate are mortised into the edges of mating panels, allowing the panels to be connected with their faces flush. Mortising also hides the mechanisms so all you see in the assembled panels is a small rose. You insert an allen wrench into the rose to operate the hook, which engages the back of a strike plate.

Surface-Mounted Hooked Cam Latch

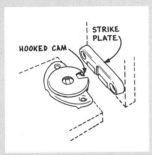

This hardware works on the same principle as the mortised hooked cam latch. Surface mounting eliminates the need to mortise.

(continued)

Knockdown Fittings—*Continued*

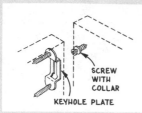

Keyhole Fitting

This fitting employs a screw with a collar below the head. A screw-mounted keyhole plate wedges between the collar and screw head. This hardware is used mostly in light modular partition systems and for hanging components from vertical surfaces.

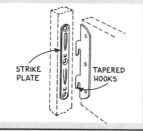

Bed Hooks

Screw-mounted steel plates have tapered hooks that wedge into slots in a countersunk strike plate. These hangers are most commonly used to attach bed rails to headboards and footboards. They are also used for booths and partitions.

Wedged Post Hangers

Used instead of bed hooks, these hangers have interlocking tabs that wedge together. Neither plate needs to be countersunk.

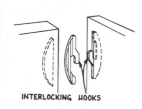

Biscuit Joiner Hooks

These fasteners consist of two identical plates with interlocking hooks. The plates are shaped to fit into a groove made with a biscuit joiner. They are barbed and are used with glue to further secure them.

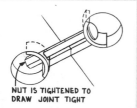

Panel Connector

Panel connectors are designed for joining laminated countertops. Semicircular pieces fit into the recesses. Tightening a nut onto a screw draws the two semicircular pieces together.

Hanger Bolt and Bracket

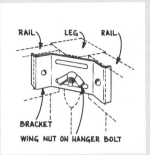

This hardware is designed to fasten table rails to legs. A bracket is screwed perpendicular to the rails. The hanger bolt has wood-screw threads for half its length and machine-screw threads along the other half. The bolt is permanently screwed into the chamfered inner corner of the leg. To affix the leg, you put the bolt through a hole in the bracket and secure it with a wing nut. Some brackets have a flange on each side that fits into a groove in the rail, making the joint more secure.

Cross Dowel

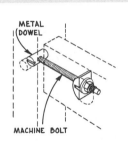

This is a strong fitting for joining frame members. You drill a hole in one member to receive a metal dowel. The dowel is threaded through its side to receive a machine bolt. A slot in one end of the dowel lets you use a screwdriver to align the threaded hole. In the version shown, the dowel is being used with a machine bolt that's hidden in the rail.

Screw and Sleeve

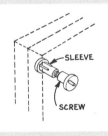

This hardware is used to join modules and cabinets together. You drill a hole through the side of both pieces to be joined. Slip a sleeve into one hole and then thread a screw into the sleeve. Both pieces have identical slotted heads so you can tighten them by using two screwdrivers together.

Twin-Block Fitting

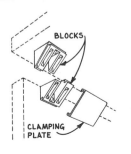

Mating blocks, either plastic or metal, are screw-mounted to panels and secured together with a connecting screw, clamping plate, or wedge. This hardware is used to assemble cabinets and other applications where panels meet at a right angle.

(continued)

Knockdown Fittings—*Continued*

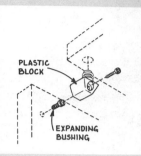

Single-Block Fitting

Also for assembling cabinets and other panels meeting at right angles, this hardware uses a plastic block that is press-fitted into one panel. The block retains a bolt that threads into a threaded insert, glue-in, or expanding bushing in the opposing panel.

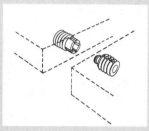

Mating Dowels

Glue-in male and female plastic dowels snap-fit together for light-duty knockdown applications.

enough to drill the pilot hole, cut the head off the nail or brad and use it as a drill.

Robert Campbell
Somerset, Pa.

PRECISE DOOR ALIGNMENT

Aligning and mounting hinges on small doors or lids can be frustrating. When I use a hinge that requires a mortise on the case but not on the door or lid, I first cut the mortise and screw the hinge to the case. Next, I close the hinge, put a drop of hot-melt glue on the unattached leaf, and lay the door in place, carefully aligned. When the glue sets in a minute or two, I add the screws.

David R. Johnson
Apple Valley, Minn.

LOW-IMPACT GLAZING POINTS

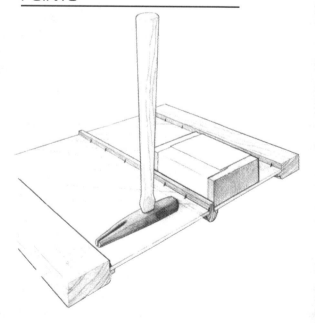

Case Connector

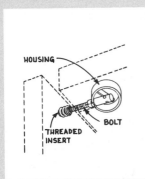

This hardware provides a bolt-tightened joint between major panels. A hidden bolt engages a threaded insert, glue-in, or expanding bushing.

A metal housing is notched to fit around a groove in the bolt. The housing doubles as a trim cap and is slotted for access to turning holes in the bolt. A variation on this hardware replaces the metal housing with a semicircular pressure plate, similar to the plate used with a cross dowel and stud bolt. A trim cap can be used with this version.

—*Jim Michaud*

When driving glazing points in place with a hammer, place a steel or lead block against the muntin to absorb the shock. Wrap the block in paper to avoid scratching the glass.

Bill Bigelow
Surry, N.H.

EMERGENCY NAILSET

Can't find your nailset? You might be able to use a nail instead. Hold the nail head on the nail to be set, with the shank perpendicular to the grain of the wood. Rap the nail head sharply to set the nail.

H. R. McDermid
Vernon, British Columbia

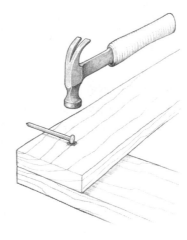

11 DUST COLLECTION

MAGNETIC MAGIC

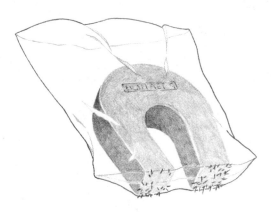

Steel wool is an excellent abrasive for rubbing out finishes. Unfortunately, however, it breaks down into little crumbs that are difficult to clean up. I solve this problem with a magnet. I wave it over the mess and it picks up the debris like magic. Well, almost like magic. The particles don't disappear; they stick to the magnet in plain sight. This cre-ates another problem. How do you clean the magnet?

The best way I've found is to not let the magnet get covered in the first place. Before waving it over the bench and uttering the magic words, I place the magnet in a plastic bag. This way, the steel wool crumbs are isolated from the magnet on the out-side of the bag. I then hold the bag over the trash can and remove the magnet. Taadaa—the steel wool par-ticles have disappeared. This trick also works for picking up spilled brads or screws. And now for my next illusion . . .

Walter J. Morrison
Northport, N.Y.

MORE MAGNETIC MAGIC

I find that I often end up finish sanding on the flat surface of my table saw. To help keep the dust to a minimum, I keep a shop-vacuum dust pickup close by while I work.

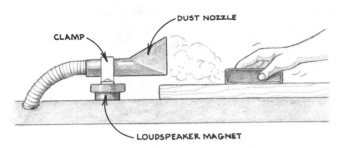

CLAMP — DUST NOZZLE

LOUDSPEAKER MAGNET

The rig I've made consists of a magnetic base with a vacuum cleaner nozzle held to it with a simple sheet-metal clamp. The magnet came from a discarded loudspeaker. Because the magnet keeps the nozzle from moving around on the cast-iron table, I can easily position the rig for optimum dust control.

Walter J. Morrison
Northport, N.Y.

IT'S A DIRTY JOB, BUT . . .

Cleaning a shop-vacuum filter is a dirty but necessary job. The key is to do it in such a way that you don't end up breathing in a cloud of extra-fine dust and creating a mess in your freshly vacuumed shop. I always clean my filter outdoors, containing the dust in a clear plastic trash bag.

I place the unit in the bag along with a stiff-bristled brush and tie the bag closed. Working from outside the bag, I hold the unit off the ground and clean the filter with the brush. Once the filter is clean, I let the dust settle before removing the unit from the bag. When finished, I tie the bag up and set it aside until the filter needs another cleaning.

Walter J. Morrison
Northport, N.Y.

BETTER FILTERING

If your shop vac has a foam or paper filter that clogs quickly with wood chips, try covering the filter with old pantyhose. This allows the larger, heavier chips to fall off into the canister when you turn the vacuum off.

Wilber Goeke
Cleveland, Wis.

ON LOAN FROM MR. HOOVER

Before purchasing any new attachments for your shop vacuum, check out the ones that came with your household machine. You may be able to borrow what you need. The

(continued on page 171)

Designing a Dust Collection System

Dust collection? That's for high-output cabinet and production shops, not my one-man shop, right?

Wrong. Even if you work wood for a hobby in your basement, the hours you spend there will be more pleasurable, safer, and a lot healthier if you install a dust collection system. You'll reduce cleanup, and more important, you'll reduce your risk of developing respiratory problems. To design a system, you need to know what type of system is right for your needs. Let's start with the collector—the heart of the system.

Types of Collectors

Although a shop vacuum should be in every shop, it should not double as a dust collector. First, it is not made for continuous duty. Second, it just doesn't move the volume of air required to be really effective. A shop vacuum is also very noisy. If you use only small bench-top tools, you may get by with one, but big mess producers like jointers and thickness planers require a dust collector.

The less-expensive models have a single-stage design. They pull dust- and debris-laden air through the eye of a radial vane impeller and then expel it into collector bags, as shown in *Dust Collectors*. The bottom bag collects big chips, and fine dust is trapped in the top bag. Single-stage collectors are compact, and they're easy to empty and clean.

Single-stage collectors may have drawbacks worth considering. The steel impellers found on some models can make sparks and trigger an explosion. For safety, look for alumimum impellers; they won't spark. Also, the impeller can clog with large chunks and stringy shavings. Finally, single-stage collectors are noisy when large particles strike impeller vanes. If the machine hose is removed, exposed impeller vanes pose a safety hazard.

A two-stage collector pulls dust and chips into the inlet. Large debris falls directly into the collector drum, and fine dust is pulled into the eye of the impeller and expelled into the collector bag, as

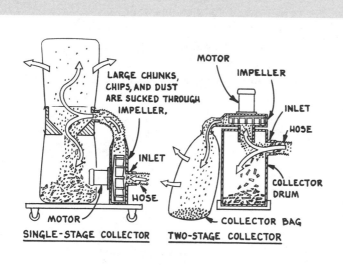

DUST COLLECTORS

shown in the drawing. Two-stage collectors are safer and quieter than single-stage models because large solids do not contact the impeller. But they cost more, are unwieldy, and take up more floor space. They are also more difficult to empty and clean.

Portable and Central Collection

The simplest approach is to set up a portable collection system. This consists of a collector that you roll around the shop, attaching it to whatever machine you are using at the time. Most collectors are mounted on casters that make it easy to move them from tool to tool. You'll spend some time connecting and disconnecting, but for the hobbyist, this is a cheap and effective way to go.

A central system uses a permanently located collector that's connected to each machine by rigid ductwork. A plus is that you can locate the noisy collector out of the way in a closet or outside. If your floor plan is etched in stone and you don't mind parting with some money, this is a worthwhile alternative.

Sizing and Laying Out a Collection System

There are several factors that must be considered when sizing a collector:

• which machines and the number of them that will run simultaneously

• the distance between machines

• the distance between the collector and the machines

Size the collector to the cubic-feet-per-minute (cfm) requirements of the largest machine you plan to hook up. (See the table "Average Exhaust Volumes in Cubic Feet per Minute" below.) The smallest collectors start

(continued)

AVERAGE EXHAUST VOLUMES IN CUBIC FEET PER MINUTE

Machine	Home Shop	Industrial
Table Saw	350	400
Jointer (to 8")	300	400
Disc Sander (to 12")	200	300
Radial Arm Saw	350	500
Band Saw	350	400
Planer (to 20")	400	775
Shaper (½" Spindle)	300	400
Shaper (1" Spindle)	500	1,000
Drill Press	150	300
Floor Sweep	350	800

Designing a Dust Collection System—*Continued*

at about 400 cfm. I recommend at least 600 cfm, which should be adequate for any tool, provided the flexible hose length is kept to no more than about 8 feet.

To size a collector for a central system, you'll need to lay out the system first so you can take all losses into account. This includes the exhaust volume requirement of machines that will run at the same time, the static pressure losses of each foot of pipe, and every elbow and fitting.

Dust collectors are designed to move a specific amount of cubic feet of air per minute at a specific static pressure. As air travels through the ductwork, it encounters friction from the walls. Static pressure is a way of measuring this friction. The main duct needs to maintain a velocity of 3,500 feet per minute (fpm) so that wood chips and dust will not settle out. It is best to be generous with your calculations, rather than ending up with an inadequate system.

Selecting Pipe and Fittings

Much controversy exists concerning plastic versus metal ductwork. Debris hurtling through plastic ductwork at 3,500 fpm can build up enough of a static charge to cause an explosion, unless the system is grounded by a continuous copper ground wire running through the duct. Attach the wire to a suitable ground. Metal ductwork is noisier and more expensive than plastic, but it is lighter in weight, more durable, and also safer.

You'll find metal air ductwork at heating ventilation and air conditioning (HVAC) supply houses. Or you can use stovepipe.

For plastic ductwork, use drain, waste, and vent (DWV) pipes and fittings, available at plumbing supply houses.

Whether you choose plastic or metal, use elbows with a long radius or a combination of two 45-degree fittings. Sharp 90-degree turns in 4-inch duct create as much resistance as 6 feet of straight duct. By eliminating as many sharp bends as possible, you reduce your collector requirements.

Blast gates at each machine are kept closed until the machine is ready to be used. They are available in plastic and metal. I recommend metal blast gates, since plastic gates wear and break easily. You can also make your own gates, with some ingenuity.

Exhaust hoods are available as aftermarket accessories for some older machines. Many new machines come with dust collection hookups standard. To rig up your own custom exhaust hoods, you can take advantage of the vast variety of HVAC and plumber's metal and plastic fittings.

Flexible hose should be kept to short lengths. The convolutions required to make it flexible create a great amount of static pressure drop. Standard hose clamps can be used to secure the connections.

Remember that dust collectors will not remove ultrafine particles from the air, so don't toss out your dust mask after you've installed your system.

—*Craig Bentzley*
   Bentzley is a professional woodworker in Chalfont, Pa.

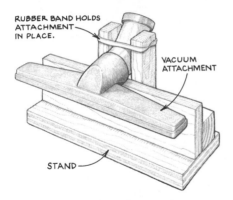

RUBBER BAND HOLDS ATTACHMENT IN PLACE.

VACUUM ATTACHMENT

STAND

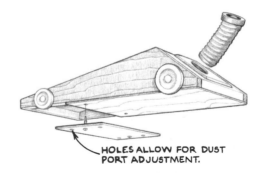

HOLES ALLOW FOR DUST PORT ADJUSTMENT.

small, round brush attachment is handy for removing sanding dust between coats of finish before using a tack cloth. The crevice tool does a good job of cleaning dust out of motors and other hard-to-get-at places.

Most home vacs use 1¼-inch-diameter hoses and fittings, the same as many shop vacs, so the parts are probably interchangeable. Or, if your shop vac has a bigger hose, you can turn a reducing plug for the end of it.

The attachment I find to be most useful is the regular floor-cleaning nozzle. It does a great job of sucking up the fine dust created by sanding on a lathe. To use the nozzle for this purpose, you'll have to build a stand for it as shown. Size the stand to fit your equipment.

Ralph S. Wilkes
Branchport, N.Y.

HOT ROD FLOOR SWEEP

I've never had much luck with the vacuum attachments that manufacturers make for floor cleaning. So I made my own from a few scraps of lumber, some odds and ends of hard-

ware, and four wooden wheels. The bottom rides about ⅜ inch above the floor and has an adjustable dust port between the front wheels. While the sweep won't pick up big shavings, it does a great job on the little stuff and it rolls right under many of the low benches and machines in my shop.

Edwin Sheriff
Birmingham, Ala.

NOT SO DUSTY

To improve the dust collection on my table saw, I used duct tape to seal all the seams around the clean-out door and between the floor and stand. I also closed the gap for the tilting arbor wheel with a piece of slotted rubber that's attached with duct tape. The suction is so strong now that it actually helps hold the wood down on the table!

Glenn Hughes
Emmaus, Pa.

SPACE-SAVING DUST COLLECTOR

I work in a small shop where every square foot is accounted for. So when it came time to install a dust collector, there wasn't a free space to put it in. Instead, I had to look for space that wasn't being used efficiently. I found two places that I could exploit—the areas under my table saw and radial arm saw. These proved ideal since the saws were the machines I wanted to hook up to the collector.

For the dust hopper, I built a plywood box that fits under the exten-sion table of the table saw. The collector motor and fan are mounted on the dust hopper, which slides open like a drawer for emptying. A length of flexible hose connects the hopper to a filter bag under the radial arm saw. The two saws are connected to the collector with sections of flexible hose with in-line blast gates to increase efficiency.

Bob Hawks
Tulsa, Okla.

POSITIVE-PRESSURE VENTILATION

Positive-pressure ventilation safely removes solvent fumes from a room more effectively than suction. If you place a fan 3 to 12 feet outside a room and aim it to blow through the doorway, the fan's cone of air will pressurize the inside of the room. An open window will allow the air and fumes to escape. The room will clear

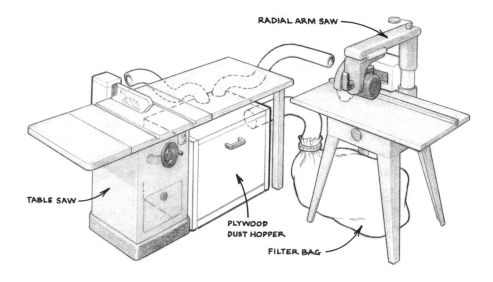

RADIAL ARM SAW

TABLE SAW

PLYWOOD DUST HOPPER

FILTER BAG

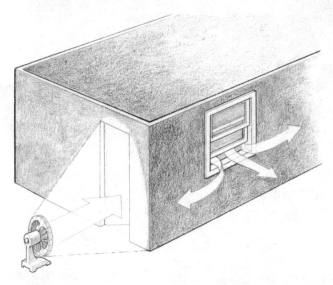

quickly and no potentially explosive gases will pass through the fan.

Steve Long
Norman, Okla.

DUST BUSTER

When I first tried my two-bag dust collector, I noticed an unacceptable amount of fine dust escaping through the top bag. Recalling a trick I'd heard, I sprayed the inside of the upper bag with a no-stick cooking spray. This treatment stopped the finer dust with no noticeable loss of efficiency in the dust-collection system.

Robert Brandt
Fort Worth, Tex.

12 TABLE SAW TRICKS

KNOWING WHEN A TABLE SAW NEEDS ALIGNMENT

For a table saw to work properly, the face of the blade must be parallel to the slots in the table. One sign that the blade is out of alignment is that the wood burns as you cut it. However, burning can be caused by a host of other problems, from feeding the wood too slowly to letting the kerf pinch together. Another indication that the saw is out of alignment is a ringing sound, or *zing,* just as you finish a cut. Also inspect the trailing corners of the workpiece (the portions of the board that were cut last). If you hear the zing and the corners look a little chewed up, it's time to realign your table saw.

Nick Engler
West Milton, Ohio

ALIGNING A SAW FENCE

Here's a quick and easy way to align your table saw rip fence with the miter gauge slots. Loosen the screws that lock the fence alignment, then press the fence against a long

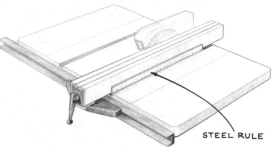

STEEL RULE

steel rule or framing square in the miter gauge slot. Retighten the screws while holding the fence tight against the rule.

David R. Johnson
Apple Valley, Minn.

HEIGHT GAUGE

The quickest way I know to set the height of a table saw (or router) is with gauge blocks. I made this one from a 3-inch length of 2 × 4, cut to the settings I most frequently use. If

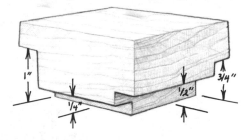

you need more settings, use another block. You can use this gauge block equally well for setting the fence to the saw blade.

L. T. Murphy
Oak Ridge, Tenn.

HALF THE FENCE IS TWICE AS GOOD

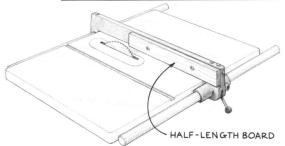

HALF-LENGTH BOARD

Wood often twists and bends when internal stresses are released during ripping. With a regular, full-length rip fence, this movement can cause the board to bind between the fence and blade, which in turn can cause a kickback. A rip fence that ends at the midpoint of the blade gives a board room to do its own thing without binding.

I converted my normal fence to half-length by bolting a short board to its side, as shown. Now the saw runs more easily and it rarely, if ever, kicks back.

Jim Turbyville
Westland, Mich.

AUXILIARY RABBETING FENCE

A dado head can make cutting rabbets on a table saw go quickly. But setting the width of cut is tedious,

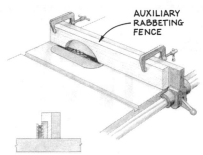

AUXILIARY RABBETING FENCE

and because the fence has to be right next to the blade, you risk damaging the fence. Instead of going through all that fuss, I clamp an auxiliary rabbeting fence to my table saw's fence.

The rabbeting fence is simply a 1¼ × 3-inch board that is as long as my regular fence. I secure it to the regular fence with C-clamps. I then set up the dado blade to cut a kerf that is slightly wider than the rabbet I want. I lower the blade beneath the table and start the saw. Then, with the auxiliary fence covering the entire blade, I raise the blade up, cutting a recess in the wood. Once the recess is cut, I adjust the fence so it exposes only enough blade to cut the necessary rabbet.

Ric Hanisch
Quakertown, Pa.

GETTING THE FIRST EDGE STRAIGHT

To get one edge straight on a board that has two irregular edges, attach a straightedge to one side with double-sided carpet tape. Then run it through the table saw with the straightedge against the fence. The tape won't damage the wood
(continued on page 178)

Tune Up Your Table Saw

In most woodworking projects, stock will pass over the table saw several times as it is shaped into its final form. This means that a well-tuned table saw is essential to well-made projects. Here are the five alignments that are critical to peak table saw performance:

• The miter gauge slots must be parallel to the blade.

• The rip fence must be parallel to the blade.

• The splitter must be in line with the blade.

• The throat plate must be flush with the table.

• The blade must stop precisely at 90 degrees when you return it to vertical.

Once you make these adjustments, you can be sure your saw will cut as true as possible. To check your saw, you'll need an accurate square and a metal rule. You can do the whole job with a good combination square. Unplug the saw before you start working.

Checking the Slots

If the miter gauge slots are not parallel to the blade, boards guided by the miter gauge will be either pushed into or pulled away from the blade, making accurate crosscutting impossible.

Use the rule or the blade from the combination square to check whether the slots are parallel to the blade. Raise the blade all the way up. Choose one tooth, and rotate the blade until that tooth is at table level toward the operator's side of the saw. Measure the distance between the tooth and the left slot as shown in *Checking the Slots*. Then rotate the blade until the chosen tooth is at table level toward the rear of the saw. Measure the distance from slot to blade. The two measurements should be equal. If they are not, you'll have to make an adjustment.

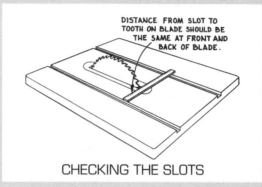

CHECKING THE SLOTS

DISTANCE FROM SLOT TO TOOTH ON BLADE SHOULD BE THE SAME AT FRONT AND BACK OF BLADE.

The means of making this adjustment varies from saw to saw. On some, you must loosen the bolts that hold the blade carriage to the table and then shift the carriage into line. On other saws the table and carriage are independent of one another, so you must loosen the bolts that hold the table to the base and then shift the table. Refer to your owner's manual for specific details.

Checking the Rip Fence

If the rip fence is not parallel to the blade, it can cause your stock to burn as it passes by the blade. In extreme cases, dangerous kickback may result.

Now that you know your slots are parallel to the blade, you can use a slot to check that your rip fence is parallel. To do this, stand a straightedge in the slot as shown in

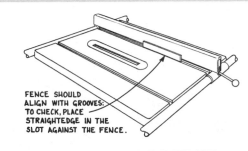

FENCE SHOULD ALIGN WITH GROOVES; TO CHECK, PLACE STRAIGHTEDGE IN THE SLOT AGAINST THE FENCE.

CHECKING THE RIP FENCE

Checking the Rip Fence. Lock the fence against the straightedge. If the fence contacts the entire length of the straightedge, you know the fence is parallel. Check this by measuring as you did to check the miter gauge slots. This time, however, measure between a tooth on the blade and the fence. Position the fence about 3 inches from the blade and lock it in place. Again, the method of adjusting the fence varies from saw to saw. On some saws, the adjustment is made via a bolt on top of the fence.

Checking the Splitter

This is another critical adjustment. If the splitter is out of line, feeding stock past it can be a problem. In an extreme situation, the stock may not be able to pass at all.

Check the splitter's alignment with the

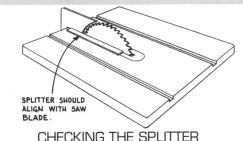

SPLITTER SHOULD ALIGN WITH SAW BLADE.

CHECKING THE SPLITTER

blade, using a rule. Hold the rule along the blade as shown in *Checking the Splitter*. The splitter should align with the rule. If it doesn't, bend it into line with a handscrew.

Checking the Throat Plate

The throat plate should be flush with the table. This isn't a critical safety factor as are the first three adjustments, but it can affect accuracy. If the throat plate is not flush with the table, stock can deflect slightly up or down as it is being cut. This can throw off a critical cut by a degree or so.

Span the throat plate with the rule as shown in *Checking the Throat Plate*. Check at the operator's side of the slot and the back of the slot. If the throat plate wobbles side to side, it is set too high. If you can see light between the plate and the rule, your plate is too low. Use a flashlight, if necessary, to check for light.

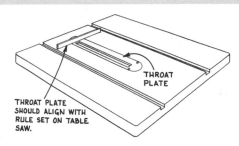

THROAT PLATE

THROAT PLATE SHOULD ALIGN WITH RULE SET ON TABLE SAW.

CHECKING THE THROAT PLATE

Many throat plates have setscrews to adjust height. If you find that vibration is constantly throwing the plate out of adjustment, coat the setscrews with a thread-locking adhesive such as Loc-tite, available at most auto-parts stores. If the throat plate

(continued)

Tune Up Your Table Saw—*Continued*

doesn't have setscrews, place shims under the plate to raise it, or file slightly to lower it.

Checking the Blade for Square

The blade should stop precisely at 90 degrees to the table when you crank it into the vertical position. Most saws have a stop mounted underneath that ensures this setting—a nice feature, but don't be lulled into a false sense of security about the blade's actual adjustment. Vibration and sawdust can throw this stop out of alignment, which in turn can cause the saw operator to become bent out of shape.

Check the stop by tilting the blade over and then returning it to vertical. Hold a square up against the blade as shown in *Checking the Blade for Square*. There should be no light between the blade and the square. Check this with a flashlight if neces-

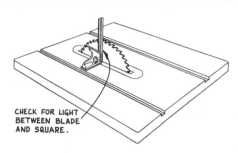

CHECK FOR LIGHT BETWEEN BLADE AND SQUARE.

CHECKING THE BLADE FOR SQUARE

sary. Your owner's manual will tell you how to adjust this stop. But before you make an adjustment, make sure there is no buildup of sawdust to prevent the carriage from coming to rest against the stop. It's a good idea to occasionally clean all the sawdust from under your saw to prevent this problem.

—Kenneth S. Burton, Jr.
Burton is a woodworking editor at Rodale Press and a studio furniture maker in Allentown, Pa.

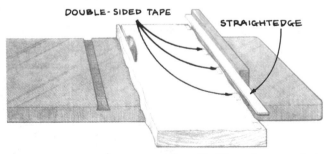

DOUBLE-SIDED TAPE

STRAIGHTEDGE

the way nails will. If you're worried about the tape coming loose in the middle of the cut, clamp the board briefly right after you stick the straightedge down. You'll be amazed at how well the tape sticks.

Stan Watson
Palm Springs, Calif.

ANOTHER WAY TO GO STRAIGHT

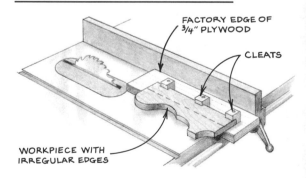

FACTORY EDGE OF 3/4" PLYWOOD

CLEATS

WORKPIECE WITH IRREGULAR EDGES

Instead of attaching a straightedge to the board, as explained above, you can attach the board to the straight factory edge of another piece of wood. This jig is simply a piece of ¾-inch plywood with a straight edge that rides against the rip fence. The hold-down cleats are rabbeted, and they fasten to the plywood with screws.

Jeff Greef
Soquel, Calif.

TABLE SAW AS JOINTER

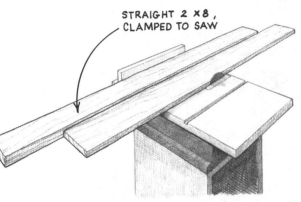

STRAIGHT 2 × 8, CLAMPED TO SAW

Here's a method I use to convert my table saw to a jointer with an effective bed length of 8 feet.

I clamp a very straight and true 8-foot-long 2 × 8 to the saw and against the regular rip fence as shown. With a triple-chip grind, 48-tooth carbide saw blade, I take shallow cuts of about ¹⁄₁₆ inch or less. Bowed stock up to 10 feet long can be easily straightened with several passes. Another advantage is that you don't have to worry about the direction of the grain as you would on a regular jointer. The 48-tooth blade produces a surface that is ready to glue without any planing.

It's important to have a good

extension table on the outfeed side of the table because the stock must pass through the saw blade without the slightest wobble—especially at the end of the cut.

Lyle E. Bohrer
Beaumont, Tex.

CHECKING A BLADE FOR SQUARE

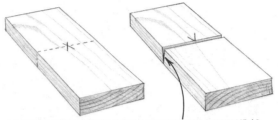

AN ERROR IN THE MITER GAUGE SETTING WILL SHOW UP AS A GAP WHEN THE PIECES ARE BUTTED TOGETHER.

To check that the blade on a table saw is set perfectly square to the table, select a scrap of wood at least 3 inches wide and 18 inches long or longer. Mark an X on one face near the middle of the board. Using the miter gauge, cut through the X. Turn one piece over and bring the cut ends together on a flat surface. If the blade is properly adjusted, the cut ends will butt together perfectly. If not, there will be a slight gap near one edge or the other.

Nick Engler
West Milton, Ohio

V-BLOCK FOR ROUND STOCK

Crosscutting round stock on a band saw or table saw is easy if you

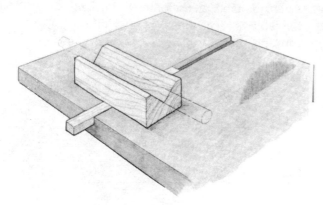

make a V-block jig with a guide strip to fit the miter gauge slot in the table.

Bill Bigelow
Surry, N.H.

COMPENSATING FOR MITER GAUGE SLOP

For a miter gauge to slide smoothly in its slot, there must be some "slop," or side-to-side play. Even the best tools have about 0.002 inch of slop; others may have 0.005 inch or more. To compensate for this, remember to push the miter gauge gently to the right or left as you cut, and *always push in the same direction.* This will make your cuts consistent.

Nick Engler
West Milton, Ohio

CROSSCUT STOP BLOCK

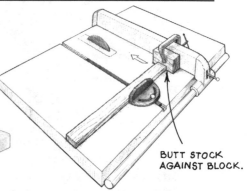

BUTT STOCK AGAINST BLOCK.

MITER GAUGE FENCE AND STOP

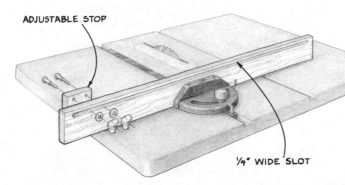

ADJUSTABLE STOP

¼" WIDE SLOT

My miter gauge auxiliary fence incorporates an adjustable stop that locks in place with wing nuts on ¼ × 2-inch carriage bolts. I use a ¾-inch plywood fence measuring 3 inches wide and 40 inches long. The ¼-inch-wide slot for the carriage bolts ends 1 inch from each end of the fence.

Bruce Levine
New York, N.Y.

When crosscutting on the table saw, it's tempting to use the rip fence as a stop by butting the end of the workpiece against it. *Don't do it.* The cutoff can bind between the fence and the blade and kick back. Instead, use an auxiliary stop for crosscutting lots of same-length pieces.

I clamp a stop block to the fence well back from the blade. This leaves a safe gap between the end of the stock and the fence when I'm making the cut.

Alvin H. Sherwood
Round Lake, Ill.

Making a Rabbeting Fence for the Table Saw

You can cut accurate rabbets on your table saw using this clamp-on rabbeting fence. The fence covers part of the cutter, eliminating the need to set up the exact width of rabbet you want.

The rabbeting fence is essentially a U-channel that straddles the saw's rip fence. Assemble it from three pieces of hardwood or high-quality plywood that are as long as your rip fence, as shown in *Rabbeting Fence*. The fence face should be at least ¼ inch wider than the widest setting of your dado cutter. This will help prevent you from accidentally dadoing the rip fence.

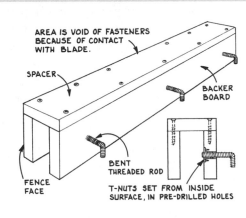

RABBETING FENCE

Fasten the channel together with screws, making sure that no fasteners are within range of the saw blade. Before you attach the backer board, set three T-nuts into its inside surface as shown. These are part of the clamping system that will hold the channel in place.

Slip the rabbeting fence over the rip fence. Bend three pieces of threaded rod into an L shape and thread them through the T-nuts to lock the rabbeting fence in place.

Once the rabbeting fence is securely locked in place, mount your dado cutter on the saw, set to its widest setting. Lower the cutter beneath the table. Slide the rabbeting fence over to cover the blade. The left face of the fence should be flush with the left side of the blade. Turn the saw on and raise the dado cutter all the way up. This will create a pocket in the fence.

To set the blade for a specific-sized rabbet, adjust the cutter height to the proper depth. Then expose a portion of the dado cutter equal to the width of the rabbet. Lock the fence in place, then cut the rabbet, guiding the piece along the fence as shown in *Cutting the Rabbets*.

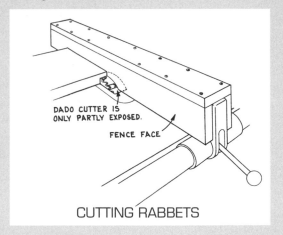

CUTTING RABBETS

—*Christopher J. Semancik*
Semancik is a professional woodworker and boat builder in Kempton, Pa.

BIGGER IS NOT NECESSARILY BETTER

To maximize the effective horse-power of any saw with a circular blade, use the smallest-diameter blade that is practical—for example, run an 8- or 9-inch blade on a 10-inch saw. Smaller-diameter blades use less energy to cut through any given material.

Why? Imagine each tooth as a lever, with the saw's arbor as the fulcrum. The longer the lever, the more mechanical advantage the wood has over the motor. As an added bonus, smaller-diameter blades are cheaper and more accurate.

David Hubbard
Baker, W. Va.

ANTI-KICKBACK HOLD-DOWN

I made a combination hold-down and anti-kickback device from a ¾-inch-thick piece of hardwood 4 inches square. In one edge, I made a 2-inch-long slot cut at 45 degrees. The slot holds a piece of Lucite, phenolic, or similar flexible material as shown. You can shim the Lucite with layers of tape to get the fit that you want. I install the guard as needed on the top edge of my auxiliary fence with hanger bolts and wing nuts.

Paul Fertell
Chester Springs, Pa.

PUSH STICK/HOLD-DOWN

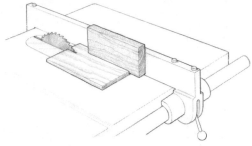

This push stick/hold-down will help you keep narrow pieces of wood under control and your fingers at a safe distance from the blade while you rip on the table saw. The ⅛- to ¼-inch heel catches the trailing end of the workpiece to push it through, while the rest of the pusher holds the narrow piece of stock down on the table.

Ric Hanisch
Quakertown, Pa.

COLLECTION PLATE

During a production run, trimming pieces to size can create a lot of small scraps. These little pieces tend to

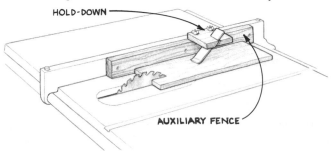

HOLD-DOWN

AUXILIARY FENCE

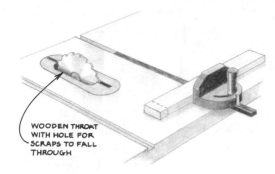

WOODEN THROAT WITH HOLE FOR SCRAPS TO FALL THROUGH

become a real hazard as they rattle around on the table saw, especially if they vibrate into the blade. To eliminate this problem, I replaced my saw's metal throat plate with one made of wood. This new plate has a hole cut in it that allows the scraps to fall into a collection bin below.

Greg Glebe
Phoenix, Ariz.

PNEUMATIC AUTOMATION

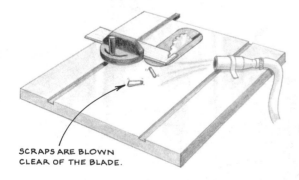

SCRAPS ARE BLOWN CLEAR OF THE BLADE.

Every once in a while I have to cut up a length of wood into a number of small pieces on the table saw. This used to scare me stiff, because about every third piece would catch between the blade and the throat plate and come whistling

back past my ear. Talk about testing your reflexes!

As a solution, I rigged up a blow gun from my air compressor to blow the small pieces clear of the blade as shown. After a little fussing, I was even able to get the pieces to blow right off the table and into a collection box on the floor.

Kenneth S. Burton, Jr.
Allentown, Pa.

WIDENING SAW KERFS

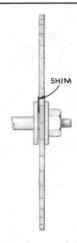

SHIM

To increase the width of the kerf of a table saw blade or a dado head a small amount, use masking tape as a shim. Apply one or more layers of tape to the blade where it comes in contact with the arbor washer. Do this on one side of the blade only, and in only one place. The tape shim will give the blade a slight wobble, which will increase the width of the kerf or dado. Remember, this is for very small increases only.

John Roccanova
Ancramdale, N.Y.

MASKING-TAPE SHIMS

When cutting tenons on the table saw, you often need to move the fence just a hair to adjust the thickness of the tenon. Instead of trying to adjust the fence in such tiny increments, I apply layers of tape to the side of my tenoning jig where it bears against the fence. Masking tape works well for a fairly thick shim, and Mylar packing tape works as a very thin shim.

Ben Erickson
Eutaw, Ala.

COVE CUTTING ON THE TABLE SAW

You can make cove cuts on the table saw by running stock past the blade at an angle. This makes use of the blade's curvature to create a curved profile. The depth of the cut is determined by the height of the blade. The width of the cut is determined by the angle of the auxiliary fence. Make the setup with the blade at the full cutting depth desired. Then drop the blade beneath the

Making Throat Plates

The standard throat plate provided with your table saw will not accommodate the width of a dado cutter. Nor will it provide the close-to-the-blade support that a fine plywood blade needs for clean cutting. While you can purchase special throat plates for these tasks, you can also make them quickly in your own shop.

Lay Out the Blank

Select a piece of hardwood or high-quality plywood that is the same thickness or slightly thinner than the stock throat plate. Trace the plate onto the blank and mark the holes for the leveling screws. Cut out the blank on the band saw about ⅛ inch outside the line. You'll trim away the excess material later for a perfect fit.

Trim the Blank to Fit

Fasten the stock throat plate to the blank with double-sided carpet tape. The plate will act as a template as you trim the blank

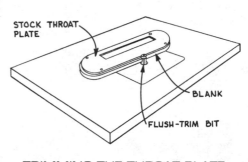

STOCK THROAT PLATE

BLANK

FLUSH-TRIM BIT

TRIMMING THE THROAT PLATE

to fit the saw. With a flush-trim bit in a table-mounted router, trim the blank flush with the plate as shown in *Trimming the Throat Plate*. Pry the plate off the blank, and check the fit of the blank on the saw. Sand it lightly if necessary to get a good fit.

Install the Leveling Screws

Most throat plates can be adjusted flush with the table surface. This feature should be included on your shop-made models,

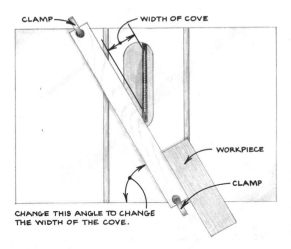

CLAMP — WIDTH OF COVE

WORKPIECE

CLAMP

CHANGE THIS ANGLE TO CHANGE
THE WIDTH OF THE COVE.

table. Make the cut in several passes, raising the blade no more than ¹⁄₁₆ inch at a time.

Jeff Greef
Soquel, Calif.

KEEP A LID ON IT

When cutting the lid off a box, I had trouble with the saw blade binding on the last cut. It was a bother to place wedges in the saw kerf to keep the lid from binding.

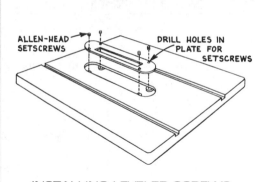

ALLEN-HEAD
SETSCREWS

DRILL HOLES IN
PLATE FOR
SETSCREWS

INSTALLING LEVELER SCREWS

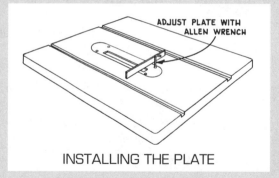

ADJUST PLATE WITH
ALLEN WRENCH

INSTALLING THE PLATE

too. Drill holes through the blank that match those for the leveling screws in the original plate. Thread allen-head setscrews down through these holes to act as levelers, as shown in *Installing Leveler Screws*.

Install the Plate

Mount the appropriate blade or cutter on the saw, and lower it all the way. Drop your new throat plate in place. Adjust the setscrews to make it level to the table.

Check this with a straightedge as shown in *Installing the Plate*. Then start the saw and slowly raise the blade up through the plate. Hold the plate down with your left hand, making sure your fingers will be well clear of the blade when it emerges.

You may also want to cut slots in the plate to accommodate the splitter or other saw guards.

—*Christopher J. Semancik*

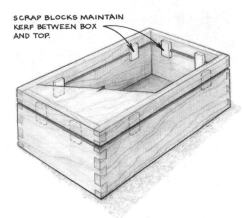

SCRAP BLOCKS MAINTAIN KERF BETWEEN BOX AND TOP.

An easy solution is to fasten blocks of scrap wood around the inside of the box on the line where you plan to cut. Attach the blocks with a drop of hot-melt glue or a piece of double-sided carpet tape. Set your saw blade to cut about ½2 inch beyond the thickness of the box side. When you cut through, the scrap blocks will hold the lid in place without binding. Then just knock off the scrap pieces, and you have your lid.

Gerald Hunt
Swartz Creek, Mich.

CUTTING PLYWOOD

Cutting a full 4 × 8-foot sheet of plywood on the table saw is an awk-ward job, even for two people. The miter gauge has to come out of its slot, and the fence may not have enough travel. My solution is to clamp a straight 2 × 4 to the underside of the plywood and let it bear against the edge of the table. It should project beyond the plywood a couple of feet on either side. The edge of the table on my Delta Unisaw is 18 inches from the blade, so I place the 2 × 4 exactly 18 inches from where I want to cut. I find I can safely get a clean, accurate cut each time.

Paul Mueller
San Francisco, Calif.

NO-CHIP INSURANCE

If you've ever crosscut plywood on the table saw, you know that the bottom side of the cut usually splinters. A good way to prevent this is to first make a shallow cut about ⅛ inch deep. Then raise the blade up enough to cut through the plywood, and make a second cut.

You'll get a substantially cleaner cut, but you still should always keep the better side of the sheet facing up.

Patrick Russo
Pattersonville, N.Y.

ALTERNATIVE NO-CHIP INSURANCE

Crosscutting with a power saw is bound to produce some tear-out. This can be reduced by putting a strip of masking tape along the line of cut. Rub it down well for good adhesion.

Jeff Greef
Soquel, Calif.

ANGLED CUTS ON PLYWOOD

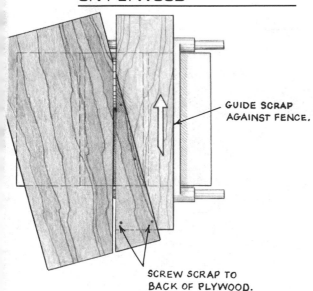

GUIDE SCRAP
AGAINST FENCE.

SCREW SCRAP TO
BACK OF PLYWOOD.

To make angled cuts on large pieces of plywood, screw a scrap piece of plywood to the back, placing it at the needed angle. Guide the scrap along the table saw fence to make the cut.

Jeff Day
Perkasie, Pa.

ADJUSTABLE SHELVES

Here's a wooden alternative to adjustable metal shelf brackets. The entire system can be made with the

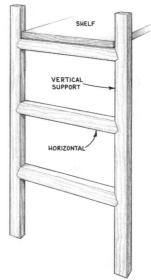

SHELF

VERTICAL
SUPPORT

HORIZONTAL

table saw. Tilt a dado head to make the cuts in the vertical supports, then cut the horizontals to fit.

Jeff Greef
Soquel, Calif.

RESAWING ON THE TABLE SAW

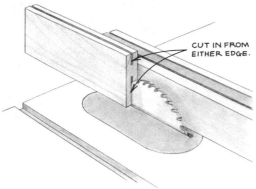

CUT IN FROM
EITHER EDGE.

Before setting up to resaw on the band saw, consider whether you can do the job on the table saw. The table saw can often be faster and more accurate.

Use a thin-kerf blade if you have

one, and set the depth of cut to 1 inch. Set the fence for a cut slightly wider than the thickness of the stock you desire. Run the stock through twice, once on each edge, keeping the same face of the board toward the fence. Then raise the blade another inch and cut again. Repeat until either the blade is at its full height or you have cut through the stock. Cutting in increments this way puts less stress on the machine than making a full-depth cut all at once.

On very wide pieces, you may not be able to cut all the way through. In this case, cut as much as possible with the table saw, then finish the cut on the band saw. The band saw blade will follow the table saw kerfs easily.

Jeff Greef
Soquel, Calif.

CUTTING CURVED PARTS PRECISELY

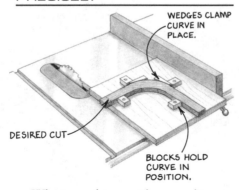

WEDGES CLAMP CURVE IN PLACE.

DESIRED CUT

BLOCKS HOLD CURVE IN POSITION.

When working with curved parts, it often is necessary to make a precise cut. This can present a problem because curved parts do not usually have straight edges to use as references. The solution is to clamp the part to a piece of plywood that has a straight edge from which you can reference. Place the curved part on the plywood so the cut you want to make is parallel to the plywood's straight edge. Screw wooden blocks to the plywood to hold the curve's position, and use wedges to clamp the piece in place. Guide the plywood along the rip fence to make the cut.

Jeff Greef
Soquel, Calif.

TAPERING ODD-SHAPED PARTS

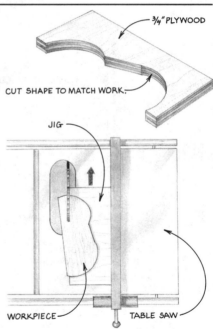

¾" PLYWOOD

CUT SHAPE TO MATCH WORK.

JIG

WORKPIECE

TABLE SAW

To cut a taper on an odd-shaped part, cut the shape into a scrap of ¾-inch plywood with parallel sides. Hold the piece in the plywood, and run both through the table saw. The portion of the piece protecting past the edge of the plywood will be cut off.

Jim Tolpin
Port Townsend, Wash.

A TAPERING JIG FOR THE TABLE SAW

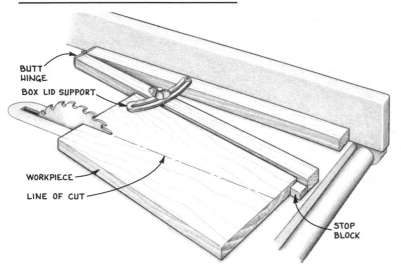

BUTT HINGE

BOX LID SUPPORT

WORKPIECE

LINE OF CUT

STOP BLOCK

You can easily make this jig for cutting tapers on your table saw. The jig consists of two legs that are joined by a hinge. A box lid support forms the adjustment mechanism and holds the legs at the required angle for tapering. A small stop at the rear of one leg prevents the work from slipping off the jig.

To use the jig, adjust the angle to match the required taper. Hold the stock against the stop, and guide the jig along the rip fence.

Jeff Greef
Soquel, Calif.

TABLE SAW MITERING JIG

I built this sliding table so that I can miter picture frames on my table saw. The jig is guided by a runner in the miter gauge slot. The secret to aligning the runner properly is to attach it to the plywood table before making the final trim cut on the table. Once the runner

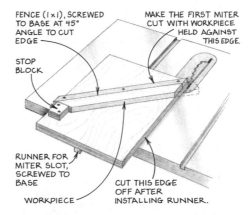

FENCE (1×1), SCREWED TO BASE AT 45° ANGLE TO CUT EDGE

MAKE THE FIRST MITER CUT WITH WORKPIECE HELD AGAINST THIS EDGE.

STOP BLOCK

RUNNER FOR MITER SLOT, SCREWED TO BASE

WORKPIECE

CUT THIS EDGE OFF AFTER INSTALLING RUNNER.

is attached, you can use it to guide the table when making that final cut.

To use the jig, make the first miter cut with the frame member held against the leading edge of the fence. Then make the second cut with the piece held against the trailing edge. You can screw the stop block down to the table at any point to control the length of the piece.

Tim Snyder
Nazareth, Pa.

AN ALTERNATE TABLE SAW MITERING JIG

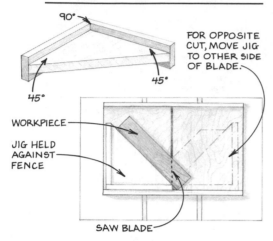

90°

FOR OPPOSITE CUT, MOVE JIG TO OTHER SIDE OF BLADE.

45°

45°

WORKPIECE

JIG HELD AGAINST FENCE

SAW BLADE

If you've made a crosscut box for your table saw, you've already got the beginnings of this mitering jig. The jig is simply a triangular fence that rides in the crosscut box as shown. Use it on either side of the blade as necessary.

Ric Hanisch
Quakertown, Pa.

TABLE SAW EXTENSION TABLES

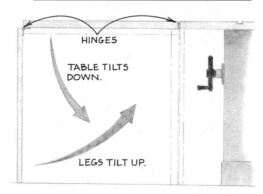

HINGES

TABLE TILTS DOWN.

LEGS TILT UP.

In my small shop, I don't have room for permanent table saw exten-sion tables, but I do like the conve-nience they afford. So I made folding extension tables that drop out of the way when they are not needed.

Jeff Greef
Soquel, Ca.

TABLE SAW TENONING JIG

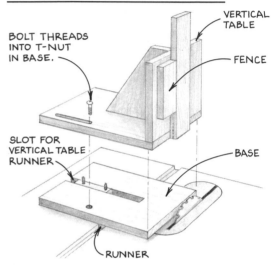

VERTICAL TABLE

BOLT THREADS INTO T-NUT IN BASE.

FENCE

SLOT FOR VERTICAL TABLE RUNNER

BASE

RUNNER

I built this tenoning jig to make cuts on the ends of parts held verti-cally. The jig rides in a miter gauge slot on a runner attached to the bot-tom. The vertical table moves on a similar slide that's set perpendicular to the blade. Secure the vertical table to the base with bolts and T-nuts mounted in the base itself.

Jeff Greef
Soquel, Calif.

MAGNETIC PICKUP

Did you ever drop the arbor nut from your table saw into the pile of sawdust beneath the machine? Depending on how big a pile is down

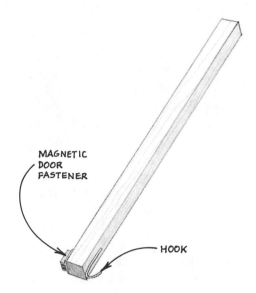

MAGNETIC
DOOR
FASTENER

HOOK

there, it could mean 20 minutes of sifting while muttering bad things under your breath. Before this happens again, make yourself a magnetic pickup. It's simply a long wooden stick with a magnet attached to one end. You don't even have to make a special trip to the hardware store for the magnet—a spare magnetic door fastener will do in a pinch. Put a hook on the other side of the stick to retrieve other fallen items, and you'll be set. Your aching knees will thank you for it.

Edwin Sheriff
Birmingham, Ala.

13 ROUTER RODEO

RING-ROUTING RIG

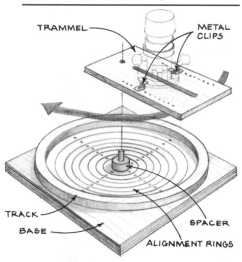

TRAMMEL — METAL CLIPS

TRACK

BASE

SPACER

ALIGNMENT RINGS

I built this jig to rout the wooden rings I use in making clocks. It works well, leaving the outside and inside of the rings concentric. The jig is essentially a router trammel with a fixed centerpoint and an outer supporting track. With it I can rout stock up to 1 inch thick.

The base is made of ¾-inch plywood. I located the center, then drew a series of concentric circles around it to aid in aligning the rings. Between these circles I drilled 3/16-inch holes for mounting screws.

After drawing the circles, I drilled a ¾-inch hole at the center of the base and glued a ¾-inch dowel in place. Over this I slipped a 1-inch-thick spacer as shown. I then attached a 24-inch-diameter, 1-inch-thick ring to the base, concentric to the center dowel.

The router trammel itself is a piece of 9/16-inch-thick oak. It has a ¾-inch hole at one end and a ¾-inch-wide slot cut down most of its length. Two rows of evenly spaced holes flank the slot. The mounting cleats for the router are bolted through these holes with carriage bolts and wing nuts. The cleats are bent from a length of ¾-inch strap iron, sold at hardware stores.

To use the jig, mount the workpiece to the base with screws driven from underneath. Then place the trammel over the dowel and clamp the router to it at the appropriate place. Rout the circle in several light passes. For fine adjustments, loosen one of the cleats and pivot the router slightly.

Ron Breadner
Owen Sound, Ontario

ROUNDING A CHEST TOP

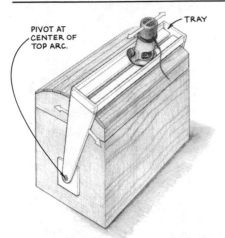

PIVOT AT CENTER OF TOP ARC.

TRAY

To round the coopered top of a chest perfectly, I made this jig for my router. I pivot a tray for my router from the center of the arc of the chest top. The bit passes through a slot in the tray bottom and trims the chest top. The router goes from end to end of the tray while the tray pivots across the top.

Bill Voyles
Vancouver, Wash.

ROUTING IN CIRCLES

I've used this jig to rout curves with radii as small as 10 inches and as long as 14 feet when making a curved door header. I can adjust the radius with great accuracy by loosening the clamp and sliding the pivot block in its slot.

Larry Humes
Bellingham, Wash.

PEGBOARD TRAMMEL WITH BUILT-IN HOLES

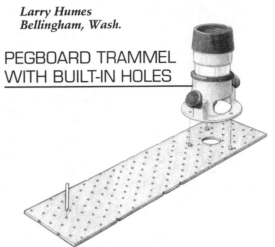

You can make a simple router trammel from a piece of pegboard. You can make the trammel as long as you want, but 24 inches seems to be a good compromise between versatility and maneuverability. Cut the pegboard at about a 30-degree angle to the lines of holes. Remove the router's baseplate and use it as a guide to drill holes in the pegboard. Countersink the mounting holes so you can attach the router with the

(continued on page 196)

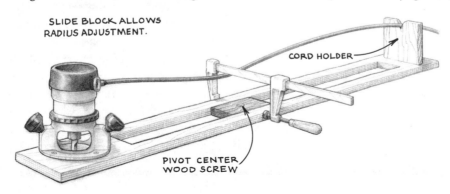

SLIDE BLOCK ALLOWS RADIUS ADJUSTMENT.

CORD HOLDER

PIVOT CENTER WOOD SCREW

Keeping Your Router Bits in Good Shape

If you are like most woodworkers, you wind up spending more for your router bits than you paid for your router. Naturally, you'll want to protect that investment by taking good care of your bits.

Carbide-tipped bits outlast high-speed steel bits many times over, but the carbide is quite brittle and must be handled and stored carefully to avoid chipping the cutting edge. And, as with any cutting tool, both steel and carbide router bits must be razor-sharp for optimum performance. A dull bit is more likely to chip, tear, or burn the wood. Also, dull bits put more stress on the router motor. And because router bits spin at high speed, a dull bit is more likely to overheat than a sharp one. The result is not only that dull bits have shorter lives, but that the router itself may not last as long.

Storing Router Bits

Don't toss a bunch of loose bits into a box or drawer where they can knock around and damage the each other's cutting edges. One way to keep bits separated is to make a simple wall-mounted storage rack. Drill a series of holes the same diameter as the bit

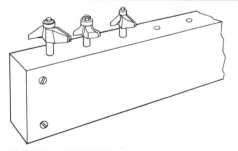

WALL-MOUNTED BIT STORAGE

shanks into the top edge of a 2 × 4, then mount the board to the wall above your bench, away from other hanging tools. Space the holes to provide about ½-inch clearance between the outside edges of each bit, as shown in *Wall-Mounted Bit Storage*.

If you prefer to store your bits in a drawer or toolbox, put them in individual containers, such as plastic pill bottles for small bits or Ziploc-type plastic sandwich bags for larger ones. Or use a piece of rigid foam packing material that's ½ to 1 inch thick. Cut the foam to fit into a drawer bottom, then poke the bits, shank-side down, into it. Another option is to cut a piece of ¾-inch-thick plywood to fit in a drawer and then drill holes in the plywood to fit the bit shanks. Don't store other tools in the same drawer or box as the router bits.

Keeping Bits Clean and Rust-Free

Router bits get coated with wood resin or pitch, which eventually hardens, reducing cutting efficiency. The newer Teflon-coated bits keep such buildup to a minimum, but even they require occasional cleaning. An all-purpose household cleaner, such as Fantastik or Formula 409, will remove light resin deposits. You can remove heavy resin buildup with spray oven cleaner.

Rust can also be a problem, especially if you live in a humid environment. To remove light rust deposits, spray the bit with WD-40, let it soak for a few minutes, then scrub lightly with a nonwoven plastic scouring pad such as Scotch-Brite. Fine (#00) steel wool also works, but you could dull the cutting edge if you're not careful.

To prevent rust and reduce resin buildup, spray the bit with a light coat of silicone lubricant after each use. Do not use petroleum-based lubricants such as machine oil, as these may leave deposits on the wood that could affect adhesion or penetration of stains, paints, and other finishes. Spray coatings made especially for rust-prone blades and bits are also available. By the way, most guide bearings are sealed, so there's no need to lubricate them.

You also can use desiccants to remove moisture from the air as a way of preventing rust. Save the small packets of silica gel desiccant that come packed with tools and electronic equipment, and put them into the drawer or toolbox with the bits. Desiccants also are available in the form of small blocks, through woodworking supply catalogs.

Sharpening Router Bits

As with any edge tool, there are two steps to sharpening a router bit—grinding and honing.

Grinding removes nicks and reestablishes the correct cutting bevel or bit profile. This involves removing a significant amount of metal. A router bit must remain in perfect rotational balance to cut effectively; both cutting edges or profiles must be sharpened equally. That means you must not remove more material from one cutting edge than from the other. Also, both cutters must have exactly the same profile. Grinding router bits is tricky business, best left to professional sharpening shops. Sometimes the most expeditious solution is to buy a new bit.

Of course, it would be impractical to send your bits out for sharpening or buy new ones each time they get a little dull. One thing you can do yourself is hone, or "dress," the cutting edge with a fine-grit sharpening stone. The honing process removes minute amounts of metal, so you won't throw your bit out of balance or change the profiles significantly.

To hone, use a flat stone or abrasive sheet for wing cutters, or a conical stone for fluted bits. Diamond and ceramic hones will sharpen carbide and steel bits—only a light touch is required. When the bit starts to lose its edge, place its flat cutting face against the stone and draw it lightly along the surface. To keep the bit in balance, give each cutting edge the same number of strokes. Hone only the cutting face of the bit, as shown in *Honing a Router Bit*. Honing the bevel or contour may change the bevel angle or bit profile on one or both cutting edges. When the bit becomes too dull to be touched up by light honing, or the cutting edge gets chipped or nicked, it's time to send the bit out for sharpening—or to get out the bit catalog.

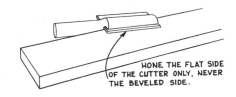

HONE THE FLAT SIDE OF THE CUTTER ONLY, NEVER THE BEVELED SIDE.

HONING A ROUTER BIT

—*Jim Barrett*
Barrett lives in Pacific Grove, Calif., where he writes about woodworking and building.

original baseplate screws. Run a nail or awl through one of the pegboard holes to establish a pivot point. If you need some odd radius, drill an extra pivot hole to suit.

Robert Tupper
Canton, S. Dak.

PRECISION PLUNGING

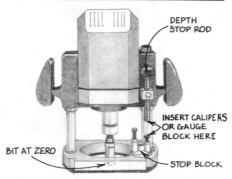

To quickly and accurately set the plunge depth on a plunge router, use either a premade gauge block or a pair of outside calipers set to the required depth. Install the bit and zero it by lowering the motor until the end of the bit is flush with the bottom of the base. Then place the gauge block or calipers on the stop turret and lower the depth stop rod to meet it. Lock the rod in place to hold the setting.

David Hubbard
Baker, W. Va.

BIT-CHANGING STAND

Changing router bits can be difficult, time-consuming, and exasperating if your router won't rest upside down on your bench.

If your router has protrusions that won't let it stand on its head, make a

simple wooden jig to hold the router upside down.

Start with a scrap piece of 2 × 4, about 7 inches long. Drill a hole for any handle or cord, then rout out a recess to match the shape of your router body. Cord holes should be large enough so that you can drop the plug end through the hole.

Clamp the jig in you bench vise to hold the router for changing bits.

Gene Payne
Sioux Falls, S. Dak.

EASY-OUT ROUTER BITS

Some router bits have a tendency to seize in the collet. The secret to freeing a bit begins when you first insert it. Push the bit all the way in, then pull it back out about ⅛ inch. Now if it won't come free when you loosen the collet, you can tap it in with a stick of wood. The bit can break free into the ⅛-inch space behind it.

Hugh Williamson
Tucson, Ariz.

SEATING ROUTER BITS

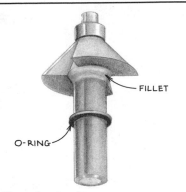

You don't always want a router bit to drop all the way down into a collet when you mount it. Sometimes, you may want the bit to extend a little farther than normal. Or you may want to keep the collet from closing around the *fillet*—the transitional area between the shaft and the cutting edges. This prevents the collet from getting a good grip on the bit. In both cases, you can easily position the router bit in the collet by slipping a small rubber *O-ring* over the shaft. Use the O-ring as a stop to keep the bit from dropping too far into the collet.

Nick Engler
West Milton, Ohio

CHEAP MILLS

Spiral-cut end mills are very good mortising bits for use in routers. The spiral flutes cut very cleanly, leaving a smooth-walled mortise. They don't last as long as carbide bits, but they're considerably cheaper. Find them at a machinist's-tool supply store.

Jeff Greef
Soquel, Calif.

ROUTER TABLE SAFETY

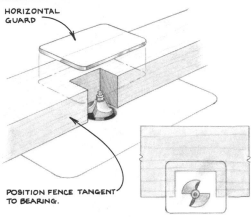

Use the fence on your router table even when cutting with a ball-bearing-guided bit: It's much safer. Position the fence so it surrounds the bit with its face tangent to the bearing. The fence will help keep your fingers away from the whirling cutter. For added safety, add a horizontal guard over the bit as shown.

Jeff Greef
Soquel, Calif.

GETTING A HANDLE ON SAFETY

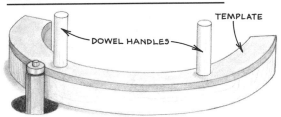

When template-routing small parts on a router table, attach dowel handles to the templates. This will keep your fingers a safe distance from the whirling cutter.

Jeff Greef
Soquel, Calif.

A HOT-MELT SOLUTION

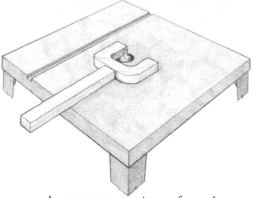

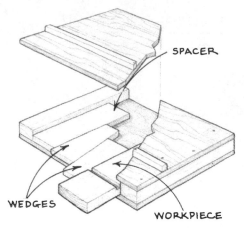

A recent project found me attempting to round-over the edges of some small pieces of wood on the router table. The key words here are *small* and *attempting*. I just couldn't bring myself to put my fingers that close to the whirling bit.

What to do? I hemmed and hawed a bit before hitting upon this solution. I tacked the small pieces to a length of scrap wood with hot-melt glue. This way I could rout them while my hands were a comfortable distance from the bit. If you apply the hot-melt glue sparingly and remove it as soon as possible, it's easy to separate the workpiece from the scrap when you're finished routing it.

Dean St. Clair
Salesville, Ohio

ROUTING SMALL PIECES EASILY

When routing dadoes or moldings on the small parts of the clocks I build, I wedge them into the boxlike jig shown in the drawing. The jig holds the small parts securely, and it's easy to line up the edge of the jig with a mark on the parts.

Ron Breadner
Owen Sound, Ontario

A SUPERIOR HOLD-DOWN

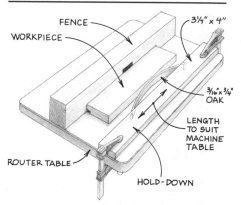

This hold-down has two advantages over the standard "featherboard." You can make it to run the full length of a fence. And it exerts constant pressure, making it easier to maintain a constant rate of feed. Use it on your router table, shaper, or even table saw for added safety.

Jim Tolpin
Port Townsend, Wash.

ANTI-SLIP INSURANCE

If you get many tool catalogs, you've probably seen the non-slip pads for routing and sanding that sell for $10 and up. Sure they work great, but ten bucks is a bit steep. What works just as well, and is often free for the asking at your local carpet warehouse, is a scrap of compressed foam carpet pad. Be sure you get the compressed foam and not the smooth. The texture of the compressed foam grips the wood better.

Rick Wright
Schnecksville, Pa.

LOUVER-ROUTING JIG

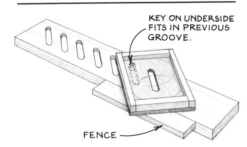

KEY ON UNDERSIDE FITS IN PREVIOUS GROOVE.

FENCE

This jig is designed to guide a router as it cuts the angled mortises for louvers in a door or shutter stile. The router rides on a ¼-inch plywood base. Scrap wood fences, screwed around the perimeter of the base, guide and stop the router appropriately. The base is screwed to a fence at the proper angle for the louvers. A wooden key, glued to the underside of the base, serves as a reference for each mortise. Start at the top of the stile and catch the key on the top corner. Rout the first mortise, then lift the jig and slide it along the stile until the key drops into the mortise you just routed. Rout the next mortise, lift and slide the jig, and so on until all the mortises are cut.

Jeff Greef
Soquel, Calif.

TWO JIGS FOR THE PRICE OF ONE

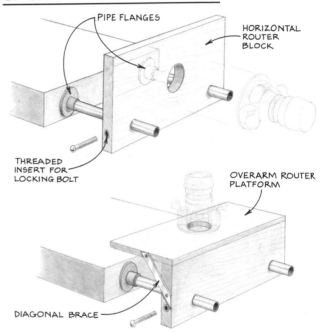

PIPE FLANGES

HORIZONTAL ROUTER BLOCK

THREADED INSERT FOR LOCKING BOLT

OVERARM ROUTER PLATFORM

DIAGONAL BRACE

This multipurpose jig hangs off one end of my workbench. It enables me to use my regular router as both an overarm router and a horizontal one. Two 1-inch pipe flanges are screwed to the end of the bench. Two 12-inch lengths of pipe are threaded into the flanges. For horizontal routing, the router is bolted to a block that rides back and forth along the pipes. Threaded inserts and bolts in the block allow me to lock

Choosing Speeds for Large Router Bits

The advent of powerful routers with variable speed control has made larger bit sizes practical. These bits include raised-panel cutters up to 3½ inches in diameter. Bit diameters of 4 and even 5 inches are also available, but in my experience these bits are too large to provide decent cuts, even when used with the largest of routers mounted in a table. I don't recommend using router bits bigger than 3½ inches. If you need larger profiles, do the work on a shaper.

Obviously, big bits need more power because they are removing more wood with each rotation. A little less obvious is that big bits need to be run at slower speeds. This is because the bigger the bit diameter, the farther the cutting edge travels with each rotation. If the speed of your router is fixed, then large-diameter bits will move the cutters much faster than smaller-diameter bits. When bit diameters get bigger than about an inch, you need to slow the rotation to use the bit safely without burning the wood.

Larger bits usually come with the manufacturer's guidelines on the maximum safe operating speed. If this information isn't available, use the table below.

Here are a few other tips for using bits safely with best results:

• Do not rout freehand with large-profile bits. Use a fence attachment for bits up to 1 inch. For larger bits, mount the router in a router table.

• For bearing-guided bits, adjust the fence on your table to just clear the bearing; don't let the bearing ride against the fence.

• Insert the bit shank fully into the collet. Then pull the bit out a little so it isn't bottomed out in the collet.

• Do not use large bits in routers with worn motor bearings or collets that are out of round. The collet must be perfectly concentric. Any minor runout in the bit shaft will be multiplied considerably at the outer edges of the bit.

—*Jim Barrett*

Bit Diameter	Maximum Safe Speed
Up to 1 inch	24,000 rpm
1¼ to 2 inches	18,000 rpm
2¼ to 2½ inches	16,000 rpm
2¾ to 3½ inches	12,000 rpm

the block in place anywhere along the pipes. For overarm routing, I made a second block to ride along the pipes. Then I added a horizontal plate to it to carry the router.

Most of the stock I work with is ½ inch, ¾ inch, 1 inch, or 1½ inches thick, so I simply made four pieces to overlay on the bench. The router stays at one height, and the overlays raise bench height to proper cutting depth. For an odd thickness, I simply shim up an overlay.

To guide the stock, I clamp fences to the workbench as needed. I wax the overlays frequently, so the stock slides nicely over them.

Bill Parrish
Norris, Tenn.

PIN ROUTER IN A HURRY

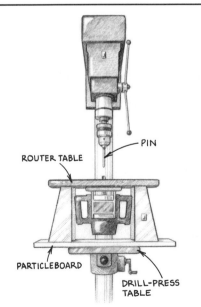

Clamp a router table to a drill-press table, and you've built a pin router! Be sure the axes of the two machines line up. A steel rod or upside-down bit in the drill serves as the pin and will rise or lower with the quill.

David Jeffrey
McKinleyville, Calif.

ROUTER TABLE MITER GAUGE

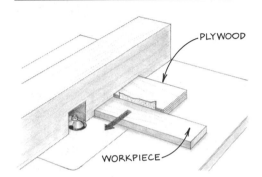

A piece of ¾-inch plywood cut square makes a good miter gauge for the router table. Hold your stock against one edge and run the other along the fence as you cut. A bit of sandpaper on the leading edge will keep your stock from slipping.

Ben Erickson
Eutaw, Ala.

ACRYLIC MOUNTING PLATES

When making mounting plates for a table-mounted router, make them from *clear* acrylic plastic. This lets you see what is going on underneath the router table as you cut. It also lets you see what you're doing when you change the bit and adjust the router.

Nick Engler
West Milton, Ohio

DROP-IN ROUTER TABLE

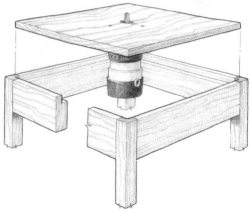

I built my router table so the table-top fits in a rabbet along the inner edge of a frame. The weight of the router keeps the top in place, but it's removable for easy installation or adjustment of the router.

H. Wesley Phillips
Greer, S.C.

ROUTING MOLDINGS SAFELY

Instead of making narrow moldings individually on a router table, rout the profile on the edge of a wider board. Then rip the molding off on the table saw.

Jeff Greef
Soquel, Calif.

MAKE SAW CUTS FIRST, ROUT LATER

Instead of routing a large molding or raised panel in several passes, use your table saw to remove the bulk of the waste first. Trace the contour of the bit onto the edge of the stock. Then place the piece in front of the

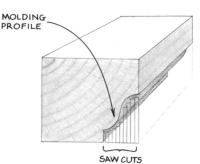

table saw blade. Set the blade to remove the waste but not to cut into the good part of the molding. It may take several passes. In some cases you can angle the blade to cut away part of the profile.

Once most of the waste is gone, rout the molding the usual way. This time, however, you'll only have to make one or two passes to finish the piece. This will save wear and tear on your router and cutter and give you a better finish cut, to boot.

Tom Groller
Palmerton, Pa.

CUSTOM-CONTOURED CABINET SCRAPERS

A router bit can clean up after itself. After I rout a molding, I use the same bit as a miniature hand scraper to clean up burns or other minor imperfections.

Daniel C. Urbanik
Washington, Pa.

PAINLESS SQUEEZE-OUT REMOVAL

I've come up with a method to remove hardened glue squeeze-out from edge-glued panels. Attach two strips of Plexiglas or ¼-inch plywood to the base of a router with double-

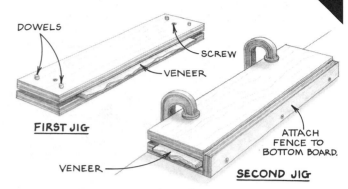

sided carpet tape. Chuck a ½-inch-wide straight bit into the router and set the depth so the bit barely grazes the surface of the stock. Run the router along the glue line and you're in business.

Ben Erickson
Eutaw, Ala.

VENEER-STRAIGHTENING JIGS

I usually buy my veneer in bulk. It's cheaper this way, and the grain and color are usually very uniform. The only drawback to this is that the edges are not trimmed straight and true when they arrive. I have to do that myself. To make this easier, I built two jigs to hold the veneer as I trim it with my router.

The first jig holds the veneer while I make the edges straight and parallel to one another. It consists of two identical pieces of plywood, screwed together at the ends. To make the jig, cut the two pieces of plywood and screw them together. My jig is about 46 inches long and 6 inches wide, but you could make yours any size to accommodate your veneer. Drill ⅜-

inch holes at either end as shown. Insert lengths of ⅜-inch dowel in the holes to keep the pieces in alignment. Keep the pieces screwed together and run both long edges over the jointer to ensure that they are true.

To use the jig, sandwich the veneer in between the pieces of plywood with the edges protruding, and tighten the screws. You can trim several pieces at once. Mount a flush-trim bit in your router and run it along both sides of the jig to trim the veneer even with the plywood.

The second jig holds the veneer while you trim its ends square. It, too, is made of two identical pieces of plywood, plus an additional piece that acts as a fence. Screw the fence to one of the larger pieces, then stack the other piece on top. Trim the ends square on the table saw.

Stack the veneer on the jig against the fence with its ends sticking out beyond the ends of the jig. Cover it with the other piece of plywood, and clamp the whole mess to your bench. Trim the ends square with your router.

Tom Groller
Palmerton, Pa.

ROUTING RECESSES FOR INLAYS

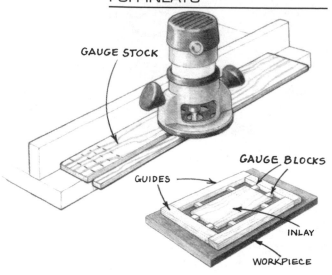

GAUGE STOCK

GAUGE BLOCKS

GUIDES

INLAY

WORKPIECE

Routing a recess for an inlay is simple if you use spacer blocks to position the router guides. With a straight bit in the router, guide the base against a fence to trim a piece of stock to the proper width (the distance from the bit to the edge of the router base). Next, crosscut this piece into short blocks and use them as spacers to position router guides around the inlay. Clamp the guides in place, remove the inlay and spacer blocks, and route the recess with the same bit you used to trim the spacers originaly. Square up the corners with a chisel.

Howard K. Gaston
Naples, Fla.

DOUBLE-FENCED DADOING JIG

Cutting dadoes in hardwood plywood on the table saw can result in a

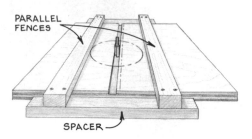

PARALLEL FENCES

SPACER

lot of tear-out. Rather than put up with this, I developed a jig that allows me to do the deed with my router. I made my jig to cut ¾-inch dadoes, but it could certainly be modified to make wider or narrower cuts. For the cutter, you should choose a straight bit that is slightly wider than one half the width of the intended dado. I use a ½-inch bit with my jig.

The jig itself consists of two parallel hardwood fences that are screwed to two spacers. The spacers should be square to the fences so you can use them to help align the jig on your workpiece. The spacing between the fences is dependent on three things:

1. the diameter of your router base

2. the diameter of the bit

3. the width of the dado you want

It can be calculated with the following formula:

$$\text{Base Diameter} + (\text{Dado Width} - \text{Bit Diameter})$$

My router base is 6 inches in diameter; therefore I made the fences 6¼ inches apart: $6 + (¾ - ½) = 6¼$.

To use the jig, lay out the positions of the dadoes first. Then measure the distance from the edge of the bit to the edge of the router base. Position the inside edge of one of the jig's fences this distance from the layout line, and clamp it down as shown.

Rout the dado in two passes, the first with the router against one fence and the second with the router against the other. If the dado is particularly deep, cut it in several shallower passes.

Tom Groller
Palmerton, Pa.

MULTIPLE RABBETS

You can make different-depth rabbets with a single bit by changing the guide bearing. In fact, with just two bits (a 1-inch and a 1½-inch-diameter) and three bearings (⅜-inch, ½-inch, and ⅝-inch) you can make six different depths of rabbet (³⁄₁₆-inch, ¼-inch, ⁵⁄₁₆-inch, ⁷⁄₁₆-inch, ½-inch, and ⁹⁄₁₆-inch).

Jeff Greef
Soquel, Calif.

ROUTING A SQUARE EDGE

When I need to square up a panel that's too large for my table saw, I simply clamp a fence across the piece and trim off the excess with a ⅜-inch or ½-inch straight bit in my router. It takes four or five passes at increasing depths of cut, but the edge is unsplintered and square. This technique also works well with veneered plywood,

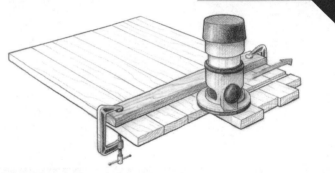

which tends to chip out when cut with a circular saw.

Bill Kearney
Douglas, Wyo.

ROUNDING ENDS OF LARGE DOWELS

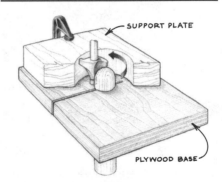

SUPPORT PLATE

PLYWOOD BASE

For a recent project I had to round the end of a 1½-inch-diameter dowel. Since I don't have a lathe, I decided to use my router instead. First, I drilled a 1½-inch hole in a piece of ¾-inch plywood. Then I sawed a slot in from the edge of the plywood through the center of the hole and past the opposite side. This way, when I put the plywood in a vise, the hole closes slightly and grips the dowel. Next, I made a support plate for the router with a 4-inch hole cut through its center.

I then mounted a ¾-inch-radius carbide-tipped piloted roundover bit in my router. With the dowel locked in the plywood and the support plate clamped on top, I rounded the dowel in three or four passes, lowering the router bit a fraction each time. As I cut, I made sure I was moving against the rotation of the cutter.

Yeung Chan
Millbrae, Calif.

ROUTING LARGE DOWELS

I needed a 4-inch-diameter dowel for a table base. I couldn't find any

Maintaining Your Router

Mechanically, routers are among the simplest of portable power tools. They're not much more than a motor with a collet attached to its shaft, into which you insert bits. As with most portable power tools, routine maintenance usually involves keeping the tool clean and free of sawdust and replacing the motor brushes when required.

Routers won't last forever, though, no matter how well they're maintained. Moving parts, such as motor bearings and collets, will eventually wear out; switches and variable-speed mechanisms may fail; cords become damaged or frayed.

To get a long life out of your router, take the time to read the owner's manual. Even if you're a veteran router user, the manual is worth a look. It contains valuable information on proper tool use, maintenance, and ordering replacement parts.

It's important to keep the router clean and to maintain the collet. Do not allow sawdust to block the air vents to the motor; this can cause overheating and premature motor failure. Vacuum or blow out the motor compartment with an air gun after each use. Because most router motors have sealed, permanently lubricated bearings, they do not require lubrication. A noisy motor or loose motor shaft usually indicates that the bearings are worn out; have them replaced or have the motor rebuilt by an authorized service center.

Learn how the collet works and keep it clean. Bits usually stick in the collet because either the collet is incorrectly assembled or it's dirty. On most routers, the collet is retained in the collet nut with a C-shaped retainer spring. When you loosen the nut, the collet expands; when you tighten the nut, it contracts, gripping the bit shank. When you remove the collet nut, the collet should come out of the router with the nut.

A worn, broken, or missing retainer spring can cause the collet to become overtightened or deformed when you tighten down the nut, in turn causing the bit to stick. Foreign matter in the collet can also lead to improper seating of the bit shank, causing the bit to spin in the collet, or creating bit runout. Runout means the bit is not spinning true, which in turn will make the router "chatter" and possibly affect the quality of cut. A worn collet can cause the same problems. If you notice scratches on the bit ready-made; so, lacking a lathe, I turned to my trusty router.

First I screwed together a 4-sided plywood box as shown. I made the box as long as the dowel I needed. In the center of each end of the box, I drilled a ⅜-inch hole. I then made a new plywood base for my router with wooden guide strips along the bottom. The strips were positioned to guide the router along the center of the box.

With the jig complete, I cut an octagonal blank for the dowel from a 4 × 4 and drilled ⅜-inch-diameter holes in the center of each end. I

shank, the collet is either worn or dirty. Disassemble and clean the collet assembly frequently. If the inside of the collet is badly scored or worn, replace it.

Make sure you use the right bits in your router. Don't use bits with large-diameter profiles on small, underpowered routers. If the bit bogs down the motor, it's too big for the tool. In some cases, you can make several light passes with a large bit, removing a small amount of wood each time, until you achieve the full depth of cut.

It's also important to provide enough electrical power to run your router. When most of us plug in a power tool, we automatically presume there's enough juice coming from the outlet. However, if the line voltage is too low for the router's rating, the motor will overheat, wearing out the brushes and possibly shortening the tool's life. This is especially true with big routers.

Most often, insufficient power can be blamed on long, thin extension cords. Electrical resistance builds up, causing a voltage drop. The higher the tool's amperage, the heavier the wire gauge must be in the cord. Recommended extension cord lengths and wire gauges are usually listed in the tool owner's manual.

Voltage at the electrical outlet should be between 102 and 135 volts. In some areas during peak electrical use, or in older houses with poor wiring, the household voltage delivered at the wall outlets may be too low to operate higher-amperage routers. If you're in doubt, you can use a voltage tester to see how much voltage is being supplied at the outlets. Also, the circuit must be fused to accommodate the maximum amp draw of the tool (up to twice the tool's rated amperage). For example, a 10-amp router may draw a maximum of 18 or 20 amps when you bog down the motor. That's enough to blow a 15-amp fuse or breaker.

Finally, if you have a plunge router, keep the plunge mechanism clean and well lubricated. A bit of silicone lubricant sprayed on the posts will keep the plunge action smooth without attracting sawdust. Side slop in the plunge assembly usually indicates worn wipers or bushings, which will affect the accuracy of cut. If this is the case, have the assembly replaced or repaired by an authorized service center. Also remember to replace worn springs.

—*Jim Barrett*

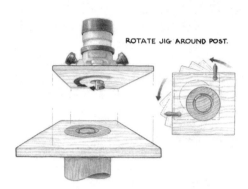

ROTATE JIG AROUND POST.

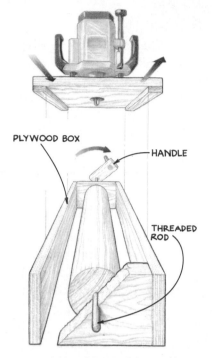

PLYWOOD BOX

HANDLE

THREADED ROD

mounted the blank in the jig with lengths of ⅜-inch threaded rod driven through the end holes. On one end I improvised a handle with which to turn the piece.

I cut the dowel with a straight bit mounted in the router. I pushed the router slowly along the jig as I cranked on the handle to rotate the blank.

Yeung Chan
Millbrae, Calif.

CUTTING ROUND HOLES IN POSTS

While making a pedestal table, I wanted to cut a round hole in the end of a large round post. I turned to my router.

First I cut a square piece of ¾-inch plywood about 4 inches bigger than

the diameter of the post. I placed the post at the center of the plywood and traced around it. I then cut out the circle on the band saw, making sure the post fit snugly but would still turn in the hole.

Next I made an auxiliary baseplate for my router from ⅜-inch plywood. At its center I drilled a hole for a ½-inch straight bit. I clamped the two pieces of plywood together so the router bit was near the center of the 4-inch hole.

To cut the hole in the end of the post, I started the router and plunged the bit to the required depth of cut. Then I slowly rotated the whole jig around the post, cutting a round recess. I withdrew the bit from the cut, shifted the router on the plywood so that the bit was slightly farther out from the center of the 4-inch hole, and made another pass. I repeated this process until the hole in the post was the right diameter. If you try this, be sure to rotate the jig against the rotation of the bit.

Yeung Chan
Millbrae, Calif.

Expanding Your Router Tool Kit

The marketplace is teeming with routers and router accessories. Here are three money-wise suggestions for expanding your router tool kit.

Three Routers in One

You can get the effect of having three routers when you have only one.

Porter-Cable makes a plunge base that accommodates most any 3½-inch-diameter router motor, regardless of make. Buy this base for hand-held plunge-routing operations, plus an extra (fixed) base to dedicate to your router table. Mount the extra fixed base on the router table's mounting plate.

Your midsized, hand-held, fixed-base router thus can be "three routers." Switch the motor from fixed base to plunge base to table-mounted base, as the job demands. One router, three very different applications. The cost of one router with two extra bases is about $150 less than that of three comparable routers.

Get Fixed-Base Precision from Your Plunge Router

For about $20, you can turn your plunge router into a fixed-base router with a "micro-adjustor." This gizmo turns the plunge router into a fixed-base machine, but one with a very precise adjusting mechanism. It makes minute adjustments to depth of cut easy to accomplish. For router-table use, this is great!

The micro-adjustor fits onto the threaded rod that links the motor to the base of a plunge router. The rod is usually equipped with a nut that prevents the motor from springing up off the plunge rod when you release the router's plunge lock. With the micro-adjustor in place, you can "screw" the motor toward the base. If a full turn of the rod lowers the bit 1/64 inch, imagine what a half-turn or quarter-turn will do.

The Pint-Sized Router

If you're in the market for a second router, think about buying a laminate trimmer—even if you don't do laminate work.

Don't let the name fool you. A laminate trimmer is simply an extra-small router. Although it is marketed for routing plastic laminates, it can be extremely handy for all sorts of woodworking.

The small-diameter base has no handles. To hold the trimmer, grip the motor barrel, which is about 3 inches in diameter. The lam trimmer has a ¼-inch collet, and you can use almost any ¼-inch shank bit in it. Because you hold a trimmer in one hand, it's easy to maneuver. The small size allows the trimmer to be used effectively in tight quarters. It can be balanced on a narrow edge more easily than a full-sized router can. It's great for all edging jobs.

One caveat: The trimmer is really just that. With a maximum rating of ¾ horsepower or less, the trimmer cannot drive big bits or make heavy cuts in dense woods. The danger is not to the bearings but to the motor itself. If it starts to bog down, the motor is under the kind of load that will pretty quickly overheat it. That will burn the commutator and destroy the motor.

—*Bill Hylton*
Hylton is coauthor of **Woodworking with the Router,** *published by Rodale Press.*

14 BAND SAW BOOGIE AND SCROLL SAW SASHAY

AUXILIARY BAND SAW TABLE

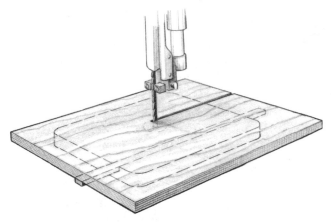

Make an auxiliary table to fit over your band saw table from a scrap of plywood. Glue a strip of wood to the underside that fits into the miter gauge slot (if your saw has one) for alignment. This "slave board," as I call it, can be clamped to the band saw table so that any number of jigs and fixtures can be attached to it without damaging the machine.

Bill Bigelow
Surry, N.H.

FINE-TUNING A BAND SAW BLADE

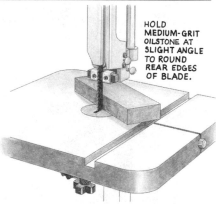

HOLD MEDIUM-GRIT OILSTONE AT SLIGHT ANGLE TO ROUND REAR EDGES OF BLADE.

Round the rear edges of your band saw blades with a medium-grit oilstone. You'll find that relieving these edges will allow you to cut tighter curves and will make backing out of cuts much easier.

Hold the stone flat on the saw table and gently touch it to the blade as the machine is running. Don't use too much pressure or you'll push the blade off the wheels. For safety, use the stone dry and vacuum the saw thoroughly both before and after the operation.

Jeff Greef
Soquel, Calif.

TWO OUT OF THREE DENTISTS RECOMMEND . . .

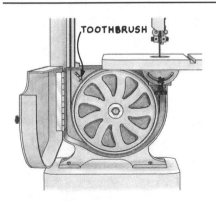

One way to prolong the life of your band saw tires is to keep them clean. This can mean simply brushing them off when you clean the inside of your machine. Or you could install a continuous cleaning system as shown. The brush is an old toothbrush. Cut the handle short and heat it to bend it to the right shape. Drill holes through the shortened handle to bolt the brush in place inside your saw. I installed a brush only on the bottom wheel of my saw, but you

might think about installing one up top, too, if your saw is in the cavity-prone years.

Kenneth S. Burton, Jr.
Allentown, Pa.

ERASERS FOR SAFETY

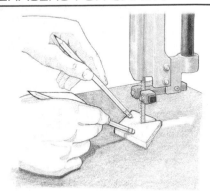

When I have to cut small pieces on the band saw, I keep my fingers away from the blade by steering the piece with the erasers on the ends of two pencils.

Glenn Hughes
Emmaus, Pa.

RELIEF CUTS

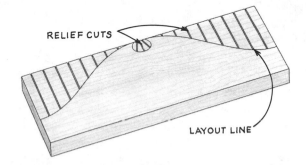

When cutting complicated ginger-bread cutouts with tight curves on the band saw, make straight relief cuts into the layout lines every ½

(continued on page 214)

A Quick Band Saw Tune-Up

The band saw is a remarkably versatile machine that many woodworkers find to be as indispensable as the table saw. It is essential for cutting curves, and it's just as likely to be used to rough out turning blanks, resaw stock, or chop scraps into kindling. However, if the band saw isn't properly adjusted, cutting kindling is the only task it will perform well. Here are four simple adjustments that will keep your band saw cutting true. It's a good idea to check these adjustments each time you use the saw. You'll definitely want to check them whenever you change the blade.

- Tension the blade.
- Track the blade.
- Square the table.
- Adjust the guides.

Be sure to unplug the saw before making any adjustments.

Tensioning the Blade

When installing a band saw blade, the first thing you do is put tension on it to hold it on the wheels. Most saws have a gauge that tells you how much tension to put on a blade of a particular width. Unfortunately, these gauges are not very accurate, and some saws don't have one at all. Instead of relying on the gauge, use it as an approximation. Tension the blade to its approximate setting, then pluck it like a guitar string. The blade should produce a clear tone, rather than a dull thud. Next, check the blade for deflection. Raise the guide all the way up

and push sideways on the blade. It should deflect no more than ¼ to ⅜ inch, as shown in *Checking Blade Tension*. Narrow blades will deflect slightly more than wide ones. Increase the tension until the blade's deflection is within the given range.

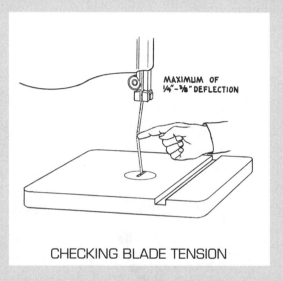

MAXIMUM OF ¼"–⅜" DEFLECTION

CHECKING BLADE TENSION

Some woodworkers advocate increasing blade tension as a cure for all the band saw's woes. While it is certainly true that the blades and saws can withstand more tension than the gauges would lead you to believe, it is not a good idea to put too much tension on blades. This practice can cause a saw's bearings to fail prematurely. And, if the saw sits idle for long periods of time, it can cause flat spots on the tires, which will result in vibration and erratic cuts. Instead of over-tensioning the blade, keep the saw tuned up to make it cut properly.

Tracking the Blade

When tracking properly, the blade rides on the middle of the wheels. Adjust tracking by tilting the top wheel in relation to the bottom one. This adjustment is usually controlled by a knob behind the upper wheel cabinet. Spin the saw by hand. Be careful not to cut your fingers on any metal burrs on the wheel. You may even want to take a few minutes to file off any nasty projections.

As you spin the wheels, adjust the tracking control until the blade is riding in the middle of the wheel. Lock the tracking control in this position. Replace the guards on the machine, then plug in the saw. Check the tracking by bumping the switch on and off to produce a short burst of power. The blade should maintain its position. Repeat this several times before running the saw under continuous power.

Squaring the Table

This is a simple adjustment that many people miss. Loosen the knobs that lock the table in place. Hold a square on the table with its blade against the saw blade, as shown in *Squaring the Table*. Square the table to the blade and lock it in place.

Under the table, there is usually a stop that you set to automatically square the table after you've had it tilted. Check and set this now.

Setting the Guides

Most saws have two similar sets of guides, one set above the table and the other

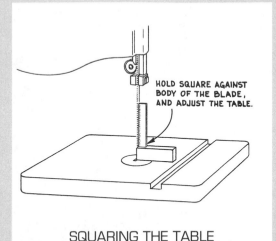

HOLD SQUARE AGAINST BODY OF THE BLADE, AND ADJUST THE TABLE.

SQUARING THE TABLE

below. Each set of guides consists of a back-up bearing and two guide blocks. The back-up bearings resist the force you exert as you push a board past the blade, while the guide blocks prevent the blade from twisting out of position. Both sets are adjusted in the same way.

Position the guard at about the halfway point between the table and the upper cabinet. Depending on how accurately the guard moves up and down, you may have to reset the guides at the extremes of the guard's travel. Set the backup bearings first. Move them forward until they almost touch the blade. Leave about a ¹⁄₃₂-inch gap between the blade and the bearings. Then set the guide blocks. Fold a small piece of paper around the blade, as shown in *Setting the Guide Blocks*. Bring the guide blocks up to gently hold the paper to the blade. Be very

(continued)

A Quick Band Saw Tune-Up—*Continued*

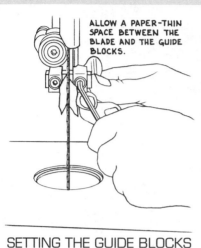

ALLOW A PAPER-THIN SPACE BETWEEN THE BLADE AND THE GUIDE BLOCKS.

SETTING THE GUIDE BLOCKS

careful not to deflect the blade one way or another with the blocks. When the blocks are in position, lock them in place.

Your saw should now be ready to run. If you have problems with the way it is cutting after this tune-up, the saw may require more-involved adjustments. These might include aligning the wheels with one another, balancing the wheels, and adjusting the drive train. See your owner's manual for further details.

—*Kenneth S. Burton, Jr.*
Burton is a woodworking editor at Rodale Press and a studio furniture maker in Allentown, Pa.

inch. As you saw, these relief cuts will allow small pieces of waste to fall away, creating more room for the blade to maneuver. This will reduce blade wear and will speed your progress.

Roy Moss
Rio Rancho, N. Mex.

SMOOTHER BAND SAW CUTS

I rip a lot of stock into very thin pieces on my band saw. The blade's narrow kerf saves wood, but the teeth marks are a real detriment. The problem? Saw teeth are not in the same plane as the rest of the saw blade; they are "set" at an angle to remove wood more quickly. Unfortunately, it also makes for a ragged cut. To lick the problem, I

removed most of the set in the teeth by squeezing the blade in a pair of smooth-jaw pliers. The blade no longer cuts as tight a curve as it did, but it leaves a satin-smooth surface.

Anson Chaney
Canby, Oreg.

BAND SAW LUMBERING

You can slice small logs into usable lumber on a band saw, using a wide blade and a simple L-shaped jig. Nail two 4-foot lengths of 2 × 6 together to make an L as shown. Cradle the log in this jig, and drive a screw up through the bottom 2 × 6 into the log to hold it in place. Using a fence to guide the jig, cut one side of the log flat. Unscrew the log, turn it 90

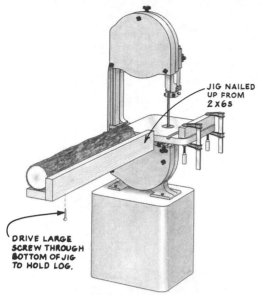

JIG NAILED UP FROM 2×6s

DRIVE LARGE SCREW THROUGH BOTTOM OF JIG TO HOLD LOG.

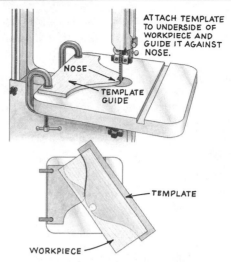

ATTACH TEMPLATE TO UNDERSIDE OF WORKPIECE AND GUIDE IT AGAINST NOSE.

NOSE

TEMPLATE GUIDE

TEMPLATE

WORKPIECE

degrees, and cut another side flat. Once you have two flat sides square to one another, remove the log from the jig. Resaw the log on the band saw, keeping one flat side on the table and the other against the fence.

Nick Engler
West Milton, Ohio

TEMPLATE CUTTING ON THE BAND SAW

If you find yourself facing a project that requires a large number of duplicate cutout parts, make a template and saw the pieces out on the band saw. The secret is in making a template guide that mounts to the saw's table as shown. I make both the guide and the templates from ¼-inch hardboard. Once you make the guide, position it on the saw surrounding the blade so that its right edge is flush with the right side of the blade. Two C-clamps hold it in place.

To use the guide, fasten a template to the underside of your stock with double-sided carpet tape. Then push it through the saw, running the edge of the template against the nose of the guide.

Kenneth S. Burton, Jr.
Allentown, Pa.

LARGE CIRCLES FROM THE BAND SAW

A recent project found me cutting large plywood disks on my band

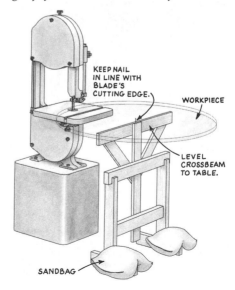

KEEP NAIL IN LINE WITH BLADE'S CUTTING EDGE.

WORKPIECE

LEVEL CROSSBEAM TO TABLE.

SANDBAG

saw. I devised this trammel jig to help get the job done. The jig clamps to a sawhorse, level with the saw table to support the work. A nail projects from the center of the jig to serve as a pivot point. The sawhorse can be moved to adjust the diameter of the circle. Sandbags sit on the horse's feet to stabilize the whole mess.

Kenneth S. Burton, Jr.
Allentown, Pa.

ONE TURNING, FOUR LEGS

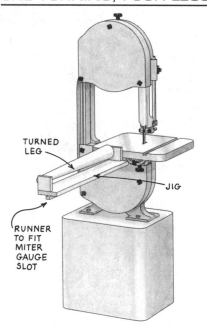

TURNED
LEG

JIG

RUNNER
TO FIT
MITER
GAUGE
SLOT

You can create elegant legs by turning a shape on the lathe, and then slicing it to create four legs. First, turn an interesting profile on the lathe. Then split the piece into quarters on the band saw by guiding the piece through the blade with the jig shown. The guide is made of ply-

wood scraps, with a runner underneath that rides in the miter gauge slot. Once you've made your cuts, pass the sawed edges over a jointer to smooth them.

Jeff Greef
Soquel, Calif.

TUBULAR TIRE TIP

Should you find yourself in need of a new set of band saw tires, you can make your own from an old inner tube. Cut a radial section from the tube as shown. Cut the tire slightly wider than your saw's wheel, stretch it around the wheel, then trim it to fit.

Kenneth S. Burton, Jr.
Allentown, Pa.

CLAMP TETHER

It used to be that when a blade snapped on my scroll saw, the blade clamps would go flying. When I finally got tired of chasing them all over the shop floor, I tethered them

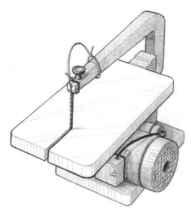

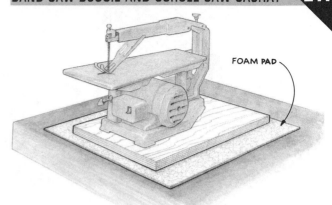

FOAM PAD

to the upper and lower saw arms with short pieces of monofilament fish line.

George Weber
Brooklyn, N.Y.

DAMPING SCROLL SAW VIBRATIONS

I didn't have room for a separate stand for my scroll saw, so I bolted it to a ¾-inch plywood base. But when I used it on top of my workbench, it vibrated so much I had to clamp it to the bench top. I solved the vibration problem by putting the saw on a routing/sanding pad—a foam pad sold by woodworking supply companies for holding small items still. The pad keeps the scroll saw from sashaying across the bench and dampens the vibrations. Now it's much easier to get accurate cuts.

Wayne Dragish
Lindwood, Pa.

15 DRILL PRESS AND DRILLS

CHUCK-KEY LEASH

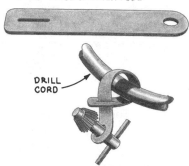

1" x 6" PIECE OF INNER TUBE

DRILL CORD

If your portable electric drill did not come with a holder for its chuck key, you can make one from a piece of inner tube. Cut the tube as shown and wrap it around the drill cord.

Ralph S. Wilkes
Branchport, N.Y.

AUXILIARY DRILL-PRESS TABLE

This removable auxiliary table clamps to the support column of a drill press and catches most of the waste, keeping the shop tidier and saving cleanup time. It's also a handy

place to put the spare bits, chuck key, and various accessories. A bonus is that it catches mortising chisels, Forstner bits, and other easily damaged tools that could fall through the hole in the metal table and strike the floor or the cast-iron base.

I made my table from ¾-inch plywood faced with plastic laminate. The slick surface makes cleaning up metal chips and oil a snap. The supporting bracket is a 16-inch-long piece of 6-inch-wide fir, which is attached to the table with wood screws. A ⅜-inch bolt clamps the table to the column as shown.

Kenneth Broun
Virginia Beach, Va.

AN EASY WAY TO ALIGN HOLES

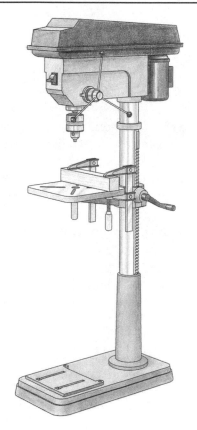

Drilling a number of holes a fixed distance from the edge of a board can be easily accomplished by clamping a fence across the drill-press table. Place the fence the necessary distance from the center of the drill bit.

Gnarly Strop
Worley's Corner, Pa.

A MAGNETIC HANG-UP

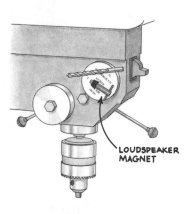

LOUDSPEAKER MAGNET

I stuck the magnet from an old loudspeaker to the side of my drill press, as shown. It comes in handy for storing the chuck key, extra bits, and other accessories.

H. R. McDermid
Vernon, British Columbia

FLOOR-MODEL CAPACITY FROM A BENCH-TOP MACHINE

If your bench-top drill press has the usual limitations, the space between the chuck and table is a foot or less. This creates an impossible situation when you need to drill the end of a longer piece. All is not lost, however. With a little work, you can expand the capacity of your small drill press to match that of its larger cousins.

Mount the drill press near the edge of the bench so its head can be swung out beyond the edge. Tighten a pipe clamp (the kind made for plastic pipe) around the column just below the head to prevent it from

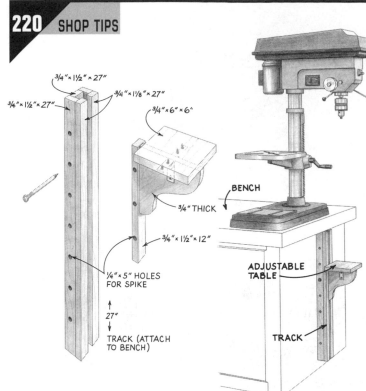

3/4" × 1/2" × 27"

3/4" × 1/8" × 27"

3/4" × 1/2" × 27"

3/4" × 6" × 6"

3/4" THICK

3/4" × 1/2" × 12"

1/4" × 5" HOLES
FOR SPIKE

27"

TRACK (ATTACH
TO BENCH)

BENCH

ADJUSTABLE
TABLE

TRACK

sliding down the column. Then loosen the head and pivot it out over the edge of the bench.

Construct an adjustable worktable against the side of the bench as shown. As you install it, make sure the center of the table is directly under the chuck, with the drill press pivoted into its new position.

Ralph S. Wilkes
Branchport, N.Y.

A DEPTH GAUGE FROM THE LOCAL GROCER

I used to rely on masking tape as a depth indicator while I drilled holes. But I had trouble removing the tape from the bit after I was through with it—there was always some residual stickiness.

I've switched to the flat, colored plastic tabs that come with bread bags or produce bags. To use them, pierce a hole in the center of the tab that is slightly smaller in diameter than that of the drill to be used. Force the drill through the rough hole and adjust the tab's location for the depth required. The rough edges of the pierced hole are irregular enough to grip the drill shank for most applications. As you work, check the position of the stop between holes. Since the tab is just a friction fit, it is somewhat easily misaligned.

Walter J. Morrison
Northport, N.Y.

PLUMBER'S HELPER

Faucet washers—the black, cold-water types—make good depth

gauges for drilling. New or used, they stretch to fit over a wide range of drill bits and hold fairly securely for repetitive operations.

Ralph S. Wilkes
Branchport, N.Y.

A WOODEN DEPTH GAUGE AND STOP

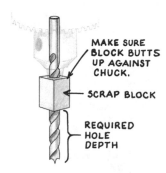

MAKE SURE BLOCK BUTTS UP AGAINST CHUCK.

SCRAP BLOCK

REQUIRED HOLE DEPTH

You can make a simple, effective stop block from a scrap of wood. Drill through the end of the block with the same size of bit you need for the job at hand. Slip the block over the bit. Then mount the bit in the drill chuck so that the amount of bit exposed matches the depth of the hole you want to bore. Plunge the bit into your workpiece until the block prevents you from going any farther.

David Page
Swarthmore, Pa.

A VARIABLE DEPTH STOP FOR THE DRILL PRESS

Should you need to drill holes at two or more depths with a single drill-press setup, place the depth stop for the deepest setting. Then

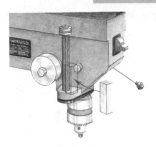

INSERT BLOCK UNDER DEPTH STOP TO ACT AS INTERMEDIATE STOP.

cut wooden spacer blocks to fit under the depth stop for the shallower holes.

Simon Watts
San Francisco, Calif.

A V-BLOCK FOR DRILLING ROUND STOCK

When drilling round pieces such as dowels, cradle them in a V-block to keep them from rolling out from under the bit. To make the block, rout a groove in a scrap with a V-grooving bit in a table-mounted router. When you go to drill a round piece, mark the hole locations with an awl or a center punch to give the drill bit a place to start.

Gnarly Strop
Worley's Corner, Pa.

Accessories for the Drill Press

The drill press can do a lot more than bore perpendicular holes to a controlled depth. A wide range of accessories are available to let you adapt this powerful, accurate tool to a variety of jobs.

An important feature that makes the drill press adaptable is the speed adjustment. All cutting accessories work best at a certain speed and feed rate. Generally, the larger the bit or cutter, and the harder the material, the slower the drill press should be run. Most manufacturers provide instructions and speed recommendations that should be followed for safety and best results.

Clamps and Jigs

For control and safety, many drill-press operations require that the work be clamped to the worktable or be controlled by a fence or jig secured to the table. Although C-clamps or specialty drill-press clamps can handle many clamping requirements, a drill-press vise is a must for holding small work, especially when drilling in metal. The vise can be bolted to the worktable through slots in its wide base—the slots allow a range of positioning on the worktable. A more sophisticated holding mechanism is the compound cross-slide vise. With its base bolted to the worktable, the cross-slide vise can position and control the work very precisely with screw-controlled east-west and north-south adjustment of the vise. With end mills and shanked emery wheels, a drill press equipped with a cross-slide vise can perform limited milling operations in metal.

A drill-press vise secured to the work-table can serve as a quick-change clamp for shop-built accessory worktables and jigs. A variety of worktables equipped with fences, stops, and holes for drum sanders can be made from plywood scraps. To the underside of the plywood, fasten and glue hardwood blocks that can be gripped securely with the drill press vise. Use a 4-inch-square block for a worktable without holes, or a pair of blocks for a worktable with holes.

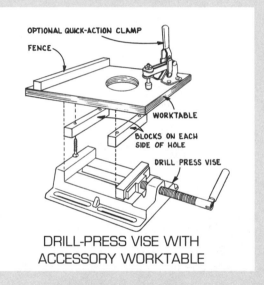

DRILL-PRESS VISE WITH
ACCESSORY WORKTABLE

Boring

A set of high-speed steel twist-drill bits, in fractional sizes from $\frac{1}{16}$ inch to $\frac{1}{2}$ inch in 64ths, is the most basic drill-press accessory. Designed for drilling metal, twist-drills are not the best bits for boring wood—they tend to wander off-center and follow grain, and they do tear wood fibers far more than bits specially designed for woodwork.

Brad-point bits are modified twist-drills

designed with a sharp centerpoint that keeps the bit from wandering. Brad-point bits also have side spurs that cut wood fibers cleanly. These bits are excellent for doweling applications and other drilling jobs requiring clean, accurate holes. Common sizes are ⅛ inch to ½ inch in 16ths and ⅝ inch to 1 inch in 8ths. Shanks of the larger bits are cut down to ⅜ inch or ½ inch to fit into drill chucks.

Spade bits, named for their flat shape, were designed as inexpensive electric-drill alternatives to hand augers. Widely used for boring through studs for wiring and plumbing runs and other carpentry jobs, spade bits of the common type were not intended for use in fine woodwork, although their sharp point does allow them to bore fairly straight in both cross grain and end grain. A great improvement over the common spade bit is a new design with side spurs that produce a much cleaner cut. Sizes range from ¼ inch to more than 1 inch in 16ths. All spade bits, even the larger bits, need to be driven at high rpm for best results.

The Forstner bit is designed with a near-full circle rim that allows it to cut very clean and straight holes through any grain direction and at any angle. Its short center spur and flat lower cutting edges leave a flat-bottomed hole. Common sizes range from ¼ inch to more than 2 inches.

Multispur bits have a circular rim and flat lower cutting edges like the Forstner bit, but they have hole-saw-like teeth on the rim to cut the larger holes for which they were designed. Common sizes range from 1 inch to 4 inches.

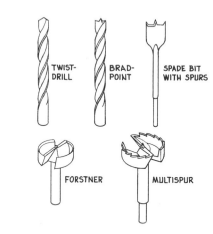

DRILL BIT TYPES

Adjustable fly cutters swing a single adjustable cutter, guided by a center pilot bit, to cut holes or wheel blanks up to 8 inches in diameter. Maximum depth of cut is about 1 inch. These must be operated at the lowest possible speed. They can be used only in drill presses, not in portable drills.

Hole saws, available in a wide range of diameters, also cut large holes or wheel blanks. As the name implies, hole saws have saw teeth that cut the circumference of the hole. Hole saws can also be used with portable drills for jobs like cutting plumbing runs through floors and joists.

Countersinks cut chamfers to recess screw heads flush with the work. The basic types are the multiflute design, for use in both wood and metal, and the Weldon pattern, with a single cutting edge better suited for clean countersinking in wood.

(continued)

Accessories for the Drill Press—*Continued*

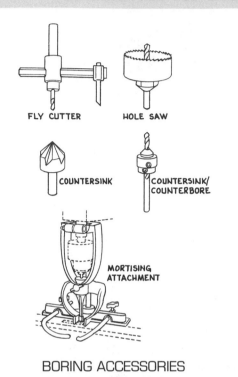

FLY CUTTER   HOLE SAW

COUNTERSINK   COUNTERSINK/COUNTERBORE

MORTISING ATTACHMENT

BORING ACCESSORIES

The countersink/counterbore drill can drill a pilot hole, enlarge the hole to accommodate the unthreaded portion of a screw shank, and countersink and counterbore the hole to accept a plug, all in one operation. In some models, the pilot hole depth, the screw shank counterbore depth, and the plug counterbore depth are all independently adjustable. Other models are adjustable as to pilot hole and plug counterbore depth, with a preset counterbore depth for the screw shank. Some models feature a tapered bit that drills the ideal pilot hole for a wood screw. The most common sizes are proportioned to handle a #5, 6, 8, 10, 12, or 14 wood screw and ¼-inch, ⅜-inch, and ½-inch plugs.

A mortising attachment bores square holes. The attachment consists of a boring bit that spins inside a square chisel. The chisel pares the sides of the mortise while the bit bores out most of the waste. The mortising attachment is secured to the quill of the drill press. It includes a fence and hold-down unit that bolts to the drill-press table. Matching chisel and bit sets are available in ¼-inch, ⁵⁄₁₆-inch, ⅜-inch, and ½-inch sizes.

LOW-TECH DEPTH STOP

When drilling holes, I use tape for a depth stop. It never slips. Wrap the tape around the bit. Leave about an inch of the tape sticking out as shown. As you near your desired depth, this "wing" of tape will begin sweeping away the wood chips around the hole. When all the chips

are swept away, you've reached your desired depth.

Aaron Blackwell
Simpsonville, S.C.

PLUG CUTTER

PLUG AND TENON
CUTTER

ROSETTE AND
WHEEL CUTTER

ROTARY PLANER

CUTTERS FOR THE DRILL PRESS

Cutters

Plug cutters can machine short plugs from the same stock as the work, for excellent grain and color matching on fine projects. Some cutters produce a slightly tapered plug for a very tight fit. The available sizes range from ¼ inch to ¾ inch in 8ths.

Dowel cutters are similar to plug cutters, and are used to cut plugs, but their longer cutting reach also allows them to cut dowels. Sizes range from ¼ inch to ¾ inch in 8ths.

The plug and tenon cutter is a new refinement of the dowel cutter. It can be used to cut plugs and dowels, but its unique spur design also allows it to machine round tenons in rail ends, leaving a clean shoulder to butt squarely against a drilled stile. Sizes are from ⅜ inch to 1 inch in 8ths.

Rosette cutters and wheel cutters spin a profiled cutter to carve rosette blocks for classic door and window trim. The tool body mounts interchangeable cutters that are available in a number of profiles—including, in some models, deep end-spur profiles that can produce wheels for wooden toys.

The rotary planer is a multiblade cutter head that can plane rough stock to uniform thickness and cut rabbets. It can be used to produce raised panels by tilting the drill-press table and using a fence to regulate the width of cut.

—Jim Michaud
*Michaud is a freelance writer and wood
worker in Swampscott, Mass.*

MORTISING FOR CIRCULAR INLAYS

To dress up some of my plainer pieces, I ornament them with one or two of those round inlays that are available from many woodworking supply catalogs. To inlay these decorative disks, I use a circle cutter in my drill press. Set the circle cutter's arm to match the radius of your inlay, and make a test cut in a scrap. Once you are satisfied with the cutter's adjustment, lay out where you want the inlay to be placed, and make the cut on the good stock. Cut only as deep as the thickness of the inlay's veneer. Remove the rest of the waste with a router, making sure the bit is set to the appropriate depth.

Tom Groller
Palmerton, Pa.

DRILLING ON THE MARK

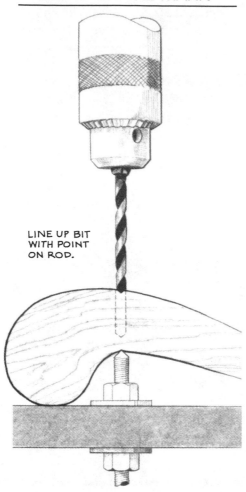

LINE UP BIT
WITH POINT
ON ROD.

Occasionally I need to drill through an irregularly shaped piece so that the hole enters and exits at exactly the right spots. I made a simple jig for my drill press that makes this difficult task easy.

I filed a point on a piece of threaded rod and cut two large washers out of thin plate steel. To drill the hole, I bolted the threaded rod through my drill-press table and carefully align the drill point over the pointed end of the rod. I then center-punch the work at the desired hole entrance and exit points. I place the exit mark on the point of the rod and line up the entrance mark with the drill.

To prevent tear-out, I drill approximately three-fourths of the way through, then flip the piece over, placing the hole over the pointed rod. I align the drill with the exit mark and finish drilling the hole from this side.

Ralph Aument
Selingsgrove, Pa.

TAMING THE WANDERING FORSTNER

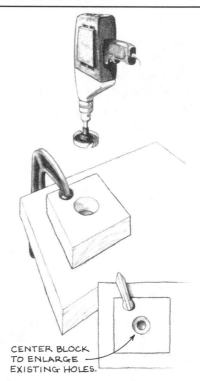

CENTER BLOCK
TO ENLARGE
EXISTING HOLES.

I find myself using Forstner bits in my portable drill as often as I do in my drill press. The problem is that the bits have a tendency to wander, especially if the brad points have been sharpened away.

My solution is to drill a hole through a small block of wood with the appropriately sized bit on the drill press. I then clamp or screw the block to the piece I want to drill. This technique is also handy for enlarging existing holes in a piece of wood. Simply center the block over the existing hole.

Glen C. Rubin
St. Marys, Ga.

DRILLING CLEAN HOLES

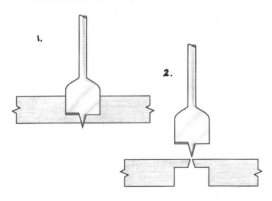

There are several methods for preventing a drill bit from tearing the wood when it exits a hole. The most common is to back up the wood with a scrap. However, this doesn't always work, particularly if the surface of the scrap is uneven or softer than the workpiece. If you use a piloted cutter bit, such as a spade bit, hole saw, or brad-point bit, there is a better method. Use a depth stop to halt the bit just as its pilot exits the

workpiece (1). Then turn the piece over and complete the hole from the other side, using the pilot hole as a guide (2).

Nick Engler
West Milton, Ohio

GETTING THE RIGHT ANGLE

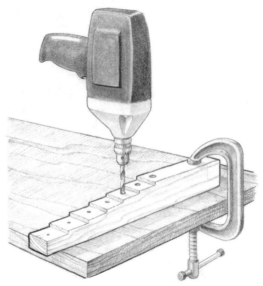

This jig is handy for drilling perpendicular holes without being limited by the throat of your drill press. Use a wood like hard maple (or even steel if the jig will be used often), and bore all of the initial holes with a drill press to make sure they are square to the base. I made my jig to accommodate drill sizes from $\frac{1}{16}$ to $\frac{1}{2}$ inch, but you can make yours to suit your needs. Be sure to hold the jig firmly when drilling, or better still, clamp it in place.

Boles Derenda
West Seneca, N.Y.

PRECISION-ANGLED HOLES

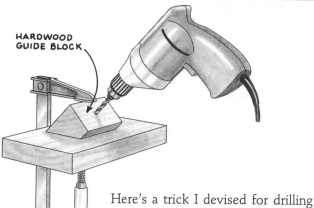

HARDWOOD GUIDE BLOCK

Here's a trick I devised for drilling precise, angled holes with a hand drill. Drill the appropriately sized hole through a block of dense hardwood (hard maple is a good choice). Use a drill press, if possible, to make sure the hole is perpendicular to the faces of the block. Then rip one face off the block on the table saw, with the blade tilted to the necessary angle. Clamp the block to your workpiece, and use it to guide the bit as you drill.

Kenneth S. Burton, Jr.
Allentown, Pa.

DRILLING IN REVERSE

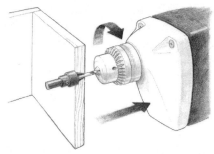

Mounting drawer pulls usually involves drilling a hole through the drawer face, then countersinking the hole on the inside of the drawer for the screw. But on shallow drawers, it can be tough to get the drill inside to countersink. In this situation, I drill through from the outside of the drawer with a combination drill and countersink bit. Once the hole goes all the way through the drawer front, remove the bit from the drill and push it through the hole from inside the drawer. Then chuck the protruding end of the bit gently in the drill as shown. Run the drill in reverse and pull it away from the drawer. This countersinks the inside end of the hole beautifully.

Paul Wagstaff
Flemington, N.J.

DIAMETER DIRECTORY

Have you ever held a dowel or a bolt up alongside a drill bit to determine its diameter? There's an easier way. Try slipping the O.O.U.D. (Object of Unknown Diameter) into the holes in your drill stand. Work your way down through the holes until you find one that is too small. The next larger hole will be the diameter you're seeking.

Ralph S. Wilkes
Branchport, N.Y.

"YANKEE" INGENUITY

I've found that the bits from my "Yankee" push drill work just as well in an electric drill. This makes them great for drilling screw holes, since they are already matched to the standard screw sizes from 4 through 12.

Rick Wright
Schnecksville, Pa.

HOLE-SAW DENTISTRY

Hole saws, particularly the inexpensive ones, often bind as they're cutting because their teeth don't have enough set. You can correct this problem, provided the saw's teeth aren't too small. Simply use a pair of needlenose pliers to increase the saw's set, gently bending alternate teeth in and out slightly.

Ralph Wilkes
Branchport, N.Y.

NO-DRILL HOLES

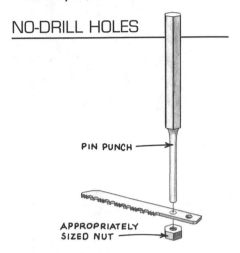

PIN PUNCH →

APPROPRIATELY
SIZED NUT →

Use a pin punch in conjunction with a nut to make holes in hard-to-drill, light-gauge metals. Make sure the inside diameter of the nut closely matches the outside diameter of the punch.

Place the nut on a solid surface. Hold the workpiece on top of the nut and the punch on top of that, centered over the nut. Strike the punch sharply with a ball-peen hammer to make the hole.

H. R. McDermid
Vernon, British Columbia

16 RADIAL ARM AND CHOP SAWS

MOUNTING A RADIAL ARM SAW OR CHOP SAW

If you have the space, the best way I've found for mounting a radial arm saw or chop saw is to build it into a counter system against a wall. The saw's table should be flush with the top of the counter. This way, long boards will have support all along their length. Extend the fence out along the counters, and you'll have a place to clamp stop blocks for production runs and other cutoff work.

Jeff Greef
Soquel, Calif.

LIMITED-SLIP CHOP SAW

To prevent moldings from slipping on the bed of a chop saw, glue strips

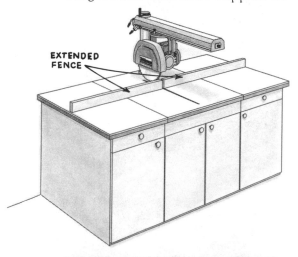

EXTENDED FENCE

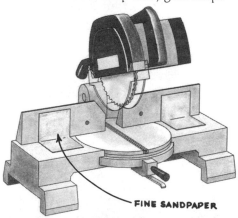

FINE SANDPAPER

of fine sandpaper to the bed and
fence. Stick the paper down with
sanding-disc adhesive, and replace it
as it wears.

Jim Tolpin
Port Townsend, Wash.

PERMANENT ADJUSTMENTS

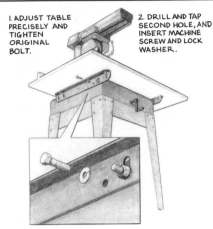

1. ADJUST TABLE PRECISELY AND TIGHTEN ORIGINAL BOLT.

2. DRILL AND TAP SECOND HOLE, AND INSERT MACHINE SCREW AND LOCK WASHER.

Some adjustments never seem to
stay adjusted. If they rely on the
clamping power of a bolt in a slot, as
is often the case with radial arm saw
tables, they can be locked securely by
drilling and tapping a second hole
next to the slotted arrangement.
Then the pieces can be locked
together with an additional bolt and
lock washer. Just make sure things
are where you want them, because
this system allows no further adjustment.

James Butterfield
Clarksville, Tenn.

KERF CONTROL

Radial arm saws cut cleanest when
the kerf in the table matches the

thickness of the blade perfectly. Over
time, however, the kerf tends to
widen, decreasing the quality of cut.
One way of fixing this problem without replacing the entire table is to fill
the widened kerf with auto-body
filler. Apply it with a putty knife.
Then, once the filler has dried, level it
to the table with a block plane.

Jeff Greef
Soquel, Calif.

DOVETAILED KERF CONTROL

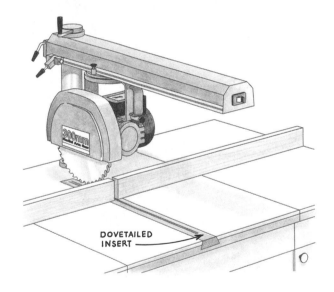

DOVETAILED INSERT

Another way to keep the kerf in
your saw table in good condition is
to make that section of table a
replaceable insert. Use a router to
mill a dovetailed slot into the table as
shown. Then make up a number of
inserts that fit snugly in the slot.
Trim them flush to the table with a
block plane if necessary.

Leave one of the inserts in the table and cut a kerf in it. When the kerf deteriorates, slip in a fresh insert and you'll be ready to go.

Jeff Greef
Soquel, Calif.

DOWELS MARK THE SPOT

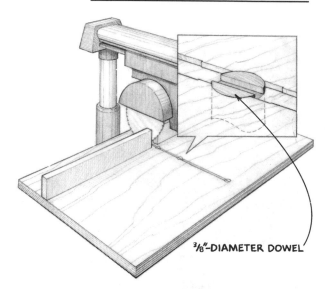

³⁄₈"-DIAMETER DOWEL

The table "rut" made by a radial arm saw blade is rarely an accurate indicator for precision trimming. It's also inadequate as a measuring point for cutoff setups. Here's a solution.

In the center of the rut, out about ¾ inch from the fence, drill a ⅜-inch-diameter hole clear through the table. Drill another hole out about one-third the length of the "rut" and a third hole at the end of the saw's travel. Drive in short dowels flush with the tabletop, and run the saw across the ends of the dowels. The kerf through the dowels will show

the exact path of the blade. When the dowels get rough, drive new ones down on top of the old ones, which will fall out the bottom of the table.

With this setup, you don't have to pull out a still-coasting blade to measure where the blade is cutting. This saves measuring tapes, and probably other things as well.

Robert M. Vaughan
Roanoke, Va.

LOW-TECH DUST COLLECTOR FOR A RADIAL ARM SAW

HOLE IN BENCH

BUCKET TO COLLECT SAWDUST

If your radial arm saw is not connected to a dust collection system, try this low-tech solution. Cut a hole behind the saw in the bench that supports it. Then create a chute from thin plywood that will direct the stream of sawdust down through the hole. Put a 5-gallon bucket on the floor below to contain the mess.

Jeff Greef
Soquel, Calif.

RADIAL ARM SAW DUST BUSTER

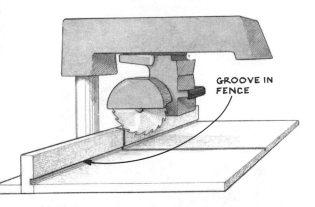

GROOVE IN FENCE

Sawdust, piling up against the radial arm saw fence, can throw off the accuracy of your cuts. To help eliminate this problem, I cut a groove into the fence at table height as shown. This gives the dust a place to go, instead of building up in the corner. A periodic vacuuming keeps the groove clear and functional. Make sure the top of the groove is lower than the top of the thinnest stock you are likely to cut on the saw.

David R. Johnson
Apple Valley, Minn.

SAFETY, SAFETY, SAFETY

Never put your arm, hand, or fingers across the path of a radial arm saw as you're making a cut. The blade could catch and come flying forward, mangling everything in its path.

Jeff Greef
Soquel, Calif.

DUST BUSTER II

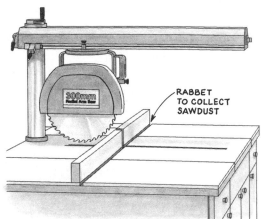

RABBET TO COLLECT SAWDUST

You can also manage sawdust by cutting a rabbet along the back edge of the saw table as shown. The rabbet will allow the dust to drop out of the way, preventing it from misaligning your work.

Jeff Greef
Soquel, Calif.

SELF-CLEANING RADIAL ARM SAW FENCE

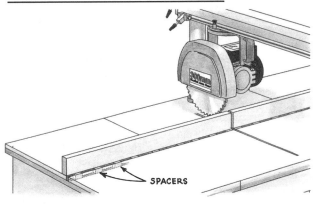

SPACERS

Another solution to sawdust buildup along a radial arm saw fence is to put several ⅛-inch-thick spacers between the fence and the table. This will let the dust drop down between the two parts, so you won't constantly have to brush it away.

Nick Engler
West Milton, Ohio

A HANDY STOP BLOCK

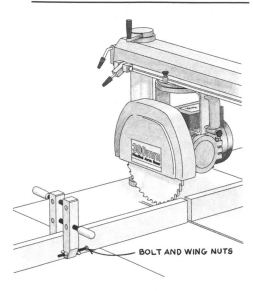

BOLT AND WING NUTS

I made this stop block for use with my radial arm and chop saws. I use it when I have to cut a number of pieces to the same length. I just clamp it along the fence at the necessary distance from the blade.

The block itself couldn't be simpler. It's just a small handscrew. In one jaw, I drilled a hole for a ¼-inch bolt. Two wing nuts hold the bolt in place. When I position the block, I measure to the bolt head. Then if I need to make a slight adjustment, I can loosen the wing nuts and shift the bolt one way or the other.

Simon Watts
San Francisco, Calif.

STOP BLOCK WITH SPACER ON THE SIDE

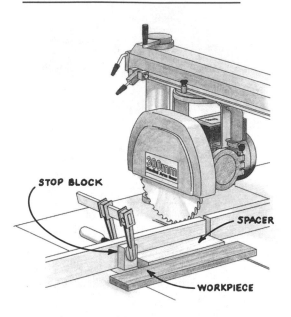

STOP BLOCK

SPACER

WORKPIECE

Nearly everyone knows how to position a stop block along a radial arm saw fence for making multiple cutoffs. But how often have you done just that, only to find you forgot to square one end of a piece you want to cut? This could mean removing the stop block, making the cut, and then struggling to reposition the block. What a pain. Fortunately, there's a better way.

Make a spacer block that is slightly wider than your stop block, as shown. Then, should you need to cut a piece where the stop block will be in the way, place the spacer against the fence. Place your workpiece against the spacer and make the cut.

Jeff Greef
Soquel, Calif.

RADIAL ARM SAW STOP AND MITER FENCE

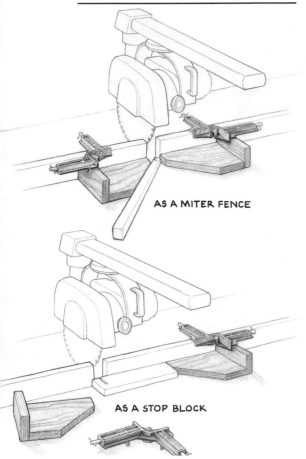

AS A MITER FENCE

AS A STOP BLOCK

A pair of Stanley #404 corner clamps holds a combination cutoff stop and miter fence to the fence of my radial arm saw, as shown. The stop/fence is made from scraps of high-quality plywood. Make the angles accurately so the miters you cut with the jig will go together well. When you need the corner clamps for holding a miter, just borrow them back.

Wayne Asper
Stroudsburg, Pa.

FINE-TUNING MITERS

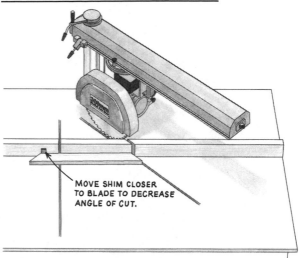

MOVE SHIM CLOSER
TO BLADE TO DECREASE
ANGLE OF CUT.

I used to have a lot of trouble setting up my radial arm saw to cut miters. No matter how much I fussed with the arm, I could never make the minute adjustments necessary to achieve a true 45-degree angle. Then I hit upon a system that allows very precise adjustments. Swing the arm over to 45 degrees and lock it in place. Then take the shortest piece to be cut, and put it in place on the table. Insert a thin shim between the workpiece and the fence. Make a test cut. If the cut needs to be adjusted, move the shim slightly. Moving the shim toward the blade will decrease the angle, while moving the shim away will increase it.

Jeff Greef
Soquel, Calif.

CUTTING TO A LINE

When I use the radial arm saw, I sometimes try to cut to a line that
(continued on page 238)

Radial Arm Saw Tune-Up

Many people think of the radial arm saw as simply a rough cutoff saw that is always out of adjustment. This may be because they have never taken the time to learn how to set one up properly. In fact, the radial arm saw can be a remarkably precise tool. To get your saw running in top form, follow these steps:

- Level the table.
- Install the fence.
- Square the blade to the table.
- Square the arm to the fence.
- Square the blade to the fence.
- Install a replaceable cutting surface.

Your owner's manual will tell you exactly how to make the adjustments on your particular saw.

CHECK THE POSITION OF THE TABLE USING A CARD AS A FEELER GAUGE.

CHECKING THE TABLE FOR LEVEL

Leveling the Table

If the table isn't level side to side, your cuts won't be perpendicular to the face of the board. If the table isn't level front to back, your cuts will be deeper on one side of the board than on the other. A dado, for example, will be deeper on one side of the board than on the other.

To check the table, remove the blade from the saw, and pivot the motor until the arbor is pointing straight down at the table, as shown in *Checking the Table for Level*. Lower the motor until the arbor is just barely above the table surface. Use a plastic-coated playing card as a gauge. There should be a slight drag on the card when you slip it between the table and the arbor. Move the motor along the arm, and pivot the arm

from side to side to check various places on the table. The drag on the card should be the same at any spot.

If the drag changes, you'll have to adjust the table. This is usually accomplished with the bolts that hold the table to the saw's base; check your owner's manual to be sure. Otherwise, you can insert shims between the table and the base.

Installing the Fence

The fence is clamped between the front and rear tables. It should not be attached to either one. Rather, it should be readily removable so you can replace or adjust it depending on the cut you are making. Ideally, for crosscutting, the fence will project ¼ inch above the workpiece, with a single kerf in it to allow the blade through. If the kerf is wider than the blade, the fence won't support the cut. This will result in tear-out at the edge of the board that is against the fence.

As the kerf widens from wear, unclamp the fence and shift it so you can cut a fresh slot. Also cut a fresh slot for making dadoes and for mitering. For ripping, install a new fence, totally free of cuts. This is to ensure that the board won't catch on the fence as you push it past the blade.

Since having a good fence is necessary for good results, you might want to make up half a dozen or so extras to keep on hand. Your owner's manual will list the proper size.

Squaring the Blade to the Table

Unless the blade is square to the table, you will not get a perpendicular cut. Hold a square on the table with its blade against the saw blade as shown in *Squaring the Blade to the Table*. Adjust the blade's tilt until it aligns with the square. Once you get the blade adjusted, some saws allow you set a stop that will hold this position. Check your manual to see how this is done.

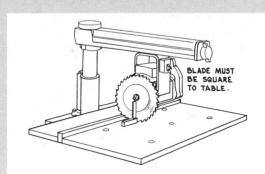

SQUARING THE BLADE TO THE TABLE

Squaring the Arm to the Fence

The arm must be set perpendicular to the fence, or else the saw will never cut square.

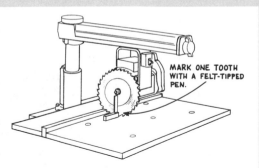

SQUARING THE ARM TO THE FENCE

Set the blade height to just clear the table. Use a felt-tipped pen to mark one blade tooth. Rotate the blade until that tooth points straight down. Hold a square against the fence with its blade touching the marked tooth, as shown in *Squaring the Arm to the Fence*. Pull the carriage out along the arm. If the arm is square to the fence, the marked tooth should stay in contact with the square. If it pulls away from the square, or if it pushes in against it, you'll need to adjust the arm. Pivot the arm to adjust it until the marked tooth maintains contact with the square for the full travel of the carriage.

Squaring the Blade to the Fence

The entire motor carriage pivots so it can be locked in the rip position, parallel to the fence. For crosscutting, however, it needs to be locked perpendicular to the fence. Hold a framing square or other large square against the fence and tilt it up so its blade is against the saw blade, as shown in *Squaring the*

(continued)

Radial Arm Saw Tune-Up—*Continued*

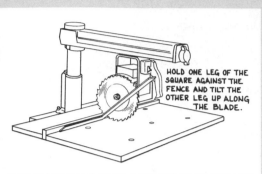

HOLD ONE LEG OF THE SQUARE AGAINST THE FENCE AND TILT THE OTHER LEG UP ALONG THE BLADE.

SQUARING THE BLADE TO THE FENCE

Blade to the Fence. Adjust the carriage until the blade aligns with the square. Again, there is probably a stop you can set to hold this adjustment.

Installing a Replaceable Cutting Surface

Just as the fence prevents tear-out at the back edge of a cut, the table prevents it on the underside. But to do this, the table must have a precise kerf cut into it. As this kerf widens from wear, it will no longer support

the cut and you'll get tear-out. Rather than replace the entire table each time the kerf widens, install a replaceable cutting surface on top of the table. This surface can be made of ¼-inch plywood.

Cut the plywood to match the size of your table. Raise the blade above the table and slip the new piece in place. Secure it with brass or copper brads. Should you inadvertently cut through one of these brads, the soft metal won't hurt your blade.

Once the new surface is secure, turn the saw on and slowly lower the blade. Cut into the surface about ¹⁄₁₆ inch deep. Pull the carriage out all the way to cut the initial kerf. This kerf should remain precise for quite a while. When you notice that it is beginning to widen from wear, replace the plywood surface.

—*Kenneth S. Burton, Jr.*
Burton is a woodworking editor at Rodale Press and a studio furniture maker in Allentown, Pa.

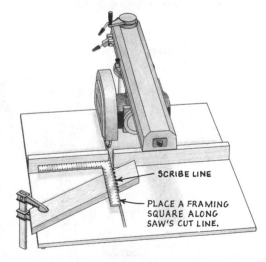

SCRIBE LINE

PLACE A FRAMING SQUARE ALONG SAW'S CUT LINE.

may not be square to the edge of the board (as when scribe-cutting stair risers or treads). Rather than adjusting the saw's arm to follow the lines, I shift the pieces to align with the saw.

Place the piece to be cut on the saw table with an accurate framing square on top of it. Hold the square against the fence, with its leg extending out along the saw's cut line. Shift the workpiece until the scribe line coincides with the leg of the square. Clamp the piece to the table, then make the cut.

David Hubbard
Baker, W. Va.

17 PLANERS AND JOINTERS

ACCURATE EDGE-GLUING

IF THE JOINTER FENCE ISN'T SQUARE, EDGES WILL BE SLIGHTLY BEVELED.

GAPS RESULT WHEN BEVELED BOARDS ARE FED THROUGH THE JOINTER THE SAME WAY.

ERRORS ARE MINIMIZED BY ALTERNATING BOARDS FACE FOR FACE AS THEY'RE JOINTED.

When you go to glue boards edge to edge, the first step is to straighten them on the jointer. Ideally the jointer fence should be dead square to the table, so the edges of a board are machined square to its faces.

I once checked this adjustment every time I used the jointer. But I recently discovered that it isn't all that critical. Now, instead of worrying about whether the fence is square to the table, I simply alternate which face of the boards I hold against the fence—the good side of the first board, the opposite side of the next one, and so on. This way, any error in the fence setting is canceled out instead of added up.

Simon Watts
San Francisco, Calif.

JUST IN CASE . . .

As you plane stock for a job, run it all through the planer at the same setting to ensure that each piece is the same thickness. When you're finished planing, mark the thickness gauge to show the exact thickness of your stock. This way, should you need an extra piece, you can easily match it to the others.

Hack Blodger
Loafer's Glory, N.C.

JOINTER PUSH STICK

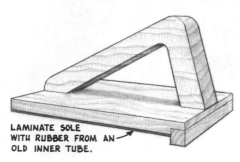

LAMINATE SOLE WITH RUBBER FROM AN OLD INNER TUBE.

Here's a push stick for use when you're face-jointing. The handle keeps your fingers up and out of harm's way, while the rubber sole provides a good grip.

Jeff Greef
Soquel, Calif.

PUSH BLOCKS WITH SOLE

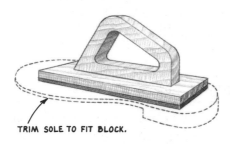

TRIM SOLE TO FIT BLOCK.

Before you discard a worn pair of shoes with crepe or nonslip rubber soles, try the soles on a flat board to see if they still have their gripping qualities. If so, save them for use on jointer push blocks. (If you have a spare, you can use it as a sanding-belt cleaner.)

Glue the sole to a backing block as shown. Make a handle to fit your hand and you're ready to go. To get the best grip, try to make the backing block as large as possible. Unless you wear enormous shoes, you'll probably end up with a block about 2½ inches wide and 8 or 9 inches long.

Ralph S. Wilkes
Branchport, N.Y.

ANOTHER JOINTER PUSH STICK

You can also use a wooden, foam-faced mason's float for a jointer push stick. The foam facing makes an excellent nonskid surface.

Jeff Day
Perkasie, Pa.

A SILENT HELPER

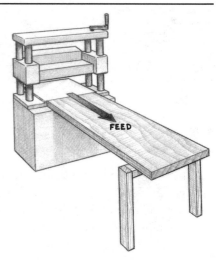

FEED

Before I built this silent helper, I used to put boards through the planer one after another, then race around the machine to catch them before they crashed to the floor. It was while running these awkward laps one day that I came upon this idea.

The helper is simply an extension

of the planer's table. It is long enough to hold several boards before they drop off the end. Now I can feed a batch of boards through without worrying about them dropping on the floor. Then, when the last one is feeding, I can stroll around the planer to collect them from my silent (and unpaid) helper.

As a further refinement, I've found that if you tip the far end of the extension up slightly, it helps keep the planer from sniping the ends of long boards.

> *Jeff Greef*
> *Soquel, Calif.*

LAZY (SUSAN) PLANING

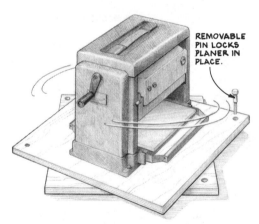

REMOVABLE PIN LOCKS PLANER IN PLACE.

After planing a number of boards on my small thickness planer, I got tired of carrying the boards around from the outfeed end to the infeed end. So I installed the planer atop a heavy-duty lazy-Susan bearing. Now when I've finished a pass, I just pivot the planer and run the boards back through to where they started. I mounted the bearing between two

squares of ¾-inch plywood and installed a removable pin to lock the planer in position while in use.

> *Tom Whalen*
> *Cohoes, N.Y.*

BEVELING UNWIELDY PIECES

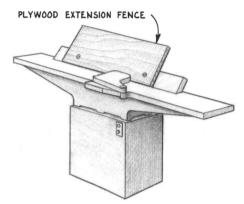

PLYWOOD EXTENSION FENCE

I once had a job making window sash. Everything went along fine until I had to bevel the bottom edge of each sash. The jointer seemed to offer the cleanest cut, but running the tall sash frames along the short jointer fence was a problem.

I overcame this difficulty by bolting a piece of plywood to the fence, effectivly increasing its height as shown.

> *Jeff Greef*
> *Soquel, Calif.*

WIDTH CONSERVATION

Occasionally, you have to straighten a board that already is close to the finish width at one end; an extra pass over the jointer might make the board too narrow. In this situation, start the cut about an inch behind

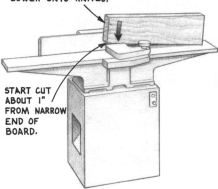

HOLD BOARD AGAINST FENCE AND GENTLY LOWER ONTO KNIVES.

START CUT ABOUT 1" FROM NARROW END OF BOARD.

the whole package over the jointer. If the grain tears, simply turn the unit around and try a pass going the opposite way.

David Page
Swarthmore, Pa.

the narrow end. Hold the piece against the fence and gently lower it onto the whirling knives. Then continue the cut from there, planing only the wider end of the board.

Jeff Greef
Soquel Calif.

EDGE-JOINTING VENEER

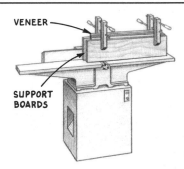

VENEER

SUPPORT BOARDS

Getting a perfectly straight cut on a piece of veneer can be a painstaking task if you use a straightedge and a knife. But it is a relatively easy job on the jointer. Sandwich several sheets of veneer between two boards as shown. The boards should be at least ¾ inch thick, 5 inches wide, and 4 inches longer than the veneer. Run

EDGE-PLANING

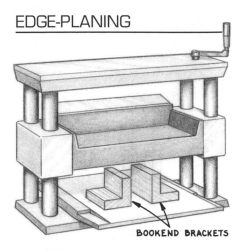

BOOKEND BRACKETS

If you need to trim a number of pieces to the same width, run them through the planer on edge. Make two bookend-style brackets, as shown, to help hold the pieces upright as you feed them through the machine.

Jeff Greef
Soquel, Calif.

MUSIC TO PLANE BY

Like to listen to music during those long, monotonous hours of planing? Buy a set of earphones that fit in your ears. Then wear your hearing protectors over them. Run the wires to your Walkman down your back to avoid having them get caught in the machinery.

Ben Erickson
Eutaw, Ala.

PLANING THIN STOCK

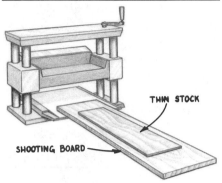

SHOOTING BOARD

THIN STOCK

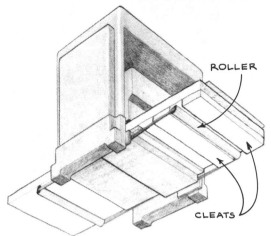

ROLLER

CLEATS

I use a small portable planer to surface stock for the Shaker boxes I make. When I first started planing down thin stock, I found the planer ate too many of the strips. After some experimenting, I devised this system.

I made a shooting board from a 6-foot length of 1-inch white pine. You can glue 150-grit sandpaper to the top surface to keep the piece being planed from slipping. Now when I have thin pieces to plane, I piggyback them on the shooting board, sending the whole mess through the machine. I find that the added support cuts down considerably on the planer's appetite.

Bill Parrish
Norris, Tenn.

PLANING THIN STOCK REVISITED

The instructions that came with my Ryobi/Sears 10-inch planer say that planing stock thinner than ½ inch is not recommended.

I use a lot of thin stock, so I made a jig that inserts into the planer and

allows me to go as thin as ⅛ inch.

The jig is 10 inches wide and 26 inches long. I made mine from ¾-inch medium-density fiberboard (MDF), which I varnished to make a smooth surface. Hardwood plywood would work, too. I fastened two wooden cleats across one end of the jig to fit over the roller on the input side of the planer. Now the thin stock just slides right through atop this slick surface.

John Neumann
Sauk Centre, Minn.

PLANING SHORT STOCK

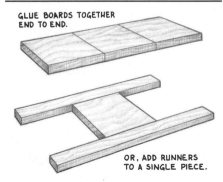

GLUE BOARDS TOGETHER END TO END.

OR, ADD RUNNERS TO A SINGLE PIECE.

After a project, I often end up with a bunch of cutoffs that are too short to plane safely but too long to throw away. As a solution, I cut the ends of the pieces square and glue them together, end to end. While I don't advise end-grain gluing for furniture work, it does just fine in less critical applications.

I glue up enough pieces to make a "board" that can be planed safely. To minimize tear-out, I try to arrange the pieces so the slope of the grain all runs the same direction.

If I have only a single short piece to plane, I glue two long runners to it as shown. These runners span the space between the planer's feed rollers, allowing the board to pass through safely.

Simon Watts
San Francisco, Calif.

PLANING END GRAIN

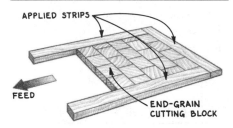

APPLIED STRIPS

FEED

END-GRAIN CUTTING BLOCK

I often make end-grain cutting boards by gluing up smaller blocks so that the end grain becomes the cutting surface. The final boards are about 10 to 12 inches square. Unfortunately, running such boards through the planer to surface them is just asking for trouble. The knives tend to catch and chew the edges of the piece to bits, sending splitters flying back out of the machine.

To prevent this kind of terror, I

glue strips around three sides of each block as shown. The two long strips span the distance between the feed rollers, in effect creating a longer board. The third strip prevents the trailing edge of the block from splintering as it is cut.

Simon Watts
San Francisco, Calif.

TAPERING ON THE PLANER

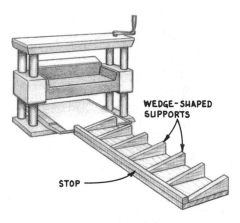

WEDGE-SHAPED SUPPORTS

STOP

You can taper pieces from side to side by running them through the planer aboard a wedge-shaped carriage, as shown. Be sure to include a stop at the lower edge of the carriage, or else the feed rollers will push the piece downhill.

Jeff Greef
Soquel, Calif.

TAPERING ON THE PLANER—TAKE 2

You can taper boards along their length with a similar jig. This time the wedges must run the length of the board, as shown. Run the jig through the planer low-end first. Be

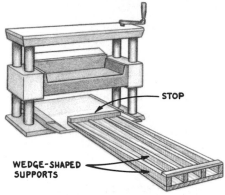

STOP

WEDGE-SHAPED
SUPPORTS

sure to include stop blocks at both
ends of the board to keep it from
shifting on the jig.

Jeff Greef
Soquel, Calif.

HONING JOINTER AND PLANER KNIVES

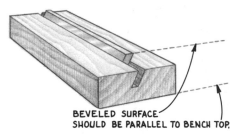

BEVELED SURFACE
SHOULD BE PARALLEL TO BENCH TOP.

Once you get your planer or jointer knives back from having them
ground, hone them with a fine oilstone (or a block of wood wrapped
with 600-grit sandpaper). Honing will
make the knives sharper, resulting in
a better cut.

Cut an angled kerf in a block of
scrap to hold the knives as you hone
them. The kerf should hold the
knives so their beveled surface is parallel to the bench top, as shown.

Tom Groller
Palmerton, Pa.

SETTING JOINTER KNIVES

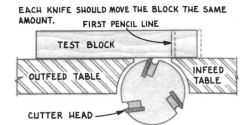

EACH KNIFE SHOULD MOVE THE BLOCK THE SAME
AMOUNT.   FIRST PENCIL LINE

TEST BLOCK

OUTFEED TABLE   INFEED TABLE

CUTTER HEAD

Here's a quick way to set jointer
knives accurately. Cut a block of
wood about ½ × 1 × 6 inches with at
least one long edge straight and
clean. Make a crisp pencil line across
one face of the block, 1 inch from an
end as shown.

Raise the infeed table until it is
level with the outfeed table. Remove
one knife at a time and replace it
with a sharp one. After you insert
each new knife, place the block on
the jointer so it bridges the tables.
Adjust the knife so it just touches the
block at either side of the table.
Tighten the bolts that lock the knife
in place.

Align the pencil mark on the block
with the edge of the infeed table as
shown. Rotate the cutter head slowly
by hand under the block. The knife
should move it forward slightly.
Mark the distance the block travels
with a second mark. Check the blade
at either side of the table to make
sure it moves the block the same
amount. Make any necessary adjustments. Set the other knives the same
way. They all should move the block
an equal distance. Once all the knives
are set, double-check to make sure all

the bolts are tight. Then make a test cut. If the jointer snipes either end of the cut, raise or lower the outfeed table to eliminate the problem.

David Page
Swarthmore, Pa.

SETTING PLANER KNIVES

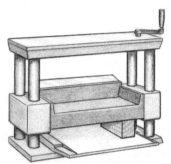

Planer knives should be set so they are parallel to the planer bed. You can use a block of wood to check this as you replace the knives in the machine.

Before you change the knives, cut a block about 2 X 3 X 4 inches. Place this on the bed under the knives, and adjust the bed until the knives just graze its surface. Leave the bed in this position for the entire time you're working on the machine. Replace the knives so that each one just touches the block along its entire length.

One problem you may discover is that planer knives tend to shift slightly as the bolts lock them in place. They usually move farther away from the cutter head. To compensate for this, place a thin piece of paper on the block when you first insert the blade. The paper will push the knife into the cutter head slightly. Then

when you tighten the blade, it will move out into its correct position. Experiment with different thicknesses of paper until you find one that, after tightening, allows the blade to just graze the block.

Jeff Greef
Soquel, Calif.

KNIFE PRESERVATION

Don't run dirty wood through your surfacing machinery. The dirt and grit will dull your knives prematurely. Before planing, give dirty boards a thorough wire brushing to clean them.

Jeff Greef
Soquel, Calif.

MAKE YOUR OWN OUTFEED ROLLERS

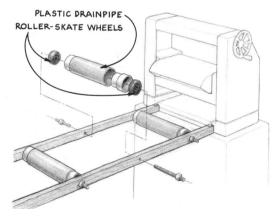

PLASTIC DRAINPIPE
ROLLER-SKATE WHEELS

I made outfeed rollers for my planer from old-fashioned steel roller-skate wheels, which happen to have the same diameter as the outside of 1½-inch plastic drainpipe. The drawing shows how I adapted the wheels to 2-inch plastic pipe. These ball-bearing roller-skate wheels run very smoothly.

Robert Schroeder
Sheboygan Falls, Wis.

QUICK-ADJUST BED ROLLERS

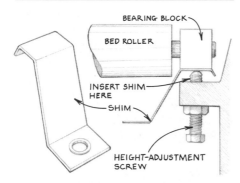

BEARING BLOCK

BED ROLLER

INSERT SHIM HERE

SHIM

HEIGHT-ADJUSTMENT SCREW

By setting planer bed rollers quite low (0.002 to 0.006 inch above the bed), you can get a supersmooth surface for a final cut. But when surfacing rough lumber, you should set the rollers higher so you won't have a tug-of-war trying to pull stock through the machine.

Make the bed rollers easy to adjust by using four shims from 0.015-inch steel shim stock (available from Small Parts, Inc., 6891 N.E. Third Avenue, P.O. Box 381736, Miami, FL 33238). Alternatively, 26-, 27-, or 28-gauge sheet metal will also work fine. The drawing shows the shims I made for my Powermatic 100 12-inch planer. The little turn-down on the end keeps the shim from backing out and may or may not be necessary on your planer.

Reach under the bed, raise the bed

roller bearing block, and simply insert the four shims over the tops of the four height-adjustment screws. The shims allow you to set your bed rollers low for fine work and quickly jack them up 0.015 inch for rough work. Remove the shims for the last two passes, and like magic you'll get a smooth cut.

Robert M. Vaughan
Roanoke, Va.

JOINTER STAND

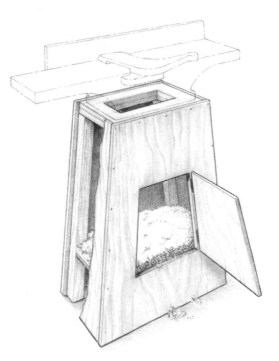

To keep jointer shavings off the floor, we built an enclosed plywood stand for our 4-inch Delta jointer. The shavings fall into the stand, and at the end of the day, we open the door and vacuum them out.

The top of the stand is made from

two layers of ¾-inch plywood, and the sides are ⅜-inch plywood, joined at the corners with 2 × 2s.

Alice & Robert Tupper
Canton, S. Dak.

YOU WON'T PAY A LOT FOR THIS ADAPTOR

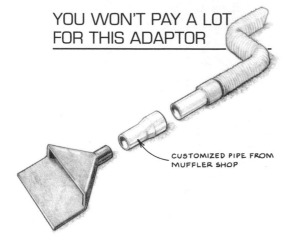

CUSTOMIZED PIPE FROM MUFFLER SHOP

Here's a tip for readers who own the Ryobi AP-10 planer. Ryobi sells a dust-hood attachment to hook up to a shop vacuum. Unfortunately, the nozzle has a 2-inch outside diameter (O.D.), which doesn't fit a standard 2¼-inch-O.D. shop-vac hose.

I took the dust hood and my shop-vac hose to a muffler shop. They took a 5-inch length of 2-inch pipe and expanded one end to fit over the dust-hood nozzle and the other end to fit my shop-vac hose. In just five minutes I had a convenient adaptor at nominal cost.

Gordon G. Ruecker
South St. Paul, Minn.

ATTACHING BOWL BLANKS

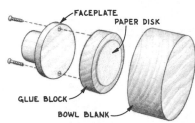

After trying several dozen different ways of attaching a bowl blank to a faceplate, I finally have settled on a method. It is a variation of the system that uses paper between the bowl and the mounting block as a release mechanism, but it is stronger because it allows actual wood-to-wood contact. I have too many bad memories of bits and pieces of bowl ricocheting around the shop after using paper alone.

Cut a mounting block to the same diameter as the faceplate. Cut a disk of paper about 1 inch less in diameter than the block. Glue the block to the bottom of the bowl blank with the paper disk centered in between. When the glue dries, you can turn the bowl. To remove the bowl from the block, first use a parting chisel to cut in about ½ inch along the joint between the two. Then stop the lathe and gently tear the bowl loose from the block.

Kenneth S. Burton, Jr.
Allentown, Pa.

ATTACHING TURNING BLANKS

You can attach turning blanks to a faceplate with hot-melt glue. Heat the faceplate and the bottom of the blank with an iron to aid in adhesion. Squirt glue on the heated surfaces, then press the two pieces together with a clamp. Leave them clamped up until the glue cools. To remove, heat the faceplate again with an iron.

Ben Erickson
Eutaw, Ala.

QUICK STICK

You can attach turning blanks to a faceplate with double-sided carpet tape. Make sure the back of the blank is flat and smooth. Clean the faceplate with steel wool to remove any oxidation. Then cover the faceplate with a layer of tape, and stick the blank on. (Thicker, cloth-backed tape works better than the thin, plastic-backed stuff.) Squeeze the two pieces together with a clamp to make sure they stay stuck. Then mount the plate on the lathe and let the shavings fly. If you're nervous about the tape giving way, bring the tailstock up against the blank as added insurance.

Your nervousness will disappear when you try to remove the blank from the plate. Double-sided tape is tenacious stuff. When I first started using this system, I broke several pieces trying to pry them free. I've since had reasonably good results with locking the spindle, then twisting the piece off.

Hack Blodger
Loafer's Glory, N.C.

PART WITH YOUR HACKSAW

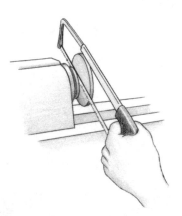

If you don't have any stock to waste and you are ready to make the final cut to separate a turning from its mount, you can do a neat job with a hacksaw. A sharp metal-cutting blade will go through the wood quickly, leaving a smooth surface that needs little sanding.

Operate the lathe at low speed until the work is almost severed, then turn it off and complete the cut with a stroke or two of the saw.

Ralph S. Wilkes
Branchport, N.Y.

TOOL REST TUNE-UP

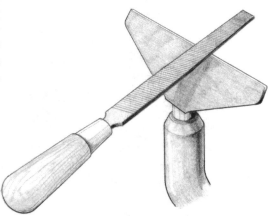

File the top edge of your lathe's tool rest occasionally to remove any nicks that might hinder smooth movement of the tools.

Bill Bigelow
Surry, N.H.

TOOL REST TUNE-UP PLUS

Rub a little paraffin on your tool rest after you file it. And rub a little on the backs of your tools, too. You'll think you have Excalibur itself in your hands as you turn.

Gnarly Strop
Worley's Corner, Pa.

MATCHING HALF-ROUND TURNINGS

GLUE HALVES TOGETHER WITH CONTACT CEMENT, THEN SPLIT WITH CHISEL TO SEPARATE.

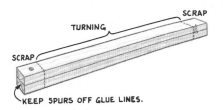

SCRAP
TURNING
SCRAP
KEEP SPURS OFF GLUE LINES.

I make matching half-round turnings for the restoration of antique clock cases. I use contact cement to glue two blanks together, back to back. After turning, I start prying the two pieces apart with a chisel, dribbling a little lacquer thinner in the resulting crack. As it grows, I add more thinner until the two halves pop apart. The two turnings are a full half-round with no loss from a saw kerf.

David R. Johnson
Apple Valley, Minn.

GUARDING AGAINST PREMATURE SPLITTING

Split-turning is a neat process that allows a turner to get two or more pieces from a single spindle. Generally, the blank is split to begin with, then glued back together to be turned. A layer of heavy paper is glued in between the pieces to facilitate separation after the turning is complete. But all too often, the paper will give way while the piece is spinning on the lathe. This can be frightening, with pieces of spindle raining down across the shop. To prevent such a disaster, there are two precautions you can take.

1. Drill a small hole in each end to locate the lathe centers. Then, when you tap the spur center into the blank, keep the spurs off the glue line(s). This will prevent the center from acting as a wedge and driving the pieces apart.

2. Allow an extra inch or so of stock at each end of the blank. Then run screws through the blank for added holding power, as shown.

Ralph S. Wilkes
Branchport, N.Y.

WHIPPING WHIP ON THE LATHE

Long, thin spindles that whip and chatter on the lathe can be tamed with a steadyrest—but you have to move the steadyrest to turn the center section. When I'm turning straight, tapered, or slightly curved surfaces, I find that they whip and chatter much less if I use a hand plane instead of a skew. After roughing out the spindle with a gouge, I set

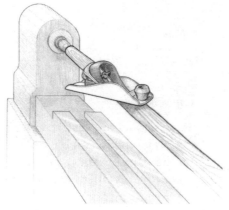

the lathe speed as low as possible and "plane" the spindle with slow, even strokes. You can experiment with blade settings, the angle of the plane to the spindle, the speed of your stroke, and the lathe speed for the results you want.

If you're still getting some chatter, try bearing down slightly on the plane or supporting the spindle from behind with your hand.

Fred Matlack
Emmaus, Pa.

TURNING TOY TIRES

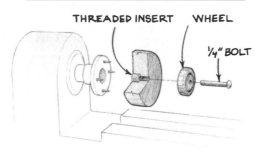

THREADED INSERT   WHEEL

¼" BOLT

If you make many toys with wheels, you'll appreciate my mandrel for turning wheels on the lathe. I rough-cut the wheels with a hole

saw that has a ¼-inch pilot bit. A ¼-inch bolt is then screwed into a threaded insert to secure the wheels quickly and easily for turning as shown.

Gordon Krupp
Northbrook, Ill.

PUTTING BACKBONE IN YOUR LATHE

The best way to stiffen up a wood lathe—the type with hollow, tubular beds—is to fill the pipes with concrete. Pop off the pipes' end caps, mix up some sand/cement mix, and fill both pipes. Let the concrete cure for a couple of weeks, then replace the caps. You'll be amazed at how much this reduces vibration.

Michael Chilquist
Pittsburgh, Pa.

VIBRATION DAMPENER

Almost every turner would like a big, massive lathe to work on. You know—the kind that won't dance around the shop when you try to turn a really off-balance chunk of firewood. Unfortunately, few of us can afford the luxury of such a cast-iron monster.

One way to get big-lathe performance from an economy model is to increase its mass. I built a hollow stand for my lathe from ¾-inch plywood. I glued and screwed all the joints for added rigidity. Once the stand was ready, I positioned it in my shop and then filled it with 700 pounds of sand. Then I bolted the 2-inch-thick oak top in place. Finally, I lag-bolted the lathe to the top. I've not been troubled by vibration since.

Gnarly Strop
Worley's Corner, Pa.

CHARRING DECORATIVE LINES

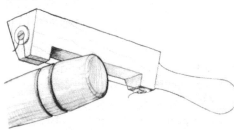

Decorative lines in tool handles and similar turned objects can be made more prominent by charring with a length of iron or steel wire held against the revolving wood. Keeping pressure on the wire soon produces enough friction heat to char a good, black line—but the wire also gets too hot to hold.

I've made a tool that enables me to do an efficient job without burning myself. The tool holds a 6-inch length of 18-gauge wire. So that wire can be tensioned or replaced, I twist its ends around screws with washers under their heads to prevent slippage.

Percy W. Blandford
Stratford-upon-Avon, England

FACEPLATE RELEASE

When I mount a faceplate or chuck on my lathe, I first slip a

WAXED PAPER WASHER

waxed paper washer on the spindle. This keeps the part from freezing on the shaft.

Bob Hawks
Tulsa, Okla.

ANOTHER FACEPLATE RELEASE

I use washers cut from an old inner tube to make the faceplates easy to break loose from my lathes.

Ralph S. Wilkes
Branchport, N.Y.

A GRANNY GEAR FOR YOUR LATHE

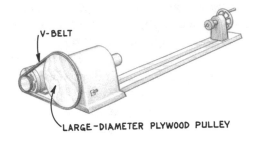

V-BELT

LARGE-DIAMETER PLYWOOD PULLEY

Need to slow your lathe way down below the limits of its step pulleys? Bolt a large-diameter (18 inches or so), ¾-inch plywood disk to the outboard faceplate. Turn the blank round and cut a V-groove in its rim. Mount a motor behind the lathe with its pulley in line with the disk. Loop a V-belt around the disk and motor pulley, and you'll be set for some serious low-speed work.

Ben Erickson
Eutaw, Ala.

LATHE TRAY

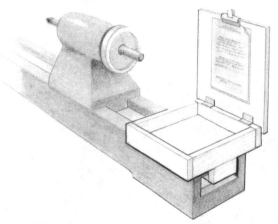

Wood turning produces a considerable amount of waste shavings and chips, causing things you put on the lathe bed to disappear. A plywood tray at the right-hand end of the lathe bed will hold calipers, gauges, and tools away from most of the clutter.

The best method for attaching the tray to the bed depends on the design of the lathe, but it should be removable in the event you need to move the tailstock to the far end of the bed.

A refinement is a plywood lid, hinged at the back. If you arrange the hinges so the lid tilts back slightly when open, it becomes a place to clip drawings or notes so you can see them while turning.

Percy W. Blandford
Stratford-upon-Avon, England

FIXED LATHE CALIPERS

Calipers are indispensable measuring tools when lathe turning, but it's time-consuming to change their setting constantly. Changing from one measurement to another and back again may also result in inaccuracy. To prevent this, make fixed calipers from scraps of ¼-inch plywood for often-used settings. Cut the openings slightly smaller than desired, then file them to the precise measurement.

Nick Engler
West Milton, Ohio

METRIC AND STANDARD CALIPERS

You may have a supply of fixed lathe calipers in your toolbox without knowing it. A set of open-end wrenches can easily double as a set of calipers for lathe work. Simply choose the size of wrench that matches the spindle diameter you want. You might even be able to use an adjustable wrench, although mine tends to slip out of adjustment when I put it down.

Hack Blodger
Loafer's Glory, N.C.

TWO-STEP FIXED CALIPERS

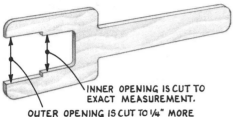

INNER OPENING IS CUT TO EXACT MEASUREMENT.

OUTER OPENING IS CUT TO 1/4" MORE THAN INNER OPENING.

When I have a number of spindles to turn to a specific diameter, I make a pair of two-step fixed calipers to determine the size as shown. The calipers measure two diameters: The inner opening is cut to the exact dimension I'm after, and the outer opening is cut about 1/16 inch larger. When I'm turning, this wider opening warns me that I'm getting close to the final diameter. Once the spindle fits into the wide opening, I make fine, finishing cuts until it just fits into the narrower space.

Nick Engler
West Milton, Ohio

TURNING PRECISE TENONS ON THE LATHE

Here's a sizing gauge for lathe-turned tenons that's faster than measuring with calipers.

Drill a hole in a piece of scrap plywood with the same bit you'll use for the mortise hole. Cut the corners off the scrap and slip it over

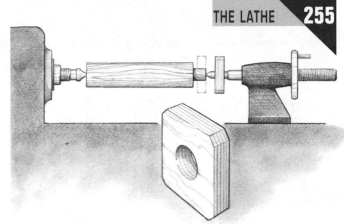

SLIP GAUGE OVER TENON TO CHECK FIT.

the tailstock center. To check the fit, slip the gauge over the tenon as you turn.

Jeff Day
Perkasie, Pa.

SPINDLE-SIZING GAUGE

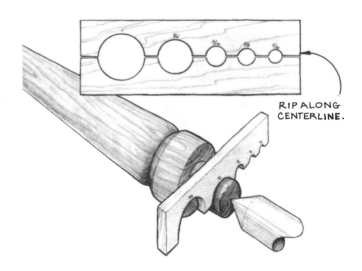

RIP ALONG CENTERLINE.

To make spindle turning go a lot faster, I came up with this sizing gauge for measuring diameters. Make the gauge by drilling different sizes of

(continued on page 258)

Turning a Mock Cabriole Leg

Country woodworkers have a long tradition of making a mock cabriole leg on the lathe. These legs look a lot like a carved cabriole leg, although they tend to be somewhat straighter. Like most country techniques, this one is simple. Old-time cabinetmakers turned a leg, remounted it on a new center, and turned it again. Because offset turning creates forms not immediately identifiable as having come from a lathe, they've made their way out of the country and into the mainstream. They've been showing up at many national turning shows lately. If you're interested in offset turnings, the best place to start is where the country cabinetmaker did—with the mock cabriole leg. From there, experiment. You'll soon discover that the sky is the limit.

Preparing a Leg Blank

Cut a piece of wood about 2 inches longer than you want the leg to be. If you're actually going to build a table, cut four pieces, each about 31 inches long. If you're just experimenting, a piece 18 inches long will be fine. The piece(s) should be about 2 to 2½ inches square in section. Cut the mortises for the aprons in the top end of the blank as shown in *Leg Mortises*. Strike diagonals across the ends of the blank to locate the centers. Mark the centers with an awl.

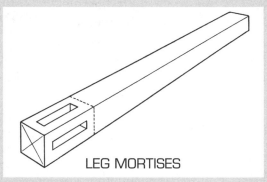

LEG MORTISES

Rough-Turning the Leg

Mount the leg between centers on the lathe. Turn it round below the mortises as

MOCK CABRIOLE LEGS

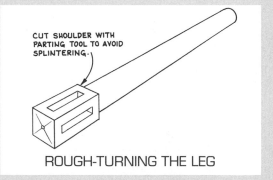

CUT SHOULDER WITH
PARTING TOOL TO AVOID
SPLINTERING.

ROUGH-TURNING THE LEG

shown in *Rough-Turning the Leg*. Try to keep the corners of the square section from splintering by first cutting in with a parting tool.

Turning the Foot

Cut in with a parting tool to mark the bottom of the leg, but don't cut in more than ¼ inch or so. Taper the foot into this cut as shown in *Turning the Foot*.

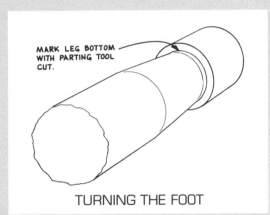

TURNING THE FOOT

Tapering the Leg

Now for the fun part. Remove the leg from the lathe. Measure its diameter immediately below the square section. Divide this figure in half. This will be the diameter of the leg at the ankle. Divide this new diameter in half. Offset the center at the bottom of the leg by this amount. In the example

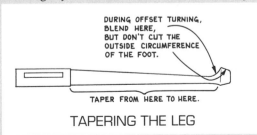

DURING OFFSET TURNING, BLEND HERE, BUT DON'T CUT THE OUTSIDE CIRCUMFERENCE OF THE FOOT.

TAPER FROM HERE TO HERE.

TAPERING THE LEG

shown, the diameter below the square section is 2 inches. So the ankle diameter is 1 inch and the offset is ½ inch. The center at the top of the leg remains in its original position.

At the foot end, measure the offset distance out from the original center along the diagonal that divides the two mortises, as shown in *Marking the Offset*. Make a mark at this point with an awl.

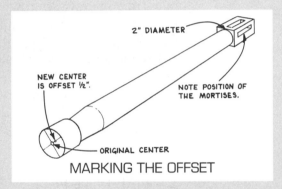

2" DIAMETER

NEW CENTER IS OFFSET ½".

NOTE POSITION OF THE MORTISES.

ORIGINAL CENTER

MARKING THE OFFSET

Remount the leg on the lathe, on the new center point. Start the lathe, and taper the leg from the square area down to the ankle at the top of the foot as shown in *Tapering the Leg*. You'll probably notice some vibration at first, since the piece is off-center. Also, the outline of the leg will start off as a blur, then it will gradually come into focus as you turn the taper.

Blend the ankle into the foot carefully, but don't cut the circumference of the foot or you'll drastically change its shape.

(continued)

Turning a Mock Cabriole Leg—*Continued*

Sanding the Leg

Sand the leg's tapered area. Be careful as you get close to the foot. It's difficult to see the offset part and you can mash your fingers. Once the taper is sanded, switch the leg back to its original centers and sand the outside of the foot. Stop the lathe. Sand by hand to touch up any parts of the transition area between the taper and the foot. Now you can use your parting tool to turn the other three legs for your table in the same manner.

—*Kenneth S. Burton, Jr.*
Burton is a woodworking editor at Rodale Press and a studio furniture maker in Allentown, Pa.

---

holes in a piece of scrap wood and then ripping the scrap along its center line.

Use the gauge as you would use a pair of calipers—keep turning until the gauge just slips down over the spindle.

Bill Bigelow
Surry, N.H.

A FINAL POLISH

As a final polish for your turnings, pick up a handful of chips from the floor around the lathe, and use them to burnish the work as it spins. Be careful not to pick up any chips that might be contaminated with abrasive dust, or you may do more harm than good.

Kenneth S. Burton, Jr.
Allentown, Pa.

PAINTING GROOVES

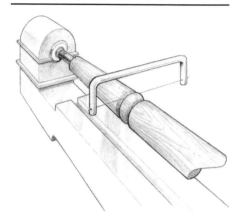

Here's a simple way to accent grooves of spindle turnings with gold or silver paint. I saturate the string with spray paint, then touch the string to the groove as the work turns slowly on the lathe.

A. J. Tryba
Benton, Ill.

MIXING YOUR OWN MILK PAINT

Many pieces of early-American furniture were finished with milk paint. Mix your own milk paint by following the recipe below.

Purchase these items from a grocery store, nursery, paint store, or building-supply store. (Because the lime is an alkali, use inert pigments that are unaffected by it. Earth pigments, such as those used to color concrete and cement, work well.) To test a color or experiment with the paint, mix a small sample using the amounts in the "Sample" column. To make enough paint to cover several chairs or a medium-sized chest or table, use the amounts in the "Working Mix" column. Blend the milk, lime, linseed oil, and cornstarch

first. Then add enough whiting or pigment to bring the mixture to the consistency of heavy cream. Let the mixture sit in a refrigerator overnight, and strain it through a cheesecloth. Stir the paint frequently as you use it. Thin it with additional milk; clean the brushes with soap and water.

Nick Engler
West Milton, Ohio

STAINING END GRAIN TO MATCH

End grain is more porous than side or face grain. So it absorbs more stain and ends up much darker than the other surfaces of a project. This can be a problem if you're after a very even-colored appearance. It's possible to use a sealer only on the end grain, but I don't always have sealer around.

MILK PAINT		
Sample	**Working Mix**	**Ingredients**
½ cup	1 quart	Whole milk or buttermilk
2 tsp.	⅓ cup	Slaked (hydrated) lime
1½ tsp.	¼ cup	Boiled linseed oil
½ tsp.	1 Tbsp.	Cornstarch
2 to 3 oz.	1 to 1½ lb.	Whiting or powdered pigments

Instead, I take advantage of the fact that the more finely sanded a surface is, the less stain it absorbs. I sand end grain a grit or so finer than face and side grain. This seems to offset the end grain's greater porosity.

Walter J. Morrison
Northport, N.Y.

AN OLD FAMILY RECIPE

This oil finish recipe was passed down to me from my father, who got it from his father, and so on. It consists of:

3 parts boiled linseed oil
1 part turpentine
1 part vinegar
¼ part Japan dryer

Combine the ingredients, and rub the mixture on just as you would any oil finish. It works well and smells like a salad.

Rick Wright
Schnecksville, Pa.

SEALING LAYERS OF FINISH

When you apply a layer of clear finish over a stain, sometimes the solvents in the finish partially dissolve the stain. As the two materials mix, the resulting mess looks cloudy and uneven. Or, when you apply one finish over another, the chemicals in the bottom layer keep the top from drying properly.

To prevent these problems, seal one layer of stain or finish with a washcoat of white shellac (a 1-pound cut) before applying a different material. Shellac is compatible with almost all other finishes. When applied between coats of incompatible materials, it keeps them from reacting together.

Nick Engler
West Milton, Ohio

START WITH A GOOD SHELLAC

A washcoat of shellac is an excellent first step in preparing projects for finishing. Dilute the shellac as it comes from the can about 1 to 1 with alcohol. Brush it on and allow it to dry. A thin cut like this will dry in about ten minutes. The shellac will stiffen any fuzz or whiskers.

Once the shellac dries, give the piece a once-over with 280-grit sandpaper. This final sanding will leave the surface glass-smooth and ready for finish. I've gone on to use a variety of finishes, including varnish, lacquer, oil, paint, and wax, with great results each time.

For best results, apply the shellac with a thick, fine-haired brush. I recommend a 2-inch-wide brush with fitch, badger, or oxhair bristles. I have such a brush just for shellac, and I leave it suspended in a jar of alcohol between uses.

Ric Hanisch
Quakertown, Pa.

PREVENTING CONTAMINATION OF FINISHES

An expensive can of paint, stain, or finish can easily be ruined by contamination. If you dip a dirty brush into the can, the old chemicals may change the color or the characteristics of the new finish. To prevent this, pour a small amount of finish into a separate container and dip the brush into this supply. Try to pour out only as much finish as you'll need for the job. When you're through, you *shouldn't* pour the leftovers back in the can.

Nick Engler
West Milton, Ohio

DETOXING YOUR PROJECTS

Before applying a water-based varnish or lacquer to a project, clean the surface with acetone or naphtha. This will dissolve any waxes or oils that might have contaminated the wood. There are many "fugitive" chemicals in a wood shop that can end up on the surface of a project from one source or another. Many finishes are unaffected by these, but water-based finishes are sensitive to oil and wax. Even body oils, deposited from the palm of your hand as you handle the wood, may prevent a water-based finish from adhering properly.

Nick Engler
West Milton, Ohio

CAJUN STEEL

To blacken steel, heat it with a torch, then dip it in a vat of used motor oil. Make sure the vat has a tight-fitting lid that you can close quickly in case of a flash fire. Such a possibility isn't likely, but it's best to be prepared. I use this technique to blacken screws to match black iron hardware.

Ric Hanisch
Quakertown, Pa.

MIXING YOUR OWN STAINS

You can use artist's oil paint to mix your own oil-based pigment stains to any color. Mix the various colors of oil paint until you get the color you're after. As you add each color to the mixture, squeeze it out of the tube in a long, even line. Measure the length of this line before blending it, and keep a careful record of how many "inches" of each color are in the mixture. This will make it possible to reproduce the color if you need it again. After you get the color you want, add equal amounts of turpentine and boiled linseed oil to the paint until it's thin and watery. Apply this mixture to the wood with a rag, as with any other pigment stain.

Nick Engler
West Milton, Ohio

MIXING YOUR OWN PASTE WAX

You can make your own paste wax by breaking up pieces of beeswax, paraffin, and carnauba wax in a glass canning jar. (These waxes are available from grocery stores, craft supply stores, and mail-order woodworking suppliers.) Add enough turpentine to cover the wax pieces. Put a

(continued on page 264)

Sorting Out Oil Finishes

Oil finishes are very popular. They are easy to apply and give consistently good results. Still, there is a lot of confusion about oil finishes. What is the best way to apply oil? What is the difference between the various "oil" finishes? Is tung oil better than linseed oil?

The cause of the confusion is that there are several different finishes marketed as "oil." Usually there is nothing on the container that really tells you what's inside.

The easiest way to understand the differences in "oil" finishes is to make them yourself and apply them. This way you'll see how simple they are and how they differ. You'll save money, too. All you need is some empty jars and a small can of each of the following: boiled linseed oil, pure tung oil, varnish or polyurethane, and paint thinner (mineral spirits).

Boiled Linseed Oil

Boiled linseed oil is one type of oil finish. Manufacturers make boiled linseed oil, not by boiling but by adding metallic dryers to raw linseed oil to make it cure faster. It's always better to use boiled linseed oil, because raw linseed oil takes many days to cure.

Apply some boiled linseed oil to a piece of wood using a cloth or brush. You can thin the oil a little with paint thinner to make it flow better, but you don't have to; it will soak into the wood just as much anyway. Keep the oil wet on the wood for at least five minutes. If any dry spots appear (caused by all the oil soaking into the wood), apply more oil until the spotting stops.

When the wood no longer soaks up oil, wipe off all the excess. It does no good to rub the oil with your hand. Rubbing just warms the oil so it cures faster; it doesn't help penetration.

Let the oil cure overnight. You will notice that the wood now feels a little rough. This is because the first coat of finish locks raised wood fibers in place. Sand off these fibers using 280-grit or finer sandpaper. Sand only enough to make the wood feel smooth.

Clean off the dust and apply another coat of boiled linseed oil in the same way you applied the first coat. Be sure to wipe off all the excess, or the finish will cure soft, causing it to smudge when you touch it. Let the oil cure overnight. Then sand the surface lightly again if it isn't smooth. You can apply a third and a fourth coat until you don't see any improvement between coats. You should end up with an imperceptibly thin finish that has an even, soft sheen. That's all there is to applying linseed oil.

Now try a couple of durability tests. First, slide a coarse object over the finish. The object will scratch the wood through the finish. Linseed oil cures too soft and too thin to provide scratch resistance. (You can usually disguise scratches by applying more oil.) Next, apply a few drops of water to the finish. Count to ten and wipe off the water. A smudge will remain. Linseed oil is not water-resistant. (To repair a water smudge, sand the wood with 280-grit or finer sandpaper and apply more oil.)

Tung Oil

Apply pure tung oil to another piece of wood in the same way you applied the linseed oil. Be sure to use *pure* tung oil. It's not the same as products called "tung oil finish" or "tung oil varnish." (See page 264 for mail-order sources for pure tung oil.)

Notice that tung oil doesn't cure nearly as fast as boiled linseed oil. Each coat can take up to three days to cure. Notice also that tung oil leaves the wood looking flat and splotchy. You have to apply at least five coats, sanding between each coat, to get a sheen approaching what you'll get after two or three coats of linseed oil.

After five or more coats, which should take several weeks to apply, do the scratch and water tests. You will find that tung oil is more scratch-resistant and much more water-resistant than linseed oil. But before concluding that tung oil is the best oil finish, try the next two types. They are also more scratch- and water-resistant than linseed oil, and they look better and are easier and quicker to apply.

Wiping Varnish

Take some varnish or polyurethane (polyurethane is actually a type of varnish) and thin it half-and-half with paint thinner. You have just made the most common "oil" finish—the same as Formby's, Hope's, Gillespie, Waterlox, Tungseal, Seal-a-Cell, Val-Oil, and Jasco. These finishes are simply varnish thinned enough so they are easy to wipe on the wood. They are not oil. Unfortunately, many of these finishes are marketed as oil or tung oil, and this causes confusion.

Apply this "wiping varnish" finish the same way you applied the linseed oil. (Again, no benefit is gained by rubbing.) You don't have to wipe off all the excess each time. This is just what you would expect from varnish. Also, just as you would expect, wiping varnish is much more scratch- and water-resistant than linseed oil. You will notice that this finish cures much glossier and quicker than boiled linseed oil, and it cures very hard. You can apply as many coats as you want to build whatever thickness you want. The greater the thickness, the more protection you get. Sand lightly between coats to remove dust nibs.

Oil/Varnish Blend

Now mix varnish or polyurethane half-and-half with one or both of the oils. If the mixture is thicker than you'd like, thin it with paint thinner. You have just made Danish oil, antique oil, and salad bowl oil. Apply this mixture the same way you applied the linseed oil.

As you would expect, this oil/varnish blend has some qualities of each of the products included. The oil part in the blend slows the curing and makes the finish soft. So you have to wipe off all the excess after each coat, or the finish will smudge. The varnish part adds some gloss and increases the resistance to scratches and water penetration. Using tung oil produces a flatter appearance, greater hardness, and more

(continued)

Sorting Out Oil Finishes—*Continued*

water resistance than using linseed oil.

You can vary the percentages of ingredients to your liking. The higher the percentage of varnish, the better chance you have of building a thickness of hard finish. The higher the percentage of oil, the more time you have to remove the excess before the finish begins to set up, and the softer it will cure.

Which Is Which

If you buy a commercial "oil" finish, you can find out which type it really is by pouring a little of the finish on a piece of glass or other nonporous surface. Let the puddle cure overnight. If it cures hard and smooth, it is wiping varnish. If it cures soft and wrinkled, it is straight oil or an oil/varnish blend.

Mail-order sources for pure tung oil:

Behlen's Tung Oil from Garrett Wade, 161 Avenue of the Americas, New York, NY 10013; (800) 221-2942.

Hope's 100% Tung Oil from Woodworker's Supply of New Mexico, 5604 Alameda Place, Albuquerque, NM 87113; (800) 645-9292.

Gray Seal Tung Oil from Gray Seal Paint Manufacturing Co., P.O. Box 33188, Louisville, KY 40232; (502) 584-8685.

—*Bob Flexner*
Flexner is the author of Understanding Wood Finishing, *published by Rodale Press. He is a professional wood finisher in Norman, Okla., and has written extensively on the topic.*

---

cover on the jar and let it sit overnight. The next morning, the beeswax and paraffin will have melted, but not the carnauba. Loosen the lid and heat the jar in a double boiler on an *electric* hotplate until all the waxes melt together. (Don't use an open flame.) As the mixture cools, it will form a creamy paste.

The proportions of the three waxes don't matter, although many woodworkers prefer to use much less carnauba than beeswax or paraffin. If there is too much carnauba, the wax will be difficult to buff out. If there's not enough, the buffed-out wax film won't be very hard or glossy.

Nick Engler
West Milton, Ohio

INEXPENSIVE PAINT STRIPPER

You can make your own paint stripper for about one-quarter the cost of brand-name strippers by mixing the following:

2 parts xylol or toluol
1 part acetone
1 part alcohol

For every gallon of mixture, add 1½ to 2 cups of paraffin shavings, and let the mixture sit overnight until the paraffin dissolves. (The paraffin makes the homemade stripper thick enough to apply with a brush.) This homemade stripper will remove paint, varnish, lacquer, shellac, and many other finishes. Like all finishing products, it should be used in a well-ventilated area. Wear gloves, goggles, and a respirator to protect yourself.

Nick Engler
West Milton, Ohio

BUBBLE-FREE POLYURETHANE APPLICATION

Discarded pantyhose or nylon stockings make an excellent applicator for urethane or polyurethane finishes, particularly on contoured surfaces or turnings. Just wad them up, dip the ball in the finish, and wipe it on. You get a nice, smooth, thin coat that dries fast and has few if any bubbles.

Brenda Johnson
Apple Valley, Minn.

AGING WOOD ARTIFICIALLY

As wood ages, the surfaces that are exposed to light and air tend to grow darker. (Only walnut and mahogany grow lighter.) This phenomenon helps to give antique furniture its lustrous patina. When making reproductions of antiques, you can create an artificial patina by applying a 10-percent solution of nitric acid (available from most chemical-supply companies). Let the acid soak into the surface of the new wood for several minutes, then warm it with a heat gun. As the temperature of the surface climbs, the wood will suddenly turn dark. Continue to apply

heat until the wood surface is dried thoroughly. When applying the acid, be sure to wear rubber gloves and a full face shield. Work outdoors or in a well-ventilated room.

Nick Engler
West Milton, Ohio

TRY PLASTIC INSTEAD OF STEEL

Try using Scotch-Brite pads instead of steel wool for cleaning up rusty metal or rubbing out a finish. These plastic pads last a long time and don't leave crumbs as the steel wool pads do.

Ric Hanisch
Quakertown, Pa.

BURNISHING A HAND-PLANED SURFACE

A hand-planed surface has a wonderful tactile quality. This is evident in traditional Japanese woodwork, where craftsmen often left the surfaces without a finish, allowing the user to feel the wood as the tools left it.

To give such a surface an added sheen, burnish it with a handful of the shavings that were peeled away by your plane.

Ric Hanisch
Quakertown, Pa.

SCRAPING OUT A FINISH

Almost anyone who has done much woodworking knows about rubbing out a finish, whether it's done with fine sandpaper, steel wool, or pumice and oil. But not as many craftsmen know how to scrape out a finish. This technique works well with lacquer finishes.

A simple hand scraper, finely honed, is all you need. Sharpen the scraper first. File the edge to remove the old burr. Then hone both faces and the edge on oilstones or waterstones to remove any file marks and remaining nicks. Make sure the edge remains square to the faces. Finally, roll a fine burr on the polished edge.

Once the scraper is sharp, you can start scraping the finish. With a light touch, hold the scraper upright and draw it toward you across the surface, leveling and scraping away any rough spots. Proceed cautiously—it is very easy to scrape right through the film. When you get the hang of it, scraping out a finish is a very efficient way to work.

David Page
Swarthmore, Pa.

RUBBING OUT WITH AUTOMOTIVE COMPOUNDS

When rubbing out shellac, lacquer, varnish, or polyurethane, try automotive rubbing compounds. These abrasive pastes level the finish faster and leave a higher gloss than traditional pumice and rottenstone. Use the orange-colored paste (equal to about 1000 grit) for a satin finish. For a high gloss, start with orange paste and finish with the white (2,000-grit). Note that to use automotive paste with open-grained woods, you must fill the pores before applying the finish. Otherwise, the paste will accumulate in the pores and appear as light-colored flecks all over the surface.

Nick Engler
West Milton, Ohio

FINISH STILTS

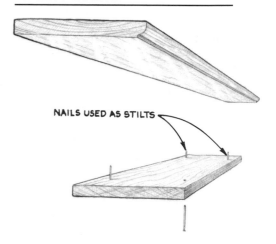

NAILS USED AS STILTS

Plaques and other flat pieces need a finish on every side to prevent cupping. Finish stilts let you finish all sides at once. To make the stilts, sharpen three or four 6d finish nails and drive them all the way through a piece of ⅜-inch plywood. To use the stilts, finish the bottom of the piece first, then lay it down on the stilts, bottom down. Finally, finish the top and edges. Protect yourself from the pointed stilts when not in use by embedding the points in a scrap of Styrofoam.

David Black
Barnwell, S.C.

SAWHORSE POINTERS

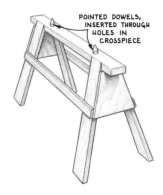

POINTED DOWELS, INSERTED THROUGH HOLES IN CROSSPIECE

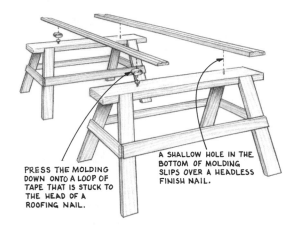

PRESS THE MOLDING DOWN ONTO A LOOP OF TAPE THAT IS STUCK TO THE HEAD OF A ROOFING NAIL.

A SHALLOW HOLE IN THE BOTTOM OF MOLDING SLIPS OVER A HEADLESS FINISH NAIL.

When I'm finishing a cabinet or other piece of furniture, I often support it on sawhorses to make it easier to work on. I've modified my horses with dowels so I can set a piece wet-side down on them without worry. I drilled two holes in each horse for pointed dowels, as shown. The dowels support the work with minimal contact.

Simon Watts
San Francisco, Calif.

HOLD THAT MOLDING

You're often better off applying a finish to molding before installing it. But holding on to thin pieces of molding can be tough. I've devised a couple of solutions.

• Drive two finish nails partway into your sawhorses and clip off their heads. Drill two shallow holes in the back of the molding to catch the nails. Rest the molding on the nails.

• For molding that is too delicate for that approach, drive two roofing nails into the horses. Stick a loop of masking tape to the nail heads. Then push the molding down onto the tape. Use a light touch with your brush to avoid dislodging the molding as you finish it.

Bill Houghton
Sebastopol, Calif.

TWO-FACED FINISHING

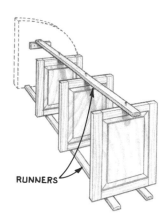

RUNNERS

Finishing both sides of a panel or door at once can be tricky. Here's how I do it. Support the doors on two runners lying on the floor. This will keep the doors up out of the dust. Secure the top of each door to another runner with nails, as shown. Anchor one end of the top runner to the wall to stabilize the setup.

Jeff Greef
Soquel, Calif.

FINISHING PICTURE FRAMES

TACKS AT CORNERS

A picture frame is an inconvenient thing to paint or varnish. It's messy to hold with your fingers and unsteady if you try to hang it from a wire.

I solve the problem by setting the frame down on my bench top for finishing, with a thumbtack at each corner to elevate it. A sheet of newspaper protects my bench from mishap.

Ralph S. Wilkes
Branchport, N.Y.

NO-SCRATCH SURFACES FOR FINISH WORK

When a project reaches the finishing stage, I protect my work surfaces from finishing materials and the project from scratches by covering the work surfaces with carpet. Because I put large projects on sawhorses for finishing, I made up carpeted, fitted

saddles for the sawhorses. I store the saddles carpeted-side down to keep them dust-free.

H. Wesley Phillips
Greer, S.C.

FREE PAINTING AIDS

I've found two uses for plastic grocery bags in painting projects. They're useful for wrapping a wet brush up in to keep it from drying out if you intend to use it later in the day. And the smaller sizes make excellent gloves to keep paint off your hands while painting or handling freshly painted objects.

Ralph S. Wilkes
Branchport, N.Y.

A MAGNETIC PICKUP

Keep a strong magnet handy in your shop. It's useful for cleaning steel wool crumbs from the corners of cabinets.

Kenneth S. Burton, Jr.
Allentown, Pa.

RECYCLING TOOTHBRUSHES

Save your old toothbrushes for the shop. They come in handy for cleaning dust out of corners and applying paint remover.

Jeff Greef
Soquel, Calif.

STICKY FINGERS

As a final step in preparing a project for finish, I wrap a few layers of masking tape (sticky-side out) around my forefinger. Then I go over the piece, picking up any stray dust particles with the tape.

Lane Olinghouse
Everett, Wash.

A FINISHING FILTER FUNNEL

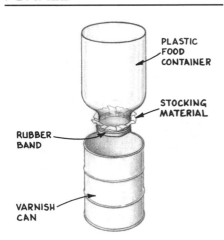

It's a good idea to strain varnish, in case any gunk might have fallen into the opened can. I use a funnel made from an inverted plastic food container that has had its bottom cut

off. I secure a piece of nylon stocking material around the jar's rim with a rubber band. Then I place the funnel over the can I'll use when applying the finish and pour the varnish in the top. The fact that the funnel's neck fits into the varnish can allows me to leave things alone while gravity does its work. This is a real advantage, since filtering is a slow process. Once finished, I discard the nylon and recycle the funnel for use next time.

Walter J. Morrison
Northport, N.Y.

TUPPERWARE FOR TACK CLOTHS

Tack cloths have a bad habit of drying out after a couple of uses. To keep a used one viable, bunch it up into a loose ball and place it in a plastic food storage container with a tight lid.

Tom Groller
Palmerton, Pa.

SOFTENING HARDENED PUTTY STICKS

Colored putty sticks are handy for filling nail holes, but they sometimes get hard with age and become difficult to use. When this happens, I soften the stick before using it by immersing an end in very hot water for about a minute. Don't submerge too much of the stick, or it will get too soft for you to hold properly.

Walter J. Morrison
Northport, N.Y.

KEEPING FINISHES FRESH

Here's an easy way to save paint or finish in a can. Just pour a thin layer of the appropriate thinner on top of the material, and cover the can. Store the can on the shelf without shaking. When you want to use the finish, stir in the thinner and the finish will be good as new.

Frank Distefano
Rochester, N.Y.

A DUST MASK STRAINER

DUST MASK

An inexpensive dust mask makes a good finish strainer. The cupped shape fits nicely over the mouth of a quart jar and acts as a reservoir as you pour the finish through.

Richard Dorn
Oelwein, Iowa

NO-NONSENSE PAINT FILTER

Old nylon pantyhose make great paint filters. Stretch a layer over the mouth of a paint can, and slowly pour the paint through into another container. The nylon will strain out any gunk that would interfere with your painting.

Jeff Greef
Soquel, Calif.

SQUEEZE PLAY

Here's another technique for keeping finishing materials from going bad in their cans. Crush the can slowly as you use its contents. Squeeze it just enough to bring the fluid level up to the top each time you use some. This will keep air out of the can and keep your finish fresh. Of course the cans won't look that great—but who cares?

Ric Hanisch
Quakertown, Pa.

A LESSON FROM A WISE OLD BIRD

According to the fable, a thirsty crow, unable to reach the water in a nearly empty pitcher, dropped in pebbles until the level rose to the brim.

Likewise, to keep the contents of a finish can from oxidizing and forming a skin, try dropping in marbles to raise its contents to the brim. This keeps out air and preserves the

finish. When you're done with the can, just rinse the marbles with mineral spirits and use them again.

Doug Kenney
South Dennis, Mass.

HANDY BRUSH CAN

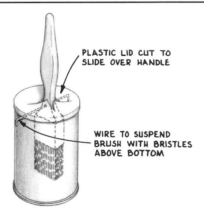

PLASTIC LID CUT TO
SLIDE OVER HANDLE

WIRE TO SUSPEND
BRUSH WITH BRISTLES
ABOVE BOTTOM

From time to time I find it convenient to leave a brush soaking in a can of thinner. But if you just plop the brush into a can, two bad things happen: The thinner evaporates, and the bristles get bent and matted.

To get around these problems, I customized an old coffee can as shown. Cut two notches opposite each other along the rim. Then cut a length of coat-hanger wire to span the can between the notches. Drill a hole through your brush handles so the wire can pass through. Locate the hole so the bristles will clear the bottom of the can by about ¼ inch. Finally, cut an X in the plastic lid so that the handles can protrude but the lid will still seal in the thinner.

Rick Wright
Schnecksville, Pa.

THREE CHEERS FOR KEROSENE

Instead of paint thinner, I use kerosene to clean my brushes. Kerosene has a low vapor pressure, so it evaporates very slowly. This keeps the air cleaner as I clean my brushes.

Simon Watts
San Francisco, Calif.

ECONOMICAL SOLVENT USAGE

To conserve solvents used for cleaning up finishing brushes, keep the fluid in a sealed can or bottle. After you clean a brush, seal the container and let it sit for a day or two. The solids will settle to the bottom, allowing you to pour off the clear solvent for reuse.

Ric Hanisch
Quakertown, Pa.

REJUVENATING OLD BRUSHES

A home brew, mixed of 2 parts xylol or toluol to 1 part each acetone and alcohol, can be used to restore an old or hardened brush. Let the brush soak in the mixture overnight to loosen the solidified paint and finish. Remove every other tooth from an old comb, and use it to scrape the crud from the bristles. Clean the brush again in fresh stripper solution, then wash the bristles with soap and water. To restore the shape of the brush, wrap the wet bristles in newspaper and masking tape. Let the brush hang, bristles down, for a week or more. When you remove the newspaper, the brush will look (and work!) like new.

Nick Engler
West Milton, Ohio

A TIP FROM MR. GOODWRENCH

To clean your hands after applying an oil-based finish, try automotive hand cleaner. The creamy stuff is designed to dissolve oil-based substances.

Jeff Greef
Soquel, Calif.

SPLATTER GUARD

Tired of having paint splatter from the lid groove when you bang the lid down on the can? Drape a rag over the can the next time you go to seal it.

Jeff Greef
Soquel, Calif.

SPLATTER PREVENTION

Instead of trying to shield yourself from paint splatter as you go to close

HOLES ALLOW PAINT TO DRAIN FROM RIM BACK INTO CAN.

a paint can, why not prevent the problem altogether? The next time you open a new can of paint, take a few seconds to punch four or five holes through the bottom of the lid groove with an 8d nail. They'll allow the paint to drain back into the can instead of collecting in the groove.

Gnarly Strop
Worley's Corner, Pa.

TOUCHING UP TEAR-OUT

To prepare a surface to be painted, you can fill any places where the grain has torn out with auto-body filler. Spread it on with a putty knife, then scrape and sand it flush after it dries.

If you've used putty to repair a routed molding, rerout the molding with the same bit to clean up the excess putty. The hardened putty cuts cleanly and will not harm your bits.

Jeff Greef
Soquel, Calif.

PHANTOM LINE REMOVAL

Chipped planer knives can leave raised lines across your stock. These lines often reappear as if by magic when you apply finish, even if you've sanded them away. To prevent this, wet the board slightly after you sand it. The crushed fibers will expand, recreating the line for you to sand away again, before you get involved with finishing.

Ric Hanisch
Quakertown, Pa.

RAISING DENTS

If you happen to dent the surface of a workpiece, don't sand out the dent—this will leave a low area in the wood. Instead, cut a piece of cloth 1 to 2 inches longer and wider than the dented area. Soak the cloth in water and lay it over the dent. Rest a hot, dry clothes iron (don't use the steam setting) on the cloth for a few moments. The water in the cloth will turn to steam. As soon as the steam stops, lift the iron off the cloth. (If you leave the iron in place too long, it may scorch the wood.) When you peel back the cloth, you'll find the dent is gone. The hot steam causes the crushed wood fibers to swell to their original shape.

Nick Engler
West Milton, Ohio

20 CARVING

CLAMP YOUR CARVINGS

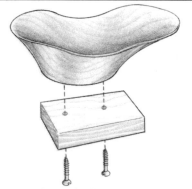

It can be a challenge to hold small pieces as you carve them. Try attaching the carving to a scrap block, then clamping the scrap to the bench or holding it in a vise. I usually attach the block with glue, or with screws if the holes are in the back of the carving and won't show.

When I use glue, I place a piece of newspaper in between the two pieces. This way I can split the scrap block off easily when I'm finished with it.

Rick Wright
Schnecksville, Pa.

DON'T THROW IN THE TOWEL

I like to carve in my family room while I watch TV. This used to create a big mess on the carpet, with chips and debris everywhere. When I got tired of cleaning up (which didn't take long), I devised a system for containing the fallout. I take a large tray and cover it with a shaggy, terrycloth towel. Then I hold my carving on top of the towel. The tray helps hold the piece in place, and the chips get caught up in the rough fabric. At the end of a session, I just shake the towel outside, where the chips aren't a problem.

Jean Scott
Floyd, Va.

GET A GRIP

To hold a carving for finishing, I use a photographer's tripod. It allows me to position the piece at any angle and at a comfortable working height.

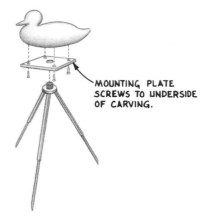

MOUNTING PLATE SCREWS TO UNDERSIDE OF CARVING.

To attach the piece to the tripod, I made a mounting plate as shown. The plate has a hole through its center, which I tapped to match the screw on the tripod, and four holes at the corners for attaching the carving.

Richard Sarbacker
Madison, Wis.

DETAILS, DETAILS, DETAILS

You can use acrylic artist's paints to add color to your carvings. They won't fade, and they can be mixed to any hue you desire. The only real drawback I've found is that they tend to obliterate fine details and burned-in lines. But excess paint is easily removed by wiping it with a rag soaked with wood alcohol. This trick has worked for me no matter how hard and dry the paint was. The alcohol won't damage your carving.

Roland Albert
Philadelphia, Pa.

COLOR TO DYE FOR

Instead of buying expensive pre-mixed stains to color your carvings, try using Rit dye instead. This water-based dye is available in the laundry section of most grocery stores. It comes in a variety of colors, which can be mixed to suit your project. Experiment with a piece of scrap until you get the color and intensity you desire.

Jean Scott
Floyd, Va.

ANOTHER USE FOR SHOE POLISH

You can use paste shoe polish to color your carvings. I rub the wax onto the work, allow it to dry, then buff the piece with a clean cloth. This produces a finish with a rich patina. If necessary, work the finish into the hard-to-reach areas with a cotton swab or a soft toothbrush.

Jean Scott
Floyd, Va.

HOMEMADE KNIVES

1"

3"

You can make carving knives from old hacksaw blades. Start by carefully breaking the blade into pieces about 4 inches long. Then make two halves of a handle. Cut a groove along one half to receive the blade, then sandwich the blade in place with epoxy and shape the handle to your liking. Finally, grind the blade on a slow grindstone and then sharpen it with a waterstone or oilstone. The result is a flexible blade that holds an edge quite well.

Rick Wright
Schnecksville, Pa.

CARVING KNIVES FOR NEXT TO NOTHING

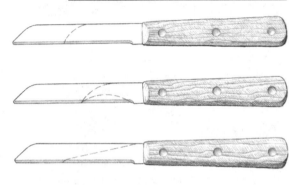

Instead of buying expensive carving knives, you can pick up small kitchen paring knives at yard sales for as little as a nickel each. They'll do the job just as well with a bit of grinding; examples of blade profiles are shown here. Look for good, firm blades that are free from rust.

Rick Wright
Schnecksville, Pa.

KEEPING AN EDGE

I came up with this trick to keep my carving tools sharp in between trips to the oilstones. I mix a handful of fine lapidary abrasive into a can of paste wax. As I work, I poke the tools into the wax instead of letting them roll around on the bench top. The fine abrasive touches up the edge each time I'm finished with a tool. A quick wipe on a shop rag, and the tool is ready to go when I need it next.

Gnarly Strop
Worley's Corner, Pa.

IMPROVED HANDLE DESIGN

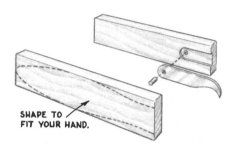

SHAPE TO FIT YOUR HAND.

I like to carve with X-Acto and Warren knife blades. But I don't like the handles that come with these blades—they roll in my hand and are generally either too big or too small to get a good grip on. So I make my own handles to fit the blades. While my shop-made handles won't allow me to change blades, I find they're easy enough to make that I can devote one handle for each blade I like.

Find a piece of hardwood about ¾ × 1 × 5 inches for the handle. Make sure both faces of the blank are smooth—you'll be gluing them together later. Mortise the blade tang into one end of the handle as shown. If the tang has a hole through it, drill a shallow, corresponding hole in the bottom of the recess as shown. Clip a ³⁄₁₆-inch-long piece from a 16d nail to fit through the blade and into the hole in the handle. This will help lock the blade in place.

Rip the handle lengthwise down the middle on the band saw. Position the blade in its mortise with the nail in place, and epoxy the two halves of the handle together with the sawed edges facing out. When the glue dries, shape the handle to fit comfortably in your hand.

Charles Holroyd
Arcadia, Calif.

EDGE PRESERVATION

Sometimes, after you've sanded a piece, you'll find you need to do a little more carving on it. Before you start cutting, be sure to clean off all the sanding dust. This dust is partly wood and partly abrasive particles. It will dull your tools in no time if you try to carve through it.

Lefty McDowell
Conyers, Ga.

ECONOMY AND SANITY

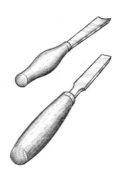

I buy my carving chisels without handles; they're cheaper that way. Then I craft my own handles from scraps of hardwood. I make each handle slightly different so that I can easily spot the tool I need. If all my chisels had similar handles, I'd go crazy looking for a specific chisel amidst the clutter on my bench.

Custis Babcock
Monterey, Pa.

HIGH-TECH TRANSFER

When I have to enlarge a pattern to lay out a carving, I use a photocopy machine that has a zoom setting. I play with the percentage of enlargement until I get a copy that is the exact size needed. Then, armed with the enlarged pattern, I glue it right to the blank with rubber cement.

Hack Blodger
Loafer's Glory, N.C.

RAPID TRANSFER

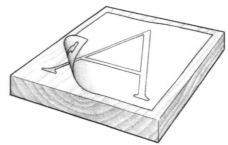

Who hasn't run across the problem of transferring a pattern from a piece of paper to a carving blank? My standard method is to trace the pattern with a soft-lead pencil. Then I turn the pattern face down on the blank and trace it again from the back with the pencil (or a blunt instrument like a crochet hook). This will transfer the graphite from the *(continued on page 280)*

Carving Decoys

Carving waterfowl decoys has challenged craftsmen for generations. Regional influences, coupled with individual carvers' styles, have produced an endless variety of decoys, ranging from the rough and crude to the elegant and lifelike. There is room for all within this unique art.

Decoys are usually carved from two pieces of wood: one for the body and one for the head. Traditional carvers worked with any soft, light, wide-grained stock they could find. White cedar, white pine, linden (basswood), and sugar pine are among the best choices. If you can't find a solid piece that's big enough, you can always glue together several smaller pieces.

Roughing Out the Body

Enlarge the patterns provided. Trace both the top and side views onto the body blank. Cut out the top view on the band saw first.

Then tape the two cutoffs back in place, recreating the square block. This will allow a uniform side-view cut. Cut out the side view.

Once the basic shape is sawed out, you can start to carve. It helps to view the body as a simple egg shape. Always cut from the egg's waist to its two tips, working with the grain as shown in *The Egg Concept*. To help keep your bearings, draw a line around the circumference of the body at its fullest point to indicate the waist. Draw a centerline around the body lengthwise to help you keep the body symmetrical.

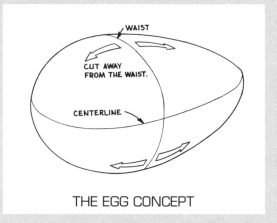

THE EGG CONCEPT

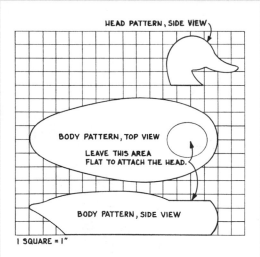

BODY AND HEAD PATTERNS

Traditional carvers usually begin to rough out the blank with a simple hatchet. Some even use the hatchet alone to carve the entire body, creating a distinctively rough and chunky bird. If necessary, choke up on the hatchet for more control. Knock off the corners, creating an octagon from the four-sided blank. Start by working toward the tail as shown in *Roughing with a Hatchet*. Then turn the piece around, and round up the breast.

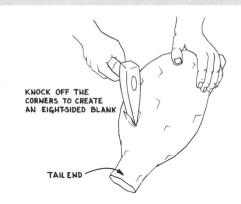

ROUGHING WITH A HATCHET

KNOCK OFF THE CORNERS TO CREATE AN EIGHT-SIDED BLANK

TAIL END

Refining the Body

Once you've roughed out the body, clamp it securely in a vise, or simply hold it to your bench with a C-clamp. Be careful not to crush the soft wood with the hard jaws. Start rounding the octagon body, blending the flats and ridges into a continuous, smooth surface. Experiment with spokeshaves, drawknives, and rasps to find which give you the best results. A rasp is especially helpful around the breast area and for working over any knots, as shown in *Refining the Body*. The neck area, where the head will attach to the body, should be left flat.

Carving the Head

The decoy head is where a carver can really lend personality and style to the project. Use a 2-inch-thick piece of the same wood you used for the body. Trace the head pattern onto the blank. Only the side profile is necessary. Make sure the grain runs from the tip of the bill through to the back of the head. Drill a hole in the waste area near the throat. This will provide relief for the band saw blade as it cuts around this tight area. Saw out the shape on the band saw.

Once the piece is cut out, draw a centerline around it. Cut off the corners and other excess material with a coping saw. Sketch the line of the bill, cheeks, and neck on the blank. Look in a field guide to get an idea of what your bird should look like.

Start carving at the back of the head, as shown in *Carving the Head*. Use a comfortable knife, a small gouge, or even a round

(continued)

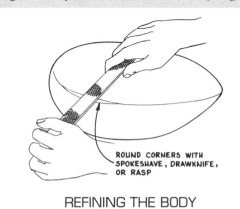

ROUND CORNERS WITH SPOKESHAVE, DRAWKNIFE, OR RASP

REFINING THE BODY

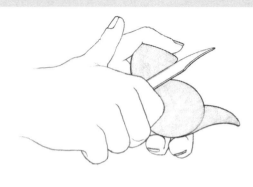

CARVING THE HEAD

Carving Decoys—*Continued*

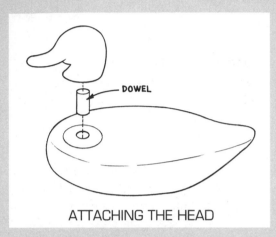

ATTACHING THE HEAD

rasp. The rasp will be handy as you work the area under the bird's bill. Slowly work the head to shape. Try to keep the edge of the beak full and blunt. When you finish carving the head, attach it to the body with a dowel and epoxy.

Once the glue dries, carve the neck area to blend the head into the body. Finish the bird with paint, varnish, or your favorite wood finish. Should you choose to paint your bird realistically, refer again to your field guide, or better yet, take a walk along a stream.

—*Christopher J. Semancik*
  Semancik is a professional woodworker and boat builder in Kempton, Pa.

front of the pattern to the blank. Be aware that this will create a mirror image of the original. If this won't do, trace the image on the back of the sheet of paper. Then place the sheet right-side up on the blank for the transfer.

You can also use carbon paper to transfer the image. Just slip a sheet between the pattern and the blank and trace away.

Jean Scott
Floyd, Va.

GIVE A CARVER ENOUGH ROPE . . .

The relief carvings I make are meant to be hung on a wall for display. I make the hangers from hemp

ROPE NAILED TO EDGE AS A FRAME AND HANGER

Rodale Press

rope, which I feel adds something to the overall design of each piece. I use glue and nails or both to attach the rope around the outside of the panel, forming a sort of frame. You can leave the rope natural or stain it to complement the carving.

Jean Scott
Floyd, Va.

SUPER TIP

To reinforce delicate parts of carvings, like fragile wing tips, coat them with a cyanoacrylate adhesive, also known as Super Glue. The glue will soak into the wood fibers and strengthen them.

George Hayduke
Moab, Utah

SYSTEMATIC SYMMETRY

Making symmetrical cabriole legs for a piece of furniture can be tough. To make it easier, I carve the legs in stages, getting each leg to a certain point before progressing. By working systematically, I find I end up with virtually identical carvings.

Custis Babcock
Monterey, Pa.

A WOOD FOR ALL SEASONS

If you're looking for a wood to carve for outdoor sculptures, I've found none better than catalpa. It is remarkably resistant to rot, it doesn't check, and it's easy to work. And when left out in the weather, it acquires a beautiful gray patina that lasts and lasts. What more could you ask for?

Its only drawback is availability. I've never found it at a lumberyard. The pieces I've worked I had cut for myself. The catalpa tree is a common ornamental in the United States. You may be able to get a piece from a local tree surgeon or lawn maintenance service.

Sam Gribbly
Catskill, N.Y.

21 HINTS, TIPS, AND WOOD SHOP WISDOM

DINNERTIME SIGNAL

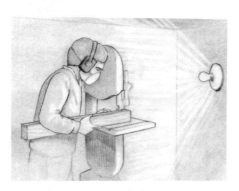

With machines running and ear protectors in place, it's pretty hard to get a woodworker's attention, even for dinner. An unexpected tap on the shoulder can be dangerous, as can flashing the overhead lights. I installed a light socket and red bulb at eye level, and when my wife flips the switch, I'm alerted to rejoin the rest of the world.

Scott W. Ball
San Antonio, Tex.

PHONE ALERT

Can't hear the phone over the roar of your machinery? Add a "fone-flasher" (Radio Shack catalog #43-177) to your phone line and attach it to any light. When the phone rings, it will flash the light on and off. Just be careful which light you set to flash. You want it to attract your attention, not distract you from the task at hand.

Ben Erickson
Eutaw, Ala.

PILOT LIGHTS

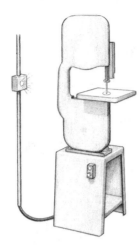

When I wired my shop, I put electric pilot lights in the lines feeding many of my machines. Now I can tell at a glance whether there is power coming to a machine without flipping the switch on and off.

These lights serve as a reminder to turn the power off at the breaker when changing blades and making adjustments and when small children visit the shop.

Ric Hanisch
Quakertown, Pa.

SHOP-VAC SURGERY

One of the first things I did to my new shop vacuum was to cut its cord off. Now before you laugh, you should realize I did it for a reason. Some vacuums come with a nice long cord, but no place to coil it. When I would take the unit outside to empty it, the cord would flop around, trip me, and get tangled in the shrubbery.

Rather than put up with this nuisance, I lopped the offensive thing off about 6 inches from the motor. Then I installed a twist-lock connector to rejoin the cord. Now I can carry the beast around without worrying about its long "tail."

Arthur Guilmette
Westport, Mass.

REMOTE TANK DRAIN

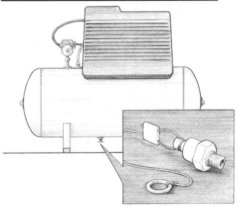

My air compressor is located out of the way, where I won't trip over it. This is great except when it comes time to drain the condensation from the tank. To solve the problem, I replaced the original drain cock with a remote tank drain valve that's designed for large trucks with air brakes (NAPA part #66164). The new valve has a 5-foot cable that I can pull to drain the tank. When I release the cable, the valve closes automatically.

Walter Colton
Wellsboro, Pa.

NO MORE BAD VIBES

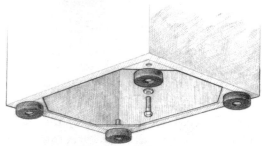

To dampen machine vibrations, I drill and then countersink hockey pucks and bolt them to the feet of the machine.

Robert M. Vaughan
Roanoke, Va.

LOW-TECH MOTOR MOUNT

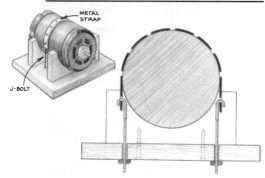

Electric motors from old washers and dryers can be useful in the shop, but they often lack a baseplate for mounting. Here's a way to solve the problem.

I make a base from ¾-inch plywood, two J-bolts, and a length of perforated iron strapping. If you can't

find J-bolts, open up the loops of eyebolts instead.

I find that one strap is usually sufficient to hold the motor in the cradle. However, you could install two straps—one at each end—if you find it necessary.

Dean St. Clair
Salesville, Ohio

NO-FUMBLE TOGGLE SWITCHES

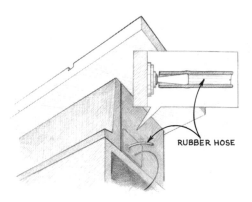

RUBBER HOSE

Recessed and short toggle switches can be improved by slipping on a short length of rubber hose with a ⅛-inch inner diameter (I.D.). The hose makes the switch easier to find and operate without fumbling.

William Guthrie
Pontiac, Mich.

EMERGENCY BELT

When a belt breaks in the middle of a job, it needs replacing right away. My method is to run cotton string between the machine's two pulleys until the grooves are half full. I then tightly wrap string around this

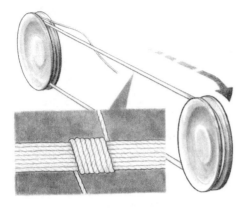

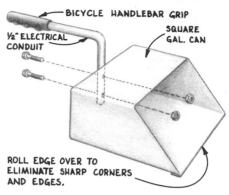

improvised belt as shown. The result is a cool-running belt that takes five minutes to make. I have four of these belts now, and they've been running more than a year with no problems.

Michael Chilquist
Pittsburgh, Pa.

CLEANING GUMMED-UP BLADES AND BITS

For cleaning gummed-up saw blades, router bits, and other parts, soak them overnight in a strong solution of Mr. Clean. The next day, they'll look brand new. Be sure to dry them thoroughly to prevent rust.

Tom Groller
Palmerton, Pa.

THE QUICKER PICKER-UPPER

Here's a dustpan that puts the best of the commercial models to shame. It holds more, and it can be adapted to suit your state of agility. Make the handle long enough, and you'll never have to bend over to scoop up a pile

of shavings again. Plus, it gives you a chance to recycle a gallon can. Practical and environmentally conscious, too—what more could you ask for?

Ron Pavelka
Orange, Calif.

IN-SHOP RECYCLING

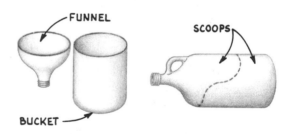

Many types of plastic bottles can be put to use in the shop. Cut the top off a bottle with a neck, and you've got a funnel. The bottom part may be useful as a small bucket. Cut a milk jug with a handle as shown, and you've got two scoops. Use your imagination—the materials are certainly the right price.

C. E. Rannefeld
Decatur, Ala.

WHEN VIEWED IN A DIFFERENT LIGHT

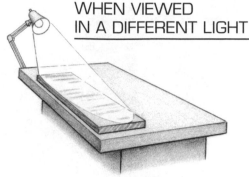

Everyone knows it's helpful to have good light in a wood shop. But beyond general lighting, many wood-workers could benefit from a small auxiliary spotlight. I keep a 50-watt bulb in a clip-on fixture by my bench.

I use this movable fixture to pro-vide raking light on the surfaces I'm working. It's amazing how apparent planer marks become when viewed this way. Scored lines, too, such as those used in laying out dovetails, pop right out. And sanding scratches are much easier to see. Once you try this trick, you'll wonder how you ever got along without it.

Ric Hanisch
Quakertown, Pa.

MAKING A THIRD EYE

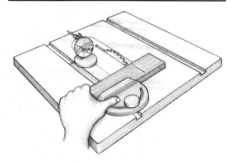

For some woodworking opera-tions, it helps to have a "third eye" to see around corners. For example, when sawing dovetails, you must monitor the cut on both the front and the back of the board. Or when lining up a cut on a table saw, you've got to use a mark on the edge of the board that faces away from you. To be able to see these things, shorten the handle of an inspection mirror (available at most auto-parts stores), and mount it in a scrap of wood as shown.

Nick Engler
West Milton, Ohio

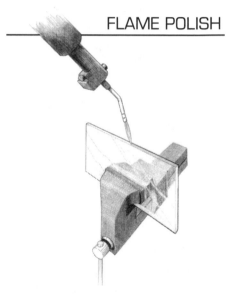

FLAME POLISH

For a professional-looking edge treatment on Plexiglas, try "flame polishing." First sand out any saw marks, then lick each edge lightly with a propane torch. The scratches disappear and the edge takes on a glossy finish. Practice on scrap to get a feel for the process.

David Black
Barnwell, S.C.

QUE SARAN, SARAN

The best way to protect a book or magazine from damage in the shop is to avoid using it there. Use a photocopy instead. If you find you must take the book into the shop, drape a piece of plastic food wrap over it. The plastic will protect the pages from dust and dirty fingers while allowing you to read.

Walter J. Morrison
Northport, N.Y.

THE PROPER LUBRICANT MAKES A WORLD OF DIFFERENCE

When drilling plastic or cutting glass, the job will be easier if you use the proper lubricant. For plastic, squirt a little water into the hole as you drill. The water will keep the plastic from melting. I keep a plant mister nearby for such occasions. Be sure to dry off the drill press carefully when you're done to prevent rusting.

When cutting regular glass, dip a wheeled glass cutter in kerosene before scoring the surface. The thin oil will keep the wheel turning and give it a better grip on the hard surface. This works only for regular glass; cutting tempered glass requires other, more-involved techniques.

Walter J. Morrison
Northport, N.Y.

THE BEST LUMBER FOR DOOR FRAMES

The best stock for door frames is that which has been quarter-sawn—

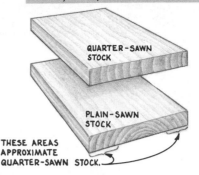

QUARTER-SAWN STOCK

PLAIN-SAWN STOCK

THESE AREAS APPROXIMATE QUARTER-SAWN STOCK.

it's the most stable. Look at the end of the board. The annual rings of quarter-sawn stock will be nearly perpendicular to the faces of the board, as shown. If you can't find a piece of true quarter-sawn lumber, you can approximate it by cutting the edges from a regular board.

Tom Groller
Palmerton, Pa.

FLATTENING WARPED BOARDS

To flatten a cupped panel or board in the summer, take it outside and place it concave-side down on the lawn. The sun will dry the exposed side somewhat, shrinking it; and the moisture from the ground will swell the underside a bit, expanding it. The result is a flatter surface.

In the winter or other dry time, place dampened newspapers on the concave side. The moisture will cause that side to swell. Check the board every half-hour. Let it warp beyond flat, then take it inside. It should then flatten out as it reaches equilibrium in the shop.

Ric Hanisch
Quakertown, Pa.

TAMING SKITTISH DOWELS

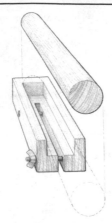

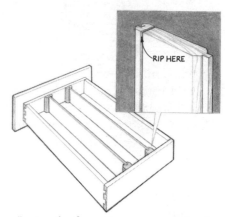

When I'm drilling or shaping round stock, like dowels, I get a good grip and a flat reference surface with a jig like the one in the drawing. I cut the width of the groove to the diameter of the dowel. The saw kerf provides just enough give for the wing nut (or screw) to clamp the jig to the dowel.

John Roccanova
Ancramdale, N.Y.

LOSING YOUR GRIP?

I put rubbery, nonslip tape (used on stair treads) on push sticks, hold-downs, the fence on a plate joiner, and the clamps on a dovetail jig.

Robert G. Brandt
Fort Worth, Tex.

GLUE-ON DRAWER DIVIDERS

It doesn't make sense to install dividers in cabinet drawers without knowing the size of the objects that will be stored there. I prefer to install the dividers on the job.

Instead of cutting grooves in the drawer parts for the dividers, I glue in separate grooved pieces as shown. I rip each one from the edge of a piece of tongue-and-groove planking, then crosscut it to match the inside height of the drawer. The width of the groove is just right for ¼-inch plywood or hardboard partitions, and the chamfered edges make the dividers look as if they were custom-made for the job.

I glue the grooved pieces in place with hot-melt glue, since the joint is under no stress. The glue's low strength allows for easy removal in case the dividers need to be changed.

Walter J. Morrison
Northport, N.Y.

NOTCHING DOWELS

Cutting slots safely and accurately in the ends of dowels can be a problem. The solution I came up with begins with drilling a hole the same size as the dowel into a block of wood. I then cut a slot in the block with the band saw. As shown, the slot runs an inch or so beyond the

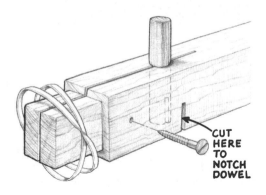

CUT HERE TO NOTCH DOWEL

hole. A rubber band squeezes the block, keeping the dowel tightly in place. (Use a screw instead if the rubber band makes you nervous.) With the dowel clamped in the block, you can easily notch it on the band saw or the table saw.

Yeung Chan
Millbrae, Calif.

STRIP O' WHEELS

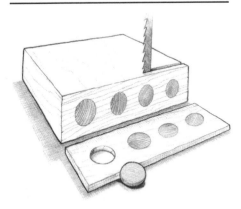

Faced with the task of making nearly a hundred ½-inch-diameter wheels for a fleet of wooden toys, I came up with the following idea. I drilled some ½-inch-diameter holes in a piece of scrap wood and drove

short pieces of ½-inch dowel into them. Then I ripped the scrap into strips the thickness of the wheels I wanted and popped the finished wheels out of the strips. This technique makes wheels that are free of rough edges.

Lawrence L. Lucas
Mount Jackson, Va.

THE MANY USES OF CARPET TAPE

Double-sided carpet tape has dozens of applications in a woodworking shop. You can use it to temporarily stick fences to tools or to stick stops to fences. When making duplicate parts, you can stick boards together to make identical cuts, drill identical holes, or sand identical edges. If you make compound (double) cuts on a band saw or scroll saw, use the tape to reassemble the workpiece after the first cut. After you've made the parts, you can use the tape to stick them together and see what the assembly will look like. The possibilities are almost limitless.

If you find that the tape holds a little too well and you can't disassemble the parts easily, drive a wooden wedge between them. Or try twisting them apart—this action sometimes breaks the bond with much less effort than simply trying to pull. If you want to be extra sure the pieces stay together, squeeze them with a clamp after applying the tape.

Nick Engler
West Milton, Ohio

FINGER ALERT!

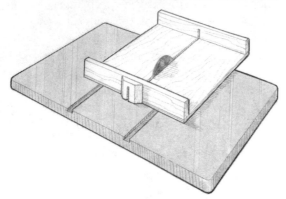

Cutoff boxes, tenoning jigs, and similar fixtures can be dangerous if you forget that the blade is going to exit from the rear of the fixture. Glue a block with angled edges over the slot where the blade comes through. It will alert you to danger if your fingers stray too close while your attention is on the cut.

John Kriegshauser
Kansas City, Mo.

RED IS FOR DANGER

Saws don't care what they cut. As a reminder, I've highlighted the danger zones near my saw blades with bright-red warning strips. I painted a band 6 inches long on each side of the blade of my radial arm saw. I then made a new insert for my table saw and painted that red, too. Finally, I masked off the rip fence and spray-painted it 3 inches in front and 4 inches behind the blade as a reminder to use a push stick when I get that close.

Charles Hirsch
Brookville, Ohio

FINGER-SAVING HANDLE

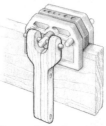

The Dowel-it doweling jig is a useful, versatile tool, but it has flaws. The handle is too small, and it hurts your fingers when you go to tighten it. After suffering this minor annoyance for years, I finally made a wooden handle long enough to apply sufficient torque painlessly. The two halves slip over the steel handle and screw together to lock in place.

April Lambert
Avon, Conn.

CIRCULAR-SAW CUTOFF BOX

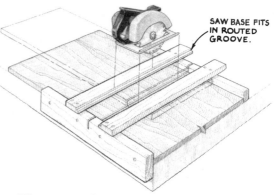

SAW BASE FITS IN ROUTED GROOVE.

This is a useful jig for anyone who does a lot of rough crosscutting but doesn't own a radial arm saw or chop saw. I find it especially handy to avoid mounting the circular saw— the saw just rides in the wooden tracks and is always free for other uses. For my purposes, a 2 × 4-foot base was convenient, but the dimensions can vary to suit your needs.

Bruce Levine
New York, N.Y.

CABINET JACK

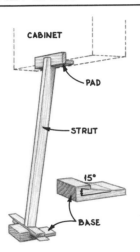

Installing wall-mounted cabinets can involve sore muscles, jury-rigged supports, and possible disaster. It is not for the faint of heart. This cabinet jack, however, can take some of the hassle out of the ordeal. Use one jack for narrow cabinets and two for wider units. Should you face a situation where you think three are necessary, it may be time to get some help.

The exact sizes of the parts aren't critical; in fact some, like the length of the strut, will change from job to job. I make the base from a piece of 2-inch stock and the rest from 1-inch. The incline on the base should be cut to about a 15-degree angle as shown. The bottom of the strut is cut square, while its top is notched to fit around

the L-shaped pad. The length of the strut should be such that the strut stands about 15 degrees from vertical with the cabinet held tightly in place.

To install a cabinet, hold it in place and brace it as shown with the jack. Rough adjustments of the cabinet position can be made by moving the base. Fine adjustments are made by driving the wedges together.

Percy W. Blandford
Stratford-upon-Avon, England

PLANING DRAWERS TO FIT

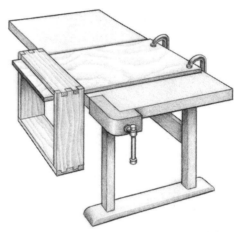

Drawers are awkward to hold when planing them to fit in a case. The best method I've found is to slip the drawer on a piece of plywood that extends out over the edge of my bench, as shown. This works best before the drawer bottom is installed, but it will work with a completed drawer as well. I try to size the plywood so it just fits in the drawer. This way the drawer won't slip around as I plane, scrape, and sand it.

David Page
Swarthmore, Pa.

PLANING DRAWERS TO FIT, TAKE 2

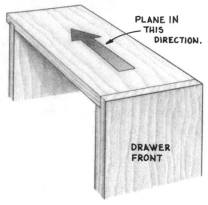

PLANE IN THIS DIRECTION.

DRAWER FRONT

When planing a drawer to fit, plane from front to back. This helps eliminate the risk of tearing the grain on the drawer front. To facilitate this, orient the grain on the drawer sides so it runs out toward the back of the drawer.

David Page
Swarthmore, Pa.

INSTALLING DRAWER FRONTS

On European-style cabinets and other pieces with separate drawer fronts, install the doors and drawer boxes first. Then, once the doors are adjusted properly, install the drawer fronts to match. Put double-sided carpet tape on the fronts of the drawer boxes, and position the drawer faces. Once you have them stuck on in the right positions, slide the drawers open and screw the faces on from inside.

Ben Erickson
Eutaw, Ala.

REPLACE YOUR DIVOTS

Occasionally, through use or mishap, templates develop dings, divots, and other deformities. Rather than remaking the template, fill the voids with auto-body filler. It sets up quickly, adheres well, and can be shaped easily to restore the template to its original shape.

Jeff Greef
Soquel, Calif.

SHIMMING YOUR WAY TO SUCCESS

If you're hanging inset doors in a cabinet, use wedge-shaped shims to position the door as you lay out the hinge locations. This way you'll be able to obtain an equal gap around all four sides of the door.

Tom Groller
Palmerton, Pa.

MAKING WEDGES

To make long, tapered wedges, start with a board that is the appropriate width. Make sure its two edges are parallel, then taper one edge of the board on the jointer. Do

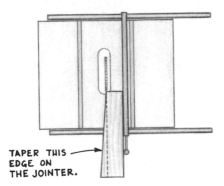

TAPER THIS EDGE ON THE JOINTER.

this by lowering the leading end of the board onto the outfeed table beyond the whirling knives and then feeding the piece through the machine. Repeat this process several times until the trailing edge is significantly narrower than the leading edge.

Once the board is tapered, set the rip fence on the table saw to match the board's narrower width. Rip the board to produce a perfectly tapered wedge.

Jeff Greef
Soquel, Calif.

PROPER LUBRICATION

When lubricating the moving parts of woodworking tools, less is better. Apply just one or two drops of oil to most joints. If you apply too much, the excess oil will mix with sawdust and make an abrasive goo that causes moving parts to wear faster. In dusty areas, you may want to use dry lubricants, such as silicone or graphite, to prevent this from happening.

There is a prevailing myth among woodworkers that WD-40 and other spray oils make good lubricants. Read the label on the can—the man-

ufacturers don't claim any lubricating properties. These sprays are penetrating oils, formulated to dissolve grease and loosen rust. If you use them to lubricate, the working parts will work well for a short time. But as the metal surfaces slide together, the spray dissolves the old grease or oil, evaporates, and leaves the joint without any lubrication at all.

Nick Engler
West Milton, Ohio

WAXING WORK SURFACES

To help workpieces slide smoothly across tables and fences, wax and buff the surfaces. Apply a coat of paste wax, then buff it out thoroughly. This leaves a film of wax, just a few molecules thick, that serves as a lubricant to help the wood slide across the tool. Remember, buffing is extremely important! If you don't buff out the wax, it will contaminate the surface of the wood and may interfere with your finish. It will also mix with fine sawdust, forming a sticky goo that will prevent the wood from sliding smoothly—exactly opposite the effect you're after.

Nick Engler
West Milton, Ohio

FOR THAT BABY-FRESH SMOOTHNESS

As an alternative to wax, you can treat your table saw's table to an occasional sprinkle of baby powder instead.

Morgan Ingalls
Walnut Grove, Mo.

SLICK TIP

Stash a piece of folded waxed paper in the pocket of your shop apron. Rub it on the soles of your hand planes and on the fences and tables of your machinery to keep things lubricated and running smoothly. You'll be amazed at the difference a little wax makes.

George Hayduke
Moab, Utah

JACK BE NIMBLE

Keep a candle or a block of paraffin in the shop to wax wooden drawer runners, sliding machine parts—anything that rubs. The wax will make things slide easily.

Jeff Greef
Soquel, Calif.

IT'S NOT JUST FOR COOKING ANYMORE

Cornstarch makes an excellent lubricant. I keep some near the table saw in a shaker with a perforated lid. Now and then I shake it over the table and fence, and the heaviest, roughest boards slide across the surface with minimal effort.

Margaret Scally
Albuquerque, N. Mex.

SWISS SPLINTER REMOVER

For most woodworkers, splinters are a fact of life. Short of giving up woodworking (not a very good option), there's not much you can do to avoid them. So you might as well be prepared for the inevitable.

The handiest tool I've found for removing splinters is the tweezers that are standard equipment on most Swiss army knives. I grind the tips as shown to facilitate the operation.

Robert Pauley
Decatur, Ga.

WOOD-SHOP MASQUERADE

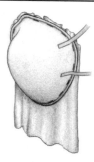

Disposable dust masks can be made bearably comfortable by lining them with clean, soft cloth like an old T-shirt. I staple the fabric around the rim of the mask as shown and tuck the remainder down into my collar to keep chips out.

Greg Glebe
Phoenix, Ariz.

FEATHERBOARDS

A featherboard is a hold-down that clamps onto a machine and pushes wood against the fence or table while still allowing it to slide in

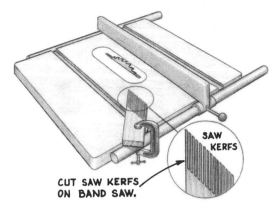

CUT SAW KERFS ON BAND SAW.

SAW KERFS

one direction. It resists backward movement of the board and thus is a guard against kickback.

Make a featherboard by starting with a piece about ¾ × 3 × 18 inches (dimensions vary to suit the application), and cut a 45-degree angle in one end. Then cut multiple kerfs in from the angled end on the band saw, as shown. The kerfs should be about ⅛ inch apart, or slightly less, and about 4 inches long. The idea is to make the resulting feathers slightly springy.

Use a piece of the stock you will be cutting to guide you as you position the featherboard. Hold the stock against the fence, and bring the featherboard up against it so the feathers flex slightly and hold the piece tight. Clamp the featherboard in place.

These simple hold-downs are particularly useful on both the router table and the table saw. On the table saw, be sure not to position it in such a way that it closes the saw kerf. This could have the unintended effect of causing kickback.

Jeff Greef
Soquel, Calif.

NO-KNOT SHOP APRON

Replace the string on your shop apron with a strip of Velcro. It makes fastening and unfastening much easier than trying to tie a knot behind your back.

William Archer
Winfield, Kans.

THINK SAFETY

When you're working around machinery, condition yourself to let things drop rather than lunging after them. It's far better to sand out a dinged corner than it is to mend a hand that has passed over a whirling blade.

Ernie Conover
Parkman, Ohio

STICKY LEVEL

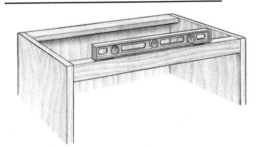

When installing cabinets, it is often necessary to balance a level precariously on the narrow edge of a unit. To keep it from falling off, attach a strip of double-sided carpet tape near each end as shown. When you are finished with the level, replace the paper backing on the tape. That way it will remain sticky through several uses.

Jim Tolpin
Port Townsend, Wash.

DISCIPLINING UNRULY TAPE

Masking tape gets old in the shop and after a while won't unroll very well. This is especially true in cold weather. As a remedy, I give a troublesome roll a 10- or 15-second zap in the microwave. After that, I find I have no trouble unrolling it.

Charles DeMaine
Red Oak, Tex.

WIRE SAVVY

Keep several scraps of #10, #12, and #14 copper wire from your latest wiring job stashed in your shop. They come in handy for poking holes in caulk tube seals, making instant hooks and hangers, and fishing the arbor nut out of the depths of your table saw.

Ric Hanisch
Quakertown, Pa.

A CABINET-SQUARING JIG

Use two sticks to help you square up cabinets and boxes. Hold them together and extend them diagonally until their ends touch the opposite inside corners of the cabinet as shown in the drawing. Mark the end of one stick on the other. Repeat the procedure across the other diagonal. If the second mark matches the first, the cabinet is square. If not, put a mark halfway between the first two marks. Clamp across the longer diagonal of the cabinet until the halfway

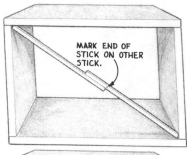

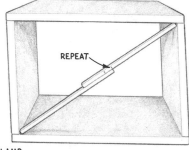

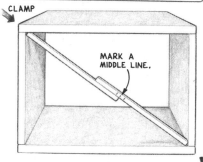

mark lines up. Check that the other diagonal is now equal, indicating that the cabinet is square.

John Roccanova
Ancramdale, N.Y.

ACCURATE SCREW HOLES

Before drilling screw holes, I punch the centerpoint with a sharp nail. This prevents the bit from wandering as I start the hole. The result: a more accurately located hole.

Jeff Greef
Soquel, Calif.

INDEX